THE
COMPLETE
IDIOT'S
GUIDE® TO

Clear
Communication

by Kris Cole

ALPHA

A Pearson Education Company

To all those on the journey of becoming better communicators. May you be rewarded for your courage, your efforts, and your perseverance.

Copyright © 2002 by Pearson Education, Inc.

International Standard Book Number: 0028642074
Library of Congress Catalog Card Number: 2001094734

04   03   02   8   7   6   5   4   3   2   1

Interpretation of the printing code: The rightmost number of the first series of numbers is the year of the book's printing; the rightmost number of the second series of numbers is the number of the book's printing. For example, a printing code of 02-1 shows that the first printing occurred in 2002.

Printed in the United States of America

Publisher
Marie Butler-Knight

Product Manager
Phil Kitchel

Managing Editor
Jennifer Chisholm

Senior Acquisitions Editor
Renee Wilmeth

Development Editor
Jennifer Moore

Production Editor
Billy Fields

Copy Editor
Jennifer Moore

Illustrator
Jody Schaeffer

Cover Designers
Mike Freeland
Kevin Spear

Book Designers
Scott Cook and Amy Adams of DesignLab

Indexer
Amy Lawrence

Layout/Proofreading
Mary Hunt
Gloria Schurick

Contents at a Glance

Part 1: Communication Begins Inside   **1**

1 The Success Sequence   3
How to be successful in your communications and your life.

2 Where It All Begins: Your Beliefs   13
Thinking your way to maximum personal and communication success.

3 We Reap What We Sow   27
Taking charge of what you say and do for better results.

4 Focus for Success   37
Making the success sequence work for you.

5 Become a Peak Performer!   45
The mindsets of peak performers.

6 The Mental Techniques of Peak Performers   55
The secrets of peak performers.

Part 2 The Dance of Communication   **67**

7 Everything We Do Is Communication   69
The dance and the obstacle course of communication.

8 Behavior Breeds Behavior   81
Pulling your own strings with empathy.

Part 3 Watch That Body Language!   **91**

9 First Impressions Count!   93
How body language can forewarn us.

10 Send the Right Signals   103
Body language is SO CLEAR!

11 Other People's Body Language   113
Reading other people's body language—are you succeeding or missing the mark?

12 Build Rapport   119
Establishing cordial relationships quickly.

Part 4 Gathering Good Information   **127**

13 Draw Out the Full Story   129
Focusing on the speaker to gather good information.

14 Ask the Right Questions   141
Questions to lose, questions to use.

15 Listen, Listen, Listen   153
   Gathering really good information and building
   relationships through reflective listening.

16 The Ten Deadly Sins of Communication   165
   The ten worst things you can do in communication
   and how to avoid them.

Part 5   Giving Good Information   175

17 Step Off with the Right Foot   177
   Introducing information so that it will be received,
   not rejected.

18 Choose Your Words for Clarity and Power   185
   Using words to generate cooperation and commitment,
   not clashes and confrontations.

19 Speak the Other Person's Language   197
   Building understanding through neuro-linguistic
   programming.

20 Speak for Yourself, Not the World   209
   Increasing your assertiveness.

21 Don't Masquerade Your Thoughts   219
   Assertion skills you can use every day.

22 Ask, Don't Tell   229
   Building harmony and cooperation and increasing your
   persuasiveness.

23 When You Say What You Like, Say Why   239
   Making feedback work for you.

24 Tune In to the Same Wavelength   249
   Recognizing and working with personality types, styles,
   and temperaments.

Part 6   Making Progress   259

25 Manage Conflicts with Aplomb   261
   Nineteen ways to reach agreement.

26 How to Deal with Difficult People   273
   Keeping cool, calm, and collected with even the most
   difficult people.

27 Win with Complaints   285
   How the professionals do it.

28 Fix It!   293
   Solving problems and making decisions.

Appendixes

A Self-Talk as an Indicator of Self-Esteem   303

B Body Language Practice   305

C Turning Closed Questions into Open Questions   307

D Some Ideas for Frames   309

E Some Word Meanings: *Order* and *Strike*   313

F How to Score the Neuro-Linguistic Programming Quiz   315

G Glossary   317

H For Further Reading   323

Index   325

Contents

Part 1: Communication Begins Inside   **1**

1 The Success Sequence   **3**

It's What's Inside That Counts 4

The Success Sequence 5

The Self-Fulfilling Prophecy 6

   Values 7

Our Thoughts 9

   Our Thoughts Lead to Actions Lead to Results 9

   Are We Stuck with Our Beliefs and Thoughts? 10

2 Where It All Begins: Your Beliefs   **13**

Our Beliefs Guide Our Actions and
Our Communications 14

Beliefs About Ourselves 14

   Self-Esteem 15

   Self-Image 17

   Self-Talk 18

Beliefs About Others 20

   Chicken or Egg? 21

   Our Psychic Mirror 22

Beliefs About the World 24

3 We Reap What We Sow   **27**

Body Language 28

   The Body Language–Mood Link 28

   The Body Language–Self-Esteem Link 30

Locus of Control, or Pulling Your Own Strings 30

Don't Just Stand There ... Do Something! 32

   Going Out on a Limb 33

   See Mistakes as Learning Experiences 33

   Fake It 'Til You Make It 34

   Act As If ... .34

4 Focus for Success **37**

The Power of STAR Goals 38
Set STAR Goals 39
Set Simple and Specific Goals *39*
Give Yourself Target Dates *40*
Make Sure the Goals Are Achievable *40*
Include Both Results and Activities *41*
Plan of Action 42
Three Steps to Success 42
Step 1: Set Your Goals *42*
Step 2: Develop Action Plans *42*
Step 3: Keep At It *43*

5 Become a Peak Performer! **45**

Peak Performers Have High Self-Esteem ... .46
... and Build Self-Esteem in Others 47
How to Pay Someone a Compliment *48*
Sunlight for the Spirit *48*
Peak Performers Have High Standards 50
The Improvement Cycle *50*
Peak Performers Take Responsibility 51
Peak Performers Stay Focused on Their Goals 52
Peak Performers Communicate and Work Effectively
    with Others 52

6 The Mental Techniques of Peak Performers **55**

Take Responsibility! 56
Focus Your Efforts Where They'll Count 56
Embrace Mistakes! 57
Focus on Solutions, Not Problems 57
A Visualization Success Story *58*
Visualize for Success 59
Reprogram Your Brain *59*
Seeing Your Way to Peak Performance *60*
A Guide to Visualization *61*
Advance with Affirmations 63
Keep Them Simple *64*
Write Them Down *64*
Guidelines for Affirmations *64*

Part 2: The Dance of Communication   67

7   Everything We Do Is Communication   69

Why Bother? 70
The Five-Part Tempo of the Communication Dance 71
The First Beat: Everything We Do Is Communication 72
The Second Beat: The Way We Begin Our Message
   Often Determines the Outcome of the Communication 73
The Third Beat: The Way We Deliver Our Message
   Always Affects the Way It Is Received................................74
The Fourth Beat: The Real Communication Is the
   Message Received, Not the Message Intended....................74
The Fifth Beat: Communication Is a Two-Way Street—
   We Have to Give as Well as Gather 75
Navigating the Obstacle Course 76
Be Aware of Communication Filters 76
Reduce Communication Barriers 79
Conquer Incompatibilities 79

8   Behavior Breeds Behavior   81

You Can Choose Your Behavior 83
Dealing With Anger 84
The Professional Approach 85
You Won't Get Anywhere Unless You Walk in the
   Other Person's Shoes 85
Understand the Other's Frame of Reference 87
Develop Empathy 89

Part 3: Watch That Body Language!   91

9   First Impressions Count!   93

The Body Speaks 94
Make Your First Impressions Count 95
Look the Part 95
Body Language—Put Your Best Foot Forward 96
Let Your Voice Ring True! 97
Put Your Best Voice Forward 97
Watch Your Tone—It Can Type You! 98

Emphasize for Clarity *100*
Perfect Your Vocal Instrument *100*

10   Send the Right Signals   **103**

Sending the Right Signals 103
Body Language Is SO CLEAR 104
  Stand *for Cooperation* 104
  Open Up 106
  Center *Your Attention* 107
  Lean *Slightly Forward* 108
  Make Eye Contact...109
  At Ease 110
  Reflect *and* Respond 110
Make It a Habit 111

11   Other People's Body Language   **113**

Reading Other People's Body Language 114
  Observe Signal Clusters 115
  Observe Movements 116
  Look Out for Negative Signals 116
  Look Out for Positive Signals 117

12   Build Rapport   **119**

The Comfortable Harmony of Rapport 120
Build Rapport Through Matching 121
  Match Body Language 121
  Match Voice 121
  Match Energy 122
Build Rapport Through Mirroring 122
Build Rapport by Identifying Commonalities 123
Test for Rapport 124

Part 4: Gathering Good Information   **127**

13   Draw Out the Full Story   **129**

Are You Guilty of Poor Listening Habits? 129
Focus on the Speaker 131
  Get the Environment Right 131
  Be Physically Involved 131

Be Mentally Involved *131*
Check It Verbally *132*
Use Your EARS! 134
Explore by Asking Open Questions *134*
Affirm to Show You're Listening *135*
Reflect Your Understanding *135*
Silence: Now Listen Some More! *135*
Closed Questions Can Be Useful 136

14 Ask the Right Questions   141

Avoid Unhelpful Questions 141
Closed and "Why" Questions *142*
Pseudo Questions *142*
Leading Questions *144*
Multiple Questions *144*
Neutral Questioning 145
Useful Kinds of Questions 146
Open Questions *146*
General Questions *146*
Probing and Clarifying Questions *146*
Unspoken Questions *147*
Tricks of the Trade 147
Help People to Be Specific *148*
Clarify Jargon *148*
Make Assumptions and "Rules" Explicit *149*
Tie Down Generalizations *149*
Help Analyze Comparisons *150*
Has Your Message Hit Home? 150

15 Listen, Listen, Listen   153

True Listening 153
How Can We Listen? Let Us Count the Ways ... .155
"Half-an-Ear" Listening *155*
"Stunned Mullet" Listening *156*
Affirmative Listening *156*
Reflective Listening *156*
Let's Get Reflective! 157
How to Listen Reflectively *158*
When to Use Reflective Listening *159*
When Not to Use Reflective Listening *160*

Five Reflective Listening Skills 160
Paraphrasing Meanings *161*
Reflecting Feelings *161*
Reflecting Facts *161*
Synthesizing *162*
Imagining Out Loud *162*

16 The Ten Deadly Sins of Communication   **165**

The Ten Deadly Sins of Communication 166
Patronizing 166
Evaluating *167*
Moralizing *167*
Playing Psychologist, or Labeling *168*
Making Sarcastic Remarks *169*
Sending Signals 169
Commanding *169*
Railroading *170*
Threatening *170*
Giving Unsolicited Advice *170*
Avoiding 171
Being Vague *171*
Diverting *171*

Part 5: Giving Good Information   **175**

17 Step Off with the Right Foot   **177**

Don't Open Your Mouth Only to Change Feet 177
Frame Your Conversations 178
Some Types of Framing Statements *179*
Practice Makes Perfect *180*
The What's-In-It-For-Me Factor 181
More Practice! *181*
Flagging 182

18 Choose Your Words for Clarity and Power   **185**

The Power of Words 185
Choose Your Words to Influence 187
Choose Neutral Words 188
Choose Positive Words 189

Choose Specific Words 190
Choose Strong Words 192
Deliver Your Words with Panache 193
Speak Clearly *193*
Use People's Names *193*
Support Your Words with Visual Aids *194*
Give Demonstrations *194*
Provide Examples/Metaphors/Analogies *194*
Use the Other Person's *195*

19 Speak the Other Person's Language   197

Neuro-Linguistic Programming 197
Four English Languages 198
Talking, but Not Communicating *198*
Visual (Seeing) Language *199*
Auditory (Hearing) Language *200*
Kinaesthetic (Feeling, Touch) Language *200*
Digital (Logical/Analytical) Language *201*
Make Your Communications Glide ...! 204
Visual Words *204*
Auditory Words *205*
Kinaesthetic Words *205*
Digital Words *206*

20 Speak for Yourself, Not the World   209

The Fight-Flight Response 210
Three Styles of Communication 211
Aggressive Communicators *211*
Passive Communicators *212*
Assertive Communicators *212*
How to Spot an Assertive Person..........................213
Developing Assertion Skills 215
Don't Trip over the Fine Line Between Assertion
  and Aggression..*215*
Watch Out for Passive Body Language *215*
Don't Masquerade Your Opinions as Facts 215
Be Explicit About Assumptions 217

21 Don't Masquerade Your Thoughts   219

Talking About Yourself Assertively 220
Own Your Messages *220*

Speak for Yourself...*220*
Own Your Feelings *220*
Open Up *221*
Don't Be Sidetracked *222*
Deal With Criticism...*222*
Find Out More *223*
One Way to Curtail a Discussion *223*
Two More Ways to Curtail a Discussion *224*
Say "No" Graciously *225*
Don't Be Bullied..*227*

22 Ask, Don't Tell   229

Telling Asks for Trouble! *230*
"I" Statements *230*
Use "I" Statements for the Small Stuff *231*
Use "I" Statements for the Big Stuff *232*
Use "I" statements for the Good Stuff....................*233*
Now Listen! *233*
For the Really Complicated Stuff, Use DELWAC *234*
And Now for the Big Stick....................................*234*
Persuade, Don't Pressure *235*
Earn Credibility *236*
Gather Good Information *236*
Give Good Information...*237*
How to Persuade *237*

23 When You Say What You Like, Say Why   239

Three Types of Feedback *240*
Positive Feedback *240*
Negative Feedback *240*
No Feedback at All *242*
Offering Feedback So It Will Be Heard *242*
Be Clear and Considerate *242*
Address Behavior, Not Interpretations or Labels *243*
Support, Don't Force *244*
By Invitation *244*
Share the Effect *244*
Balance It *244*
Asking for Useful Feedback *244*

Receiving Feedback 245
Dealing With Criticism *247*
Accepting Praise *248*

24 Tune In to the Same Wavelength   249

Find Out People's Main Needs 250
People Who Need to Achieve *250*
People Who Need Relationships *250*
People Who Need Power *250*
Work With People's Metaprograms 251
Avoiders and Seekers *251*
Some People "Just Know," Others Need to Be Told *252*
Matchers and Mismatchers *253*
Lone Rangers and Musketeers *253*
Take Personality into Account 253
Four Preferences for Dealing With Information 254
Thinkers *254*
Feelers *255*
Intuitors *255*
Sensors *255*
Four Types of People 255
Dominant Directors *255*
Interacting Socializers *256*
Steady Relaters *256*
Conscientious Thinkers *257*
Four Temperaments 257
Analysts *257*
Legalists *257*
Realists *258*
Empathists *258*

Part 6: Making Progress   259

25 Manage Conflicts with Aplomb   261

Bring Problems into the Open 262
Five Approaches to Conflict 262
Collaboration *262*
Force *263*
Avoidance *263*

    Accommodation 264
    Compromise 264
  Think It Through First 265
    Go for Win–Win 266
  Twenty Ideas for Resolving Conflicts 266

26 How to Deal With Difficult People   273

  Ten Principles to Bear in Mind 274
    1. Let Difficult People Know You've Heard Them and
      Understood Their Point 274
    2. Don't Take It Personally 274
    3. They're Probably Doing the Best They Can 274
    4. Keep Your Cool 275
    5. Filter What You're Hearing 275
    6. Remember Your ABCs 275
    7. Don't Lose Sleep over Chronically Difficult People 275
    8. We Can't Change Someone's Personality 276
    9. Focus on a Good Outcome 276
    10. Fix It 277
  The General Strategy 277
    Name That Behavior 277
    Step Into Their Moccasins 277
    Pre-Call the Problem 278
    Will Speaking Hurt or Help? 278
  Recognize Anyone? 279
    Complainers 279
    Back-Stabbers and Gossips 280
    Showoffs 281
    Sarcastic People 281
    Unreliable People 281
    Those Who Must Be Obeyed 282
    Bullies 282

27 Win with Complaints   285

  Welcome Complaints 286
    Complaints Are Feedback 286
    Complaints Are Warnings 287
    Complaints Are Opportunities 287

Dealing With a Complaint 287
L-L-A-R-A-A 287
Gather Good Information 288
Give Good Information 288
Make Progress 289
Dealing With Angry Customers 289
Dealing With Habitual Complainers 292

28 Fix It!   **293**

How Much Effort? 293
Approach Problems Positively 294
State the Problem 294
Outline the Problem 295
List Your Options 297
Visualize Your Options 298
Evaluate Your Results 298
Making Decisions 299
Involving Others 299
Don't Let Your Brain Trip You Up! 300
Capitalize on Your Creativity 300
Know Your Stuff 301
Stick With It 301
Brainstorm 301
Work Backward 301
Imagine 301
Sleep On It 302

Appendixes

A Self-Talk as an Indicator of Self-Esteem   **303**

B Body Language Practice   **305**

C Turning Closed Questions into Open Questions 307

D Some Ideas for Frames   **309**

E Some Word Meanings: *Order* and *Strike*   **313**

F **How to Score the Neuro-Linguistic Programming Quiz**   **315**

G **Glossary**   **317**

H **For Further Reading**   **323**

Index   **325**

Foreword

Virginia Satir, the acclaimed psychoanalyst and therapist, said "Once a human being has arrived on this earth, communication is the largest single factor determining what kinds of relationships he makes with others and what happens to him."

I couldn't agree more.

Think how many times you've been hurt by a supposed joke. Think of the number of marriages and parent-child relationships that founder on issues of communication. (That classic cry of the teenager "Its pointless talking to you, you just don't understand!") Think how bewildered ordinary people can be by their dealings with medical professionals ("was that good news or bad?") and how quelled from asking more by a "doctor knows best" attitude.

Think how confusing official letters can be; the ones where you get to the end and still have no idea what you're supposed to do. And the forms with instructions that may as well be in a foreign language, not to mention so-called instruction books!

Turning the tables, are you blameless in communication?

Perhaps you've given someone a performance appraisal and left him or her no wiser about what you *really* meant. Perhaps you've lost a sale because you drowned the customer with too much irrelevant information. Perhaps you've taken a message and not passed on how urgent it was, given instructions and left out key steps, or got a friend lost because of poor directions …

Every day we cause and deal with communication mishaps and disasters. So how do we change? How can we improve our ability to communicate?

Then there's the issue of making your message stand out from the tidal wave of information that is engulfing today's world. How do you make your message compelling? How do you make it memorable? How do you make it persuasive?

This book holds answers to these questions.

This book will teach you how to manage your words, your mind, and your body in order to manage your communications; how to give and gather good information; how to use communication to deal with difficult people, manage conflicts and complaints, and solve problems. You will improve and perfect your communication skills and see the results immediately in every sphere of your life.

Using plenty of humor and the latest research—and sprinkling all with sound common sense—Kris Cole will show you how to improve your life by communicating effectively. Her book is a model of the principles it covers. So take a leaf out of Kris's book and learn to communicate with confidence!

Jane Hemstritch

Managing Partner of Accenture's Communications and High Technology Market Unit

Jane Hemstritch is the Managing Partner of Accenture's Communications and High Technology Market Unit in Australia and New Zealand, a unit employing over 300 professionals and serving clients in the Telecommunications, Electronics and High Tech, and Media and Entertainment sectors.

Jane's areas of specialization include: change strategy, planning and implementation, organization and job design, process facilitation, curriculum planning, training design, and development and training evaluation and support.

Prior to assuming this role Jane developed and led Accenture's Change Management practice in the Asia Pacific; a practice employing some 500 professionals in 11 countries.

Introduction

It's no secret that clear communication is an essential element of success.

Do you ever suspect you could achieve more, have more satisfying friendships and relationships, or get more of what you want? Do you want to be able to write clear and convincing letters and reports, organize your thoughts, and deal with difficult people? Do you want to be able to figure out what people are *really* saying, understand where others are "coming from," or coolly and calmly take charge of tense and tricky communication situations? If so, this book is for you!

We'll skip the fancy theories and fluff and get straight to the heart of clear communication. You'll discover practical ideas to help you communicate clearly in a range of everyday situations. You'll find out how to get inside other peoples' heads, so you can communicate clearly and persuasively, and inside your own head, so you can take charge of your communications to achieve the results you really want. You'll find out how to build satisfying relationships that get things done. You'll learn lots of sensible, easy-to-apply tips and ideas that really work.

This no-nonsense guide to clear communication will give you a whole new perspective on how to make the most of yourself. It will last you a lifetime.

How to Use This Book

You can use this guide as a handy reference. Whenever a particular communication challenge arises, you can dip into it for help. The table of contents will help you locate the specific information you need quickly.

Better still, you can start by reading it cover to cover to get an overall feel for what you can do to improve your communication every day. The six sections build on each other, beginning by explaining the source of all your communications and your results, the dance of communication, and your all-important body language. We then move into how to gather good information, how to give good information, and, that accomplished, how to make sure your communications actually achieve something.

Part 1, "Communication Begins Inside," explains the source of all your communications—your values, beliefs, and thoughts—and how you can manage them for your success. It explains the Success Sequence: how your values, beliefs, and thoughts control your actions—what you say and do—and how you reap the results you sow. You'll learn how to make the Success Sequence work for you and how to apply the secrets of peak performers to achieve the goals you want.

Part 2, "The Dance of Communication," explains the five-part tempo of the communication dance, examines the things that can trip you up, and shows you how to avoid them. You'll find out how to enter another person's world temporarily in order make the communication dance more graceful and harmonious.

Part 3, "Watch That Body Language!" explains how to improve your communication by making a good first impression and ensuring your body sends the signals you intend. You'll find out how to read other people's silent messages and learn to develop a sense of comfortable harmony with people quickly.

In Part 4, "Gathering Good Information," you'll discover how *not* to listen and how to *really* listen, plus you'll get some pointers on how to ask questions to draw people out.

In Part 5, "Giving Good Information," you'll learn how to introduce information so that it will be received, not rejected; how to choose your words for maximum influence; and how to use techniques from the field of neuro-linguistic programming to communicate at deep levels by speaking the other person's "language." We'll also look at some assertion skills you can use every day to make sure you give clear information about what you want and need without stepping on the others person's toes.

Part 5 also explains how to give and receive feedback in a way that helps, not hurts, and how to identify other people's personalities so that you can better understand how they operate and what they need so that you can communicate more successfully with them.

In Part 6, "Making Progress," you'll discover the master principles for dealing with difficult people, resolving conflict, problems, and complaints, and producing decisions that work.

Extras

As you read this book, you'll come across the following boxes, which contain information that'll help you become a crystal clear communicator:

Foot in Mouth

Hopefully these boxes will help you keep your foot *out* of your mouth. They serve to warn you about potential communication hazards and offer tips for what to do instead.

Famous Last Words

Probably not famous, and definitely not the last word on the matter, these boxes define important communication concepts that you'll come across as you read the book.

Silver Tongue

I'm not the first person to think and write about how to communicate clearly. These boxes contain quotes by people from all walks of life about the importance of communication in our lives.

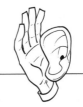

Listen to This

You'll find true stories and other concrete information in these boxes that will help you see the real-world effects of good—and bad—communication.

A Word to the Wise

In these boxes you'll find tips, advice, and helpful hints to help you communicate clearly.

Acknowledgments

I have many people to thank:

Thank you to all the authors of interpersonal skills and self-development books and seminars whose ideas I've borrowed, adapted, or built on.

Thank you, Alan Hyde, for teaching me about fact, fantasy, and folklore; and Graham Andrewartha, for your insights into the basics of communication.

Thank you, Jeff McComas, for the statistical information on the voice, and for teaching me about the importance of our "vocal instrument."

Thank you, Janet Chin, for helping me understand Asian body language. Thank you to the people at Tandanya for your information on Australian Aboriginal people's body language. Thank you, Irene Low and Dr. Lor Wai Tan, for your help with *ting*.

Thank you, Rob Meates, for your insights on feedback and on the "taking responsibility model," and Bob Donaldson, for your insights on "the mirror."

Thank you, Hilary Kahn, for teaching me about "perfect practice."

Thank you, Ilse Jamonts, for unlocking the door to effective communication.

Thank you to the hundreds of people who have attended workshops I've led, for your thought-provoking questions, for offering your ideas, opinions, experience, and insights, and for helping me think things through and reach and test conclusions.

Thank you, Ted Gannan, my first editor at Prentice Hall, for teaching me so much, and all the other fine editors at what is now Pearson Education—you're a terrific crowd to work with! I would particularly like to say thank to Pat Evans for your support on this project and to Nella Soeterboeck for nursing and guiding it to fruition. And finally, a big thank you to Jennifer Moore. I feel privileged to have had you editing this book.

Trademarks

Part 1

Communication Begins Inside

The source of all your communications and how to manage them for your success.

Abraham Lincoln, the sixteenth President of the United States, said, "If I had eight hours to chop down a tree, I'd spend six sharpening my axe." In communication, sharpening your axe is learning about and developing yourself—what's inside. This shines through in all your communications.

Have you ever wondered why you don't see things the same way as your next-door neighbor or best friend? Or how someone who seems so much like you in so many ways can be so different in others? It's because of what's inside.

In this part of the book, you'll discover what makes you tick and why you say and do the things you say and do. You'll see just how important it is to get your mental approach right, not just to communicate well, but to succeed in other areas of your life, too. You'll also learn the secrets of peak performers and how to apply them.

Chapter 1

The Success Sequence

In This Chapter

➤ What makes us all different

➤ What makes you who *you* are

➤ How our beliefs, values, and thoughts shape our destiny

➤ How our subconscious works to protect our psyches

➤ What all this has to do with how we communicate

Do you know that people are about 80 percent water? That's right—you and I are about 80 percent identical! In fact, we're more identical than this. We share more than 99.6 percent of our DNA. If we're so similar, what makes us all so incredibly different?

What truly makes us different is not how tall we are or what color our hair is. It's things we can't see or touch. What makes us different is what's inside: "up here" in our heads and "in here" in our hearts—our values, beliefs, and thoughts.

In this chapter, you'll discover how what's "up here" in your head and "in here" in your heart either works forcefully to help you attain your deepest desires or keeps them a mere distant dream. You'll find out what the Success Sequence and self-fulfilling prophecy are and how they can support or sabotage your goals. You'll learn how to adjust your beliefs and thoughts to shape your destiny.

It's What's Inside That Counts

Many of our values, beliefs, and thoughts are established during childhood by our parents, siblings, friends, and early experiences. As we live our lives, we expand on them and adjust them according to what life, the society we live in, and our culture teaches us. Unless we take the time to examine these deeply ingrained values, beliefs, and thoughts, often we don't even realize we have them!

Silver Tongue

"Reality is merely an illusion, albeit a persistent one."

—Albert Einstein

Our values, beliefs, and thoughts make us who we are. They become our mental models that define us as people. They are the lenses through which we view the world. They color what we see and hear, how we think about it, and what we conclude. They influence the way we communicate with others—what we say and how we say it—and how we perceive what others communicate to us. They silently guide our actions and the way we live our lives and communicate with others.

The truth is, there is no reality! We each construct our own, inside our heads and in our hearts. We communicate to others and filter others' communications to us in ways that reflect and support our values, beliefs, and thoughts.

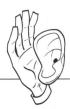

Listen to This

Helga was a child during World War II. Her well off family lost everything. They didn't have many things that we consider essential today and on many occasions didn't even have enough food to eat. During her formative years, Helga was poor.

Today, nearly 80 years old, Helga is a wealthy woman. Although she can buy anything she wants, she doesn't. She saves for "a rainy day." When she goes to a restaurant, she fills her purse with bread rolls and her coat pockets with mints from the checkout counter—even though she can buy all the bread she needs and doesn't eat mints!

Why does Helga behave as if she's poor when she really has plenty of money? She still thinks of herself as poor. This affects how she lives her life and communicates with others. What is Helga really—rich or poor?

We each see truth and reality from our own perspective. Others see it from a different perspective: theirs. Whether it is objectively true or not is irrelevant; we each have our own realities and our own truths, and we behave accordingly.

William James, often called the father of modern psychology, said that "Belief creates the actual fact." We subconsciously behave in ways that ensure our beliefs come true and gather information that supports our beliefs. Whether these beliefs are "right" or "wrong" is really irrelevant.

The Success Sequence

What determines how well we communicate and how successful we are? Luck? The circumstances we are born into? Perhaps these have something to do with it.

More important, though, are our own values, beliefs, and thoughts. These construct our reality and are a direct cause of what we say and do next. They can spell the difference between giving it a go and giving up.

Foot in Mouth

We each construct our own reality. The painfully thin person with anorexia looks in the mirror and sees someone who is hideously overweight. The child who "knows" he can't catch a ball will seldom catch it.

What beliefs might be holding you back?

The Success Sequence.

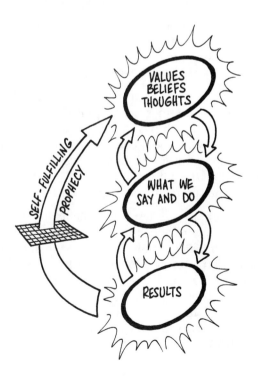

Our values, beliefs, and thoughts are the seeds of everything we do and say. And what we do and say largely determines the results we reap. These results, in turn, reinforce our values, beliefs, and thoughts. This is the Success Sequence.

Silver Tongue

"Man often becomes what he believes himself to be. If I keep on saying to myself that I cannot do a certain thing, it is possible that I may end by really becoming incapable of doing it. On the contrary, if I have the belief that I can do it, I shall surely acquire the capacity to do it even if I may not have it at the beginning."

—Mahatma Gandhi

Epictetus, the Roman philosopher, is credited with describing the Success Sequence like this: "Our life is what our thoughts make it." The best athletes demonstrate an understanding of this principal when they tell us that limits are in our heads not in our arms or muscles. In other words, what we believe leads to our actions, and our actions determine the results we get. It's a self-fulfilling prophecy: If we believe we can do something, we will be more likely to act in such a way that we will get the results we want. Similarly, if we believe we can't do something, we will tend to act in such a way we aren't able to achieve our goals.

Our values, beliefs, and thoughts combine to guide our actions and communications and, as the Success Sequence shows us, to determine the results we get.

The Self-Fulfilling Prophecy

Our values, beliefs, and thoughts shape what we say and do, determining the results we get. These results, in turn, confirm our values, beliefs, and thoughts. They become *self-fulfilling prophecies*.

Have you ever noticed that we see what we expect to see? This is another form of self-fulfilling prophecy. It's easy to see things that confirm what we already "know." What about conflicting information? Easy. We ignore it! If it's so insistent we can't ignore it, we twist it a bit, so it fits in with our beliefs. This preserves our psyches from *cognitive dissonance*.

Famous Last Words

A **self-fulfilling prophecy** is a belief that continually reinforces and strengthens itself. For example, if you expect a person to be friendly, you will treat her differently than if you expect her to be unfriendly. The way you treat her influences how she responds to you. This will confirm and strengthen your initial belief.

The brain, in its quest for predictability and conformity, will ignore or bend any information that contradicts our beliefs. For example, a woman who firmly believes that other people don't like her will not just overlook our efforts to be friendly, her brain won't even register them. This is an unconscious and rapid process. "Mustn't let that self-image of being disliked crumble," says her *subconscious*. "Must make sure that self-talk comes true!"

Our subconscious contains thoughts and information just below the threshold of our awareness. Unlike our conscious mind, which only works when we're awake and can deal with only one or two things at a time, our subconscious works all the time, collecting and processing information. It can deal with an infinite number of things simultaneously. Our subconscious doesn't only direct our communications and behavior; it also acts as a filter, letting in information that supports our beliefs and keeping out information that doesn't.

This means we go through life seeing what confirms our mental models and ignoring what contradicts them. If we can't ignore incompatible information, we will reinterpret it so that it fits in with our mental models. This becomes a loop—a self-fulfilling prophecy. The more we act on our beliefs, the more evidence we produce to validate them.

Famous Last Words

Cognitive dissonance is the term psychologists use to describe the feelings of acute discomfort and confusion we experience when faced with information that challenges our deeply held beliefs. We are programmed to protect ourselves by ignoring it. If we can't ignore it, we mold it to mesh with what we already believe.

There is nothing sinister in this. It's completely natural. Our subconscious works hard to avoid cognitive dissonance by sifting incoming information to select things that support our beliefs. It isn't surprising, then, that miscommunications, conflicts, and misunderstanding can so easily occur.

This is why, if you want to improve your communication and your destiny, it's important to know what your values, beliefs, and thoughts are.

Surprisingly, many people don't!

They act as if what is "true" for them is true for everyone. Yet this can't be so since we each have different experiences and backgrounds, different values, beliefs, and thoughts.

Many of our values, beliefs, and thoughts are "hidden" from us in our subconscious. Nevertheless, they control our communications and our actions and, through them, the results we achieve. It stands to reason, then, that the more we understand about ourselves, the more we will be able to take conscious control of the way we communicate with others and respond to events, people, and situations.

Famous Last Words

Values are deeply and strongly held beliefs and principles about what is right and wrong, good and bad, important and unimportant, what should and shouldn't be.

Values

What's important to you? It all depends on your *values*.

Some people value living a life filled with people, fun, and excitement—they'll party any time! Others value ideas, being alone, and learning new things—they prefer to read a good book. Yet others value helping people and prefer to use their time lending a hand to those who need it.

What do you value? Check off the things that are important to you from the following list. Of those you've selected, circle the 10 most important to you. Then whittle these down to your five core values. These values guide your behavior.

What Do You Value?

- Acceptance
- Winning
- Being polite
- Physical fitness
- Justice
- Being in control
- Feeling important
- Honesty
- Being respected
- Having authority
- Taking risks
- Peace
- Self-discipline
- Imagination
- Logic
- Health
- Being lucky
- Integrity
- Quality
- Tenacity
- Affection
- Reliability
- Being liked
- Looking good
- Helping others
- Being knowledgeable
- Learning new skills
- Working hard
- Being neat and tidy
- Being alone
- Being on time
- Conserving resources

- Participating
- Being logical
- Love
- Wisdom
- Communication
- Success
- Competition
- Friendship
- Humor
- Beauty
- Consideration
- Creativity
- Participating
- Decisiveness
- Security
- Prosperity
- Loyalty
- Having fun
- Being responsible
- Being generous
- Following tradition
- Service
- Doing my duty
- Being committed
- Feeling fulfilled
- Humility
- Talent
- Adaptability
- Compassion
- Contribution
- Adventure
- Having courage

- Wealth
- Optimism
- Spontaneity
- Innocence
- Being articulate
- Giving and receiving affection
- Behaving in a professional manner
- Being responsible for others
- Having lots of friends
- Peaceful relationship with others
- Being honest
- Following a religion
- Being relaxed and informal
- Freedom of action
- Cooperating with others
- Standing up for my beliefs
- Being correct and formal
- Being enterprising
- Behaving with dignity
- Excellence
- Truth
- Orderliness
- Taking the initiative
- Perfection
- Efficiency
- Intelligence
- Tolerance
- Being practical

Although values are neither right nor wrong, most of us behave as if they are! In fact, it's often difficult to understand or accept where a person with very different values to our own is "coming from." This is why differences in values often lead to problems in communication and conflicts between people.

Our Thoughts

Our brain is the most complex object scientists have yet to find in the universe, far more advanced than the most powerful computer we could possibly build. The average person's brain has about 100 billion *neurons*, or cells. They can connect with countless others; in fact, up to 1,000 trillion connections and probably more are possible. This is greater than the known number of atoms in the universe. It means we can think a limitless number of thoughts!

When we think, speak, or take any action, electrical and chemical connections between specific neurons are established. These connections are called *neural pathways*. The more often we think a thought the more likely we are to think it again because we establish, and then strengthen, these neural pathways.

Once a neural pathway is established, whether as a value, a belief, or paradigm, it becomes difficult (but not impossible) to change (see Chapter 2, "Where It All Begins," for more on paradigms). Do yourself a favor: Do a check-up from the neck-up! Make sure your thoughts support you if you want to achieve positive results and crystal clear communication.

A Word to the Wise

Know which values are important to you and to others close to you. Recognize the right of other people to hold the values they hold. Agreeing to disagree can save us a lot of irritation and prevent a lot of arguments.

Our Thoughts Lead to Actions Lead to Results

Someone once said that there are only two things we have to do: We have to die, and we have to live until we die. We make up all the rest.

When you have a chore to do that you dislike— say, washing the dishes—how do you approach it? Do you say to yourself, "Yuck, I *have to* do the dishes"? Or do you say, "I *want to* do these dishes now so they're out of the way"?

Whether we choose to say *want to* or *have to* makes a big difference in the way we approach a task. When we *have to* do something, we usually do it reluctantly and half-heartedly. And what sort of results does this approach lead to?

Silver Tongue

"Those neurons that fire together wire together. Every thought we have makes new connections as well as reconstructs old ones. We can change our brain function ourselves and the patterns of our behavior."

—Evian Gordon, brain scientist

When we approach a task because we *want to* do it, it's with energy and enthusiasm. We do it whole-heartedly. The results reflect that, too.

Silver Tongue

"The highest possible stage in human culture is when we recognize that we ought to control our thoughts."

—Charles Darwin

Silver Tongue

"There is nothing so easy but that it becomes difficult when you do it reluctantly."

—Roman comic dramatist Terence

We may never reach the point where we enjoy washing the dishes; but we can feel satisfied once they're done and, because of this, we can want to wash the dishes. Or we can enjoy how tidy the kitchen looks and want to do the dishes for that reason. Or we might want to do the dishes so we can enjoy the rest of the day without worrying about them. Select a reason that works for you!

Are We Stuck with Our Beliefs and Thoughts?

Twentieth-century author and journalist Walter Lippmann said, "We are all captives of the pictures in our head—our belief that the world we have experienced is the world that really exists." How captive are we, really?

Viktor Frankl, the Austrian neurologist, psychiatrist, and Holocaust survivor, said, "Our greatest freedom is the freedom to choose our attitudes."

How can we do this? Here's what Confucius had to say:

By three methods we learn wisdom: The first is by reflection, which is noblest. The second is by imitation, which is easiest. The third is by experience, which is bitterest.

We can examine our thoughts and beliefs. Upon reflection, are our beliefs realistic or lacking in evidence? Are they sensible or silly?

Sometimes, beliefs are destructive and serve no useful purpose and we need to replace them with beliefs that are useful and in our own best interests.

We examine Confucius's first method for learning wisdom—reflection—more in the next chapter, and his second and third methods—imitation and experience—in Chapter 3, "We Reap What We Sow," and Chapter 4, "Focus for Success," respectively.

The Least You Need to Know

➤ Over 99 percent of our DNA is the same as everyone else's. Our beliefs, values, and thoughts make us different from one another.

➤ Our beliefs, values, and thoughts guide our actions and our communications.

➤ Our personal reality is shaped by our thoughts, beliefs, and actions, which also filter how we perceive and respond to "our world."

➤ Our subconscious works to preserve our deeply held beliefs and values even when the facts contradict them.

➤ Our beliefs, values, and thoughts become a self-fulfilling prophecy because our subconscious continually finds ways to verify them.

➤ In guiding our actions and communications, our beliefs, values, and thoughts also determine our success and our destiny.

Chapter 2

Where It All Begins: Your Beliefs

In This Chapter

➤ Where our values and beliefs come from

➤ How our beliefs about ourselves direct our behavior

➤ How our beliefs about others affect their behavior and communications

➤ How to think your way into the results you want

Do your thoughts, values, and beliefs support you, or do they sabotage you?

We've seen how communication begins on the inside, with our thoughts, values, and beliefs. The Success Sequence illustrates how they direct our communications and guide our actions, and in this way, influence how successful we are in reaching our goals.

To smooth our path in life and clear the way for successful communication, we need to understand our beliefs, values, and thoughts, where they came from, and how we can alter them to improve our fortunes.

In this chapter, you'll find out more about how what's inside the top box of the Success Sequence—what's in your head and your heart—can help you succeed in your communications and your life. You'll learn how to think your way to maximum personal and communication success.

Taking control of our values, beliefs, and thoughts is the first step in the Success Sequence.

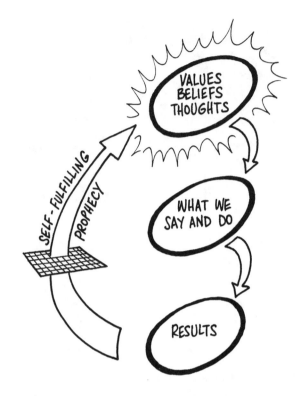

Our Beliefs Guide Our Actions and Our Communications

Our beliefs guide our actions and communications. That makes sense—why would we do something that goes against our beliefs?

Silver Tongue

"Man is made by his beliefs. As he believes, so he is."

—Bhagavad Gita

Beliefs About Ourselves

Friedrich von Schiller, the eighteenth-century German dramatist and poet, said, "Every man stamps his value on himself. Man is made great or small by his own will." There is no doubt that the beliefs we hold about ourselves are central to the way we communicate.

What messages about yourself did you grow up with? What messages are you raising your kids with?

Stupid!	Clever!
Clumsy!	Sweet!
Naughty!	Nice!

When people we care about continually send us messages, they have a way of "sticking" and coming true. Whether these messages are nice or nasty, true or false, our subconscious absorbs them and guides us to behave as if they were true. This is another form of the *self-fulfilling prophecy*.

It's as if we say to ourselves, "Oh, so this how I am! Okay, this is how I'll be!" Our beliefs about ourselves are the source of our sense of *self-esteem* and become part of our self-image.

Self-Esteem

How do you think of yourself? Do you like yourself? Do you think you're a valuable, important person? Do you believe you deserve the best? How comfortable are you with who you are? This is your *self-esteem*.

Our level of self-esteem reflects our feelings of self-respect and self-worth, the value we place on ourselves as people, and the expectations we have of ourselves and for ourselves.

People with high self-esteem feel comfortable and confident. They are able to communicate clearly with others. People with low self-esteem feel unworthy and uncomfortable. They lack the self-confidence to say what's on their mind. Their communications are fuzzy.

Famous Last Words

Our **self-esteem** is our feelings of respect and self-worth. It's how we value ourselves.

To get a sense of your level of self-esteem, place a check mark on the scale on the quiz below which best describes you. For example, if you are more likely to act with confidence most of the time, but not all of the time, then you might place an *x* under the 4 on the line below. But if you act with little confidence more often than not, you'd put an *x* under the 2.

How High Is Your Self-Esteem?

Do you	5 4 3 2 1	
Act with confidence	⊢———————⊣	Act with little confidence
Make your own decisions?	⊢———————⊣	Let others make them for you?
Look for answers to problems?	⊢———————⊣	Let problems defeat you?
Take risks?	⊢———————⊣	Play it safe?
Take action?	⊢———————⊣	Give up?
Control your moods and thoughts yourself?	⊢———————⊣	Let someone else's bad mood affect your good mood?

Do you	5 4 3 2 1	
Feel exhilarated when you work hard?	|—————|	Feel exhausted, as if you haven't accomplished any-thing, when you work hard?
Accept responsibility?	|—————|	Make excuses, find fault, lay blame.
Measure yourself against your own standards?	|—————|	Measure yourself against other's standards?
Speak up, set limits, voice your thoughts honestly?	|—————|	Swallow your opinions, your thoughts, your wishes?
Stand straight and look people in the eye?	|—————|	Slouch, with downcast eyes, looking sideways at people?
Respond flexibly to changing circumstances?	|—————|	Hold on to what you've always done and thought because it's easy and comfortable.
Act with integrity?	|—————|	Do whatever is expedient?
Feel self-confident and self-assured?	|—————|	Feel shy, nervous, and awkward?

Silver Tongue

"Achieving starts with believing."
—Norman Vincent Peale

If most of your check marks are fours and fives, this indicates you have a high level of self-esteem. If they're mostly ones and twos, it indicates you need to lift your level of self-esteem.

Having low self-esteem is like driving through life with your hand brake on, even when you're driving uphill!

The view we hold of ourselves, whether positive, nega-tive, or indifferent, is our constant companion. It guides our thoughts, our actions, and our communica-tions. It plays a central role in our success—in our communications and in our lives.

Are you concerned that if you have high self-esteem you'll seem arrogant?

High Self-Esteem	Arrogance
Self-aware	Self-absorbed
Self-confident	Self-conscious
Self-assured	Self-centered

Arrogant people think only of themselves. People with high self-esteem have a high regard for others, not just themselves. They understand the saying: "We each have something to learn; we each have something to teach." If you balance self-respect with respect for others, you needn't worry that people will find you arrogant.

Here are some ideas for giving yourself a self-esteem boost!

➤ Instead of blaming others, take responsibility for what you say and do, for achieving your goals, and for enjoying your life.

➤ Instead of focusing on your faults, think positive thoughts that build your confidence and make you feel good, competent, and self-sufficient.

➤ Instead of spending time with negative people, or people who constantly criticize you or make you feel bad about yourself, associate with positive people who have high self-esteem and who make you feel good about yourself.

➤ Instead of wasting time, participate in activities you enjoy.

➤ Instead of being critical of yourself and others, look for something likeable in yourself and in everyone you know and meet.

➤ Instead of trying to change others, focus on being the person you want to be.

➤ Instead of living in the future or the past, live in the present.

➤ Instead of saying "I can't do this" or "I don't know anything about this," read, attend seminars, learn from others—do whatever you can to develop your talents and skills.

A Word to the Wise

The most important thought you can ever hold is: "I matter."

➤ Instead of focusing on your failures, acknowledge and celebrate your achievements and successes.

➤ Instead of over-eating, over-drinking, or under-exercising, take care of yourself—you deserve it!

➤ Instead of saying "Oh, it's nothing, really," and dismissing compliments, accept them. Say "Thank you!" and enjoy praise without embarrassment.

Famous Last Words

Our **self-image** is how we see ourselves; the view we hold of ourselves that describes us and defines us. What's inside the person *you* see in *your* mirror?

Self-Image

Our *self-image* flows from our self-esteem. It is how we see ourselves: as competent or helpless, shy or friendly, gentle or severe, kind or cruel, smart or dumb, dependable or haphazard.

With high self-esteem and a strong self-image, our options multiply. We have more choices in any situation.

Our self-image and self-esteem are apparent to others even before we speak—it's in the way we dress, the way we carry ourselves, the way we make eye contact, the way we sit. This is how self-esteem and self-image set up the communication rhythm before the dance of communication even begins.

Self-Talk

Do you ever talk to yourself? Don't worry if you do.

Psychologists estimate that we talk to ourselves 60,000 times a day. This *self-talk*, the silent messages we continually give ourselves, directly reflects our self-esteem and self-image and strongly influences our day-to-day behavior.

It either builds us up or belittles us. It supports us or sabotages us. It can give us the "all clear" to do a great job (as expected) or instruct us to "pull in the reins" so that our efforts fall short (as expected).

Famous Last Words

Self-talk is the often unconscious messages we give ourselves about ourselves that shape our behavior.

Silver Tongue

Watch your thoughts; they become words.

Watch your words; they become actions.

Watch your actions; they become habits.

Watch your habits; they become character.

Watch your character; it becomes your destiny.

—Frank Outlaw

Try this little exercise. Write down your answers.

What do you say to yourself

➤ when you've just made a mistake in front of others?

➤ when you're doing something for the first time and finding it difficult?

➤ when you've forgotten to do something you promised to do?

➤ when you join a group of people you've never met before?

➤ when the boss calls you in and you don't know why?

➤ when you trip walking down the road?

➤ when you're running late for an important appointment?

➤ when you can't balance your check book?

➤ when you've done something particularly well?

What you've just written down will give you an idea of the sort of self-talk you usually use (see Appendix A, "Self-Talk as an Indicator of Self-Esteem," for more on self-talk and self-esteem).

A good way to assess your level of self-esteem is to listen to your self-talk. What are you telling yourself? Are you sending yourself downbeat, destructive, or disapproving messages? Or are you sending yourself energizing, encouraging, and enlivening messages?

The loudest voice you'll ever hear is your own.

We know from the self-fulfilling prophecy that our self-talk comes true. Richard Bach, author *of Jonathan Livingston Seagull,* put it this way: "Argue for your limitations and sure enough, they're yours."

Henry Ford, founder of the Ford Motor Company, said it like this:

> "Whether you think you can or think you can't—you're right."

Whether you're right or whether you're wrong is irrelevant. You will always believe your self-talk and obey it. Why are our self-image and self-talk so powerful? Because whether we know it or not, we behave according to our self-image and follow the instructions our self-talk gives us. Build your self-esteem (and improve your results) with positive self-talk.

Self-talk is a two-way street. It reflects our level of self-esteem, and we can use it to change our self-esteem. Listen to your self-talk and stop negative instructions to yourself when you hear them. Replace them with something positive. You have to think positively in order to act positively in order to achieve positive results.

Foot in Mouth

Watch your language when you talk to yourself! The part of us that makes sure we behave according to our values and beliefs and obeys our self-talk is our creative subconscious. It has a way of ignoring negatives, so program it with what you *do* want, not what you *don't* want!

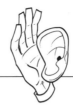

Listen to This

Karl Wallenda, the famous high-wire performer, fell to his death in 1978 while walking the tightrope in Puerto Rico. Karl's wife believed he was the victim of negative self-talk and negative thinking. All he thought about for three months prior to the accident was falling. "It was the first time he'd ever thought about that and it seemed to me he put all his energies into not falling rather than into walking the tightrope."

In their book, *Leaders: Strategies for Taking Charge*, Warren Bennis and Burt Nanus call this the "Wallenda Factor."

If you want to stay calm in difficult situations, program yourself through your self-talk to stay calm and not get nervous. When you want to remember to do something, use your self-talk to remember not to forget.

Our creative subconscious follows instructions. What instructions are you giving yours?

Beliefs About Others

Just as our beliefs about ourselves affect our approach to life, our communications, and our success, so do our beliefs about others.

Silver Tongue

"Treat people as if they were what they ought to be and you help them to become what they are capable of being."

—Johann Wolfgang von Goethe

In 1847, the 12-year-old son of a handloom weaver emigrated from Scotland to the United States. He built a steel empire employing thousands of people and became one of the wealthiest and most influential people in America. His name was Andrew Carnegie. He was known for his ability to identify and develop people's talents. How did he do it? This is what he said:

Men are developed the same way gold is mined. Several tons of dirt must be moved to get one ounce of gold. But one doesn't go into the mine looking for the dirt. One goes in looking for the gold.

If we look for the gold in those around us, we will find it. Whose gold do you mine and polish?

Chicken or Egg?

In Aesop's Fables there is a story about a philosopher sitting outside his home on a hill overlooking Athens. He is approached by a traveler. "Excuse me," said the traveler, "I'm just moving to Athens and I wondered if you could tell me what the people here are like."

"Where are you from?" asked the philosopher. "I'm from Sardis," said the traveler, "and I don't mind saying, I'm glad to be leaving the place. The people of Sardis are unfriendly, untrustworthy, and unhelpful. I'm really hoping I'll find a better sort of person here in Athens."

"Well, my friend," said the philosopher, "I'm sorry to report that you will find the people of Athens much the same as the people of Sardis." Disappointed, the traveler went on his way.

Later in the day, another traveler approached the philosopher and asked the same question, saying, "I'm just moving here from Sardis and if the people of Athens are even half as wonderful as the people there, I'll be a happy man. In Sardis, everyone is as friendly, honest, and helpful as the day is long."

"My friend, I'm happy to report that you'll find the people of Athens much the same as the people of Sardis," said the philosopher. In good spirits, the second traveler went on his way.

Silver Tongue

"I don't like that man. I'm going to have to get to know him better."

—Abraham Lincoln

Silver Tongue

"The world is a looking glass and gives back to every man the reflection of his own face."

—William Thackeray

The philosopher in the fable was illustrating a simple principle related to the self-fulfilling prophecy and our beliefs about others: We see in others whatever we expect to see (whether it's there or not!).

Which comes first—the chicken or the egg? Are people unfriendly to the first traveler from Sardis, causing him to see people as unfriendly? Or does he expect them to be unfriendly and treat them as if they will be unfriendly, which makes it more likely they will act this way toward him? If they are unfriendly toward the first traveler, why would they be friendly toward the second? How could the people of Athens act one way to one traveler and a different way to the other?

What is your attitude to others? How do you treat them? Do you generate the responses you expect? Which of the travelers from Sardis is most like you?

Our Psychic Mirror

Sometimes, we see ourselves reflected in the world around us. Psychologists call this *projection*.

Famous Last Words

Projection occurs when, rather than admit we have a characteristic or quality, we unconsciously cast it onto someone else.

Projection can manifest itself in three different ways. The first way is when we see in other people one of our own characteristics that we don't realize we have.

Have you ever known someone who says or does something that really irritates or even angers you? Or have you ever felt strongly drawn to a person because of an admirable quality you saw in them?

The stronger the feeling, the greater the chance a mirror is operating—we're seeing an *unrecognized characteristic in ourselves* and, rather than claim it as ours, we attach it to someone else.

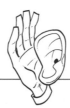

Listen to This

At the age of 50, Mike resented being unappreciated and undervalued by colleagues and friends. It drove him wild!

One day he recalled how his father had always favored his younger brother, continually praising his cleverness (Mike felt he was more clever) and his athletic abilities (Mike felt he was more athletic). The attention his younger brother received from their father made Mike feel left out and unloved. These feelings became a part of his self-image.

As an adult, whenever he felt someone was being appreciated more than he was or someone wasn't recognizing how clever and able he was, he felt very hurt. This happened so often that his communications with those around him became quite destructive.

Once he recognized the link, the "here we go again!" feelings of not being appreciated by others just as his father hadn't appreciated him, he was able to deal more effectively with those he felt were not recognizing or appreciating his talents. He was also able to see that most people did appreciate him and he was just being super-sensitive.

➤ "She's so selfish!" can mean: "I'm really self-ish but I don't want to admit it."

➤ "They are such friendly, warm people" can mean: "I'm friendly and warm, too, but I don't want to boast, even to myself."

➤ "You need to watch people carefully because they'll cheat given half a chance" can mean: "I cheat whenever I have a chance."

Silver Tongue

"None of us sees the world as it is. We see the world as we are."

—The Talmud

Are there times when you feel infuriated, more so than circumstances would seem called for? To paraphrase the English Lord Julian of Norwich: "If there is something we criticize in another, we should first examine it and see whether it would be best criticized in ourselves."

Listen to This

When Beth was a child, whenever she tried to explain something, her father would cut her off with: "I'll have no excuses from you, young lady!" Beth felt this was very unfair since she sometimes had a very good reason for doing what she did or a good explanation why something happened.

As an adult, whenever one of her friends or colleagues tried to explain something that had gone wrong, she felt herself feeling unspeakably angry and heard herself cutting off their explanations, often quite rudely.

When she recognized the connection, she was able to temper her responses and deal more effectively with people when a problem arose.

The second way that projection can manifest itself in our lives is in *situations* that we find ourselves in. Those situations, just like other people, can be mirrors to us. Do you ever find yourself in a recurring situation that makes you very uncomfortable or infuriates you?

The third kind of projection involves seeing our own *unrecognized desires in other people*. Sometimes when we become very angry with someone for doing something, a look in our psychic mirror might tell us that we would really like to do the same, but we don't let ourselves. So when someone else does it, it drives us wild with anger!

We can think of mirrors as irrational triggers. These people and situations often tell us a lot about ourselves. They don't affect others nearly as much as they affect us!

If you don't take the time to recognize your irrational triggers, the things that make you "see red," they can surface unexpectedly and spoil your communications and relationships with others.

Beliefs About the World

As we go through life, we organize our experiences and beliefs about others, ourselves, and the world into *paradigms*, or world views, which are unique for each of us. Like our values, they are often buried deep in our subconscious.

These deeply held mind-sets are the lenses through which we see, interpret, and experience our world. They guide our thoughts, our attitudes, our actions, and, ultimately, how successful we are in our communications and our lives.

You'll remember from science class that we once thought the world was flat—that was our paradigm about the world at the time. But we've come to see that the paradigm is incorrect. Paradigms can be true once and then not true, or never true at all. Either way, they can cause trouble and limit us and hold us back if we hang on to them or just accept them without question.

Our paradigms can be up-to-date and helpful. Or they can be self-limiting, embarrassing, and prevent progress. Whichever they are, we assume they represent truth and reality and seldom question them.

Famous Last Words

Paradigms are our beliefs about the world and how it operates. These mind-sets and mental models guide our behavior and are generally unconscious and unquestioned.

Here are some paradigm prisons:

➤ "I think I may say without contradiction that, when the Paris Exhibition closes, electric light will close with it and no more will be heard of it."—Professor Erasmus Wilson, Oxford University

➤ "Louis Pasteur's theory of germs is ridiculous fiction."—Pierre Pachet, Professor of Physiology at Toulouse, 1872

➤ "This 'telephone'… device is inherently of no value to us."—Western Union internal memo, 1876

➤ "Heavier than air flying machines are impossible." —Lord Kelvin, President of the Royal Society, 1895

➤ "Airplanes are interesting toys but of no military value."—Marechal Ferdinand Foch, Professor of Strategy, École supérieure de Guerre

➤ "Everything that can be invented has been invented." —Charles H. Duell, Commissioner, U.S. Office of Patents, 1899

➤ "Sensible and responsible women do not want to vote."—Grover Cleveland, U.S. President

➤ "There is no likelihood that man can ever tap the power of the atom."—Robert Miliham, Nobel Prize in Physics, 1923

➤ "The wireless music box has no imaginable commercial value. Who would pay for messages sent to nobody in particular?"—David Sarnoff's associates, responding to his urgings for investment in the radio in the 1920s

➤ "Who the hell wants to hear actors talk?"—Harry M. Warner, Warner Brothers, 1927

➤ "I think there is a world market for maybe five computers."—Thomas Watson Sr., Chairman of IBM, 1943

➤ "The concept is interesting and well formed but, to earn better than a C grade, the idea must be feasible." —Yale University Management Professor to student Fred Smith's proposal for a reliable overnight delivery service. Smith went on to found Federal Express.

➤ "There is no reason anyone would want a computer in their home."—Ken Olson, president, chair, and founder of Digital Equipment Corporation, 1977

➤ "640K ought to be enough for anybody."—Bill Gates, computer software tycoon, 1981

What lenses color your world?

The Least You Need to Know

➤ Listen to your self-talk and make sure it lifts you up, not pulls you down.

➤ When you talk to yourself, mind your tongue—your self-talk can come true.

➤ We usually generate the responses in others we expect, so expect the best.

➤ Find ways to "polish people's gold."

➤ We can alter our lives by altering our attitudes.

Chapter 3

We Reap What We Sow

In This Chapter

➤ How your body language can make you happy or sad

➤ How your body language can lift or lower your self-esteem

➤ How not to let other people or events dictate your mood, your behavior, or your communications

➤ Four ways to use your behavior to get better results

You'll recall from Chapter 1, "The Success Sequence," that the second of Confucius's ways to learn wisdom is through our behavior. This is also the second way to make sure we harvest the result we want, in all the facets of our life, including our communications.

Our behavior leads to our results and influences our attitudes. In this way, the three elements of the Success Sequence are closely linked and dependent on each other.

Our behavior is important for a third reason: It announces who we *really* are. Good intentions alone aren't enough—we need to follow through.

In this chapter, we explore your behavior, which is the second part of the Success Sequence. You'll learn how to take charge of what you say and do for better results all around.

Taking charge of what you say and do is the second step of the Success Sequence.

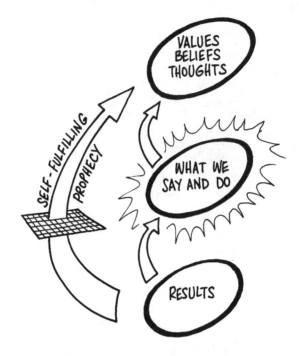

Eleanor Roosevelt pointed out that our philosophy is not best expressed in words; it is expressed in the choices we make. "In the long run," she said, "we shape our lives and we shape ourselves. The process never ends until the day we die. And the choices we make are ultimately our responsibility."

Silver Tongue

"One's philosophy is not best expressed in words; it is expressed in the choices one makes. In the long run, we shape our lives and we shape ourselves. The process never ends until the day we die. And the choices we make are ultimately our responsibility."

—Eleanor Roosevelt

There is no doubt that what we say and do is important, and we have choices in what we say and do. The choices we make generate results, which create our destiny.

Body Language

Our body language links our thoughts with our results in two important ways: through our mood and our self-esteem.

The Body Language–Mood Link

How do you sit when you're miserable? When you're excited? When you're absolutely fascinated by what someone is telling you?

It's no secret that our body language reflects how we're feeling and, often, what we're thinking.

Body–Mind Experiment

If you don't think your body language affects your mood, try the following experiment.

First, hang your head and slouch. That's right—do all the things you're not supposed to do! Cave your chest in, look down at the floor, and say in a soft, sad voice: "I'm so happy. This is the best day of my life."

How do you feel? If you went through the rest of the day with this body language, it's easy to predict it wouldn't be a good one!

Now stand or sit straight and tall. Head up, stomach in, chest out. Look up and say in a loud, clear, confident voice: "I'm so miserable. I hate what I'm doing and I hate where I am!"

How do you feel now?

Most people's feelings and actions follow their body language, not their words. If you kept the happy, confident body language for the rest of the day, you'd probably love the results!

Our body language *reflects* how we feel. It also *affects* how we feel. Body language is a two-way street.

A Word to the Wise

The mind–body connection is very powerful. If you're feeling a bit low, change your body language. Smile! Hold your head up and stand or sit straight and tall. This will improve the way you feel and act, so you'll get better results.

Listen to This

William Fry Jr., M.D., has researched the power of humor for 30 years. He says laughter is a total body experience, an "internal massage." It involves all our body's systems, including muscles, nerves, brain, and digestion. After being stimulated and exercised by laughter, the body goes into deep relaxation.

Like jogging, laughter is good aerobic exercise. It aerates the lungs, relaxes the muscles, nerves and heart, expands breathing and circulation, and enhances oxygen intake and expenditure.

Around 100 to 200 laughs, he says, equals 10 minutes rowing or jogging.

Here's another chicken or egg puzzle: When we feel happy, we smile. When we smile, we feel happy because smiling triggers our body to release endorphins. These are so-called "feel good" chemicals that flow through our bodies and make us feel happy. So we smile.

Which came first?

Laughing releases even more endorphins than smiling! It also releases enkephalins, which are natural pain suppressors. Aim to have a good laugh at least once a day. You'll get better results!

The Body Language–Self-Esteem Link

Our body language doesn't just affect and reflect our mood. It also affects and reflects our level of self-esteem.

Foot in Mouth

Don't sabotage your mood, your results, or your destiny with sad, weak, uncertain, or self-deprecating body language.

Have you ever noticed that people with low self-esteem often try to make themselves appear smaller, as if they don't believe they deserve to take up their full space? They slouch, they let their chest cave in, they drop their head. Their body language says, "I'm not very confident and I don't like myself much." Their actions reflect this, too. So do the results they get.

Too bad. Standing up straight and tall and taking up their own space would make a big difference.

High self-esteem does more than just lead to attractive body language and constructive actions. It also helps us choose our actions and our communications.

Locus of Control, or Pulling Your Own Strings

"He makes me mad" is a phrase we have all heard. Is it possible that someone else can force us to be angry? Must we respond to others as they treat us? Or do we have more say in the matter?

Eleanor Roosevelt pointed out that no one can make us feel inferior without our consent. No one can make us feel angry without our consent either! No one can make us feel *anything* without our consent.

To some people, it doesn't matter whether it's rainy or sunny—they carry their own weather with them. It's more than just "looking on the bright side" or having a "positive mental attitude." It's about *locus of control:*

Famous Last Words

No, it isn't a grasshopper! **Locus of control** is about where our behavior is directed from—inside ourselves, or outside, by other people or events.

who "pulls our strings." We can control our own thoughts and what we say and do, or we can let someone else or outside events control them.

People who carry their own weather with them don't need sunshine to be happy. They don't need to receive excellent service to be in a good mood, and poor service doesn't put them in a bad mood. Their locus of control is internal. *They* take charge of their feelings; *they* decide what they'll say and do.

Others give away their locus of control; they allow *other people* to control their behavior and determine whether they'll be happy or sad, pleasant or unpleasant, respectful or rude. These people have given up their freedom of choice. Their locus of control is external.

The good news is we can choose what we reap by choosing what we sow.

If someone is rude to us, we have choices. Two choices—to be rude in return, or to be polite. In any communication we have options and each has predictable results because we reap what we sow.

When we're in control, we can choose to be polite to someone who is rude to us. When we're not in control—if we're "rude right back" or dissolve into a puddle of tears—the other person is in control. We've allowed the rude person to choose our response for us.

People with high self-esteem have an internal locus of control. They decide what they say and do.

People with low self-esteem have an external locus of control. They let others choose their behavior. Others can pull our strings only if we let them.

If you want to retain control and choose the way you act and communicate, keep your locus of control internal. This means you will never have to say, "He makes me mad." You can choose not to allow someone to anger you but to notice that his behavior is annoying and carry on with your day, unaffected. This is the more powerful position from which you can retain control over many of the communication situations, especially the difficult ones, in which you find yourself.

Beliefs, body language, high self-esteem, and an internal locus of control are important, but they won't bring results by themselves.

A Word to the Wise

Carry your weather with you. Choose your communications and your actions. You'll feel better about yourself and get better results.

Silver Tongue

"I, not events, have the power to make me happy or unhappy today. I can choose which it shall be. Yesterday is dead, tomorrow hasn't arrived yet. I have just one day, today, and I'm going to be happy in it."

—Groucho Marx

Don't Just Stand There ... Do Something!

To win the lottery, achieve a goal, or make a friend, we need to take some positive action. Or nothing will happen.

Will any action do? Of course not! Aimless action will get us where we want to be only by sheer coincidence! If we want to achieve something specific, we need a specific goal so that we can take specific action. As the saying goes, "If you don't care where you're going, any road will get you there."

Silver Tongue

"It's better to light a small candle than curse the darkness."

—Confucius

To generate the results we're after, we need a clear goal. And it might as well be a worthwhile and challenging one. Why? Because we get what we focus on. So set your sights high! (We'll look at how to set clear goals in the next chapter.)

Listen to This

Have you heard the one about the woman who had five young children to bring up on her own? She loved her children very much and was the best mother she knew how to be—helping them with their homework, cooking healthy meals for them, and working at two jobs so she could provide for them. Each night she prayed that she would win the lottery so that she could buy her children all the little extras she would love to give them but couldn't afford.

Before she knew it, her children were grown. They'd all left home and she was alone. Reflecting on how much she had sacrificed for the sake of her family, she suddenly felt sad and a little angry. That night when she prayed she said, "God, I've done my best. I've been a good mother and a God-fearing woman. Why haven't you helped me out? Why haven't you let me win the lottery just once? Even a small win? After all, I've done my bit!"

Suddenly, the house shook. Thunder crashed and lightning flashed. A deep voice said, "The least you could have done was buy a lottery ticket!"

Going Out on a Limb

Sometimes, taking action means doing things we've never done before—trying new things, communicating in new ways, learning, extending our skills. We step out of our *comfort zone*, that nice, safe place where we do the same old comfortable things and communicate in the same old comfortable ways. At least we know what the results will be! But as the saying goes, *out on a limb is where the fruit is.*

When we're in our comfort zone we don't challenge our self-image or work at our cutting edge. We don't "push the envelope." But if we stay in our comfort zones, we won't make any progress. As the saying goes, "If we continue to do what we've always done, we'll continue to get what we've always got."

Stepping out of our comfort zone can make us uncomfortable. We're taking a risk. We have no guarantees of success. All we know is that, by trying something different, we'll get a different result.

Peak performers stretch themselves all the time. How often do you extend to try something different or difficult?

Famous Last Words

Our **comfort zone** is our haven of habit. It's that nice, safe feeling we get when we take no risks, do the same old thing, and don't stick our neck out—and don't learn anything, do anything different, or make any major advances, either.

See Mistakes as Learning Experiences

Of course, taking action and stepping out of our comfort zone can mean making mistakes. The more we try new things, the more likely we are to make mistakes. But which of us was born fully skilled and talented, anyway?

To achieve success at anything, we have to make a lot of mistakes. Did you walk correctly at your first attempt? You probably fell flat on your face or your bottom—most babies do! Did you hit the tennis ball, bat the baseball, or sink the basketball on your first attempt? Not likely! How many mistakes do you reckon you made before becoming proficient at anything you are now good at?

If we use mistakes as excuses to give up, we'll never get anywhere. It's a good thing Thomas Edison didn't give up the first 2,999 times he tried to make a bulb light or we might not have electric lights today. He didn't say "Gee, this won't work," but "This won't work *yet.*"

Abe Lincoln, elected sixteenth President of the United States in 1860, didn't give up politics even though he had been defeated for Congress twice (1843 and 1848), the Senate twice (1855 and 1858), and Vice President once (1856). R.H. Macy's store in

New York failed seven times before it caught on. Bob Dylan didn't give up singing even though he was booed off his high school stage when singing in a talent show. Chuck Yeager, combat pilot and the first person to break the sound barrier, didn't give up flying even though he threw up quite spectacularly on his first flight. Babe Ruth may have hit more home runs than anyone but he also struck out more times.

That's no doubt why successful people make more mistakes.

There are smart mistakes and foolish mistakes, though. Smart ones offer lots of potential. Drawing a wise conclusion from a foolish choice and contemplating what we've done wrong so we don't repeat it are smart mistakes. With smart mistakes, we learn the lessons we've already paid for. Foolish mistakes are doing the same thing over and over, even though it doesn't get us what we want.

There is no such thing as a bed of roses! Failure is part of success. In short—mistakes are inevitable; learning from them is optional.

Foot in Mouth

Don't let a mistake be your excuse for giving up. See it as feedback on how you're doing.

Fake It 'Til You Make It

Robert the Bruce, the thirteenth-century Scottish revolutionary and king, said, "If at first you don't succeed, try, try again." That's excellent advice, provided we try something different. If we keep doing the same thing, our results won't change at all.

Silver Tongue

"Do something. If it works, do more of it. If it doesn't, do something else."

—Franklin D Roosevelt

What should we do when we do "something else"? If we don't know, we can always fake it. In other words, keep trying different things out until you find one that works. Then refine that until you're fully satisfied with the results you're getting.

Act As If ...

William James taught us the *Act As If* principle. He said, "Act as if what you do makes a difference. It does."

He also said, "If you want a quality, act as if you already had it."

There is a third way to use the *Act As If* principle. If you don't know what to say or do in a situation, think of someone you know who would know exactly what to say or do. What would this be? Step mentally into their shoes and *Act As If* you're them.

This will at least start you moving in the right direction. It might even produce the precise result you hope for. You will then have this new behavior as part of your repertoire—your self-image will grow to include being a person who knows what to say or do in this type of situation. Your self-esteem will lift and the Success Sequence will spiral upwards.

What we say and do is guided by our values, beliefs, and thoughts. To make what we say and do more powerful, our values, beliefs, and thoughts must be positive, supportive, and realistic. Then we need to focus our attention and efforts on the results we're after. The next chapter looks at goals more closely.

The Least You Need to Know

➤ Our body language both *reflects* our state of mind and *affects* it.

➤ Have a good laugh every day for your humor *and* your health.

➤ Don't unthinkingly react to other people or events. Pull your own strings and be in charge of your communications.

➤ Step out of your comfort zone to improve your performance and results.

➤ See mistakes as learning opportunities.

➤ Use the *Act As If* principle to harvest the results you want.

Chapter 4

Focus for Success

In This Chapter

➤ The power of goals

➤ The kind of goals that will make you a star

➤ Three steps to reaching your goals

➤ The importance of choosing excellence

Confucius was wise. In previous chapters, we covered the first and second ways he said we could seek wisdom, and I bet you already feel smarter! In this chapter, we'll turn to his third way to wisdom: experience, or by paying attention to our results. To get anywhere, we need to know what we want to achieve and keep it firmly in mind.

You'll find out how to set great goals, focus on them, and direct what you say and do towards achieving them. You'll learn the final key to making the Success Sequence work for you.

The third and final step of the Success Sequence is getting the results you want and using those results to get even more great results.

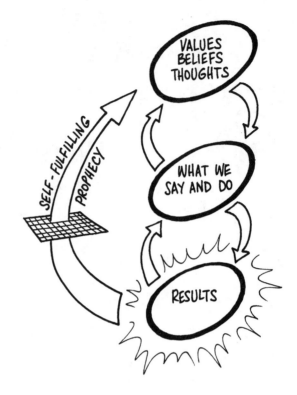

Foot in Mouth

William Jennings Bryan, the nineteenth-century U.S. lawyer, orator, and politician, said, "Destiny is not a matter of chance. It is a matter of choice. It is not a thing to be waited for. It is a thing to be achieved."

If you don't set clear goals, you're putting your destiny in the hands of others or leaving it to pure chance.

The Power of STAR Goals

A goal is our glimpse of the future—a future of our own choosing that we're creating every day. Identifying what we want to achieve, what we want to be like, and how we want to live our lives, gives us meaning and purpose.

Goals allow us to tune our actions and our communications so they will lead us to the results we want. Are you getting all the results you want?

We've seen that, to generate more of what we want, we first need positive, empowering beliefs about others and ourselves. We need clear and specific goals to aim for. And we need to take action aimed at achieving the results we want.

If what we're doing and how we're doing it isn't achieving the results we want, we need to adjust what we're doing and keep adjusting it until we get the results we're after.

Set STAR Goals

Use STAR goals to turn yourself into the kind of star you want to be.

S—Set simple and specific goals.

T—Give yourself target dates.

A—Make sure the goals are achievable.

R—Include both end results and activities needed to get there.

I'll discuss each step of the STAR goal system in the sections that follow.

Set Simple and Specific Goals

Keep your goals positive, short, and uncomplicated.

Did you ever hear the saying "All things are created twice—first in the mind"?

Create crystal clear goals for yourself. Simple and specific goals will fast-track your progress. You can see them clearly in your mind's eye, which makes it easier to achieve them. And easier to get feedback on how you're doing.

Measurable goals are the clearest of all. As much as possible, express your goals in measurable terms. This makes them even more precise and that much easier for your subconscious to get to work on them. You will be able to identify all sorts of opportunities and sources of help to draw on as you work toward them.

As the saying goes, "Inch by inch it's a cinch. Mile by mile it's a trial." If your goals are very ambitious (large) or far away (years ahead), divide them up into smaller steps, or milestones, along the way.

It's easy to keep these smaller goals constantly in the back of our minds. They become part of us and embed themselves into our subconscious. We will automatically focus our energies and our efforts on achieving them. We'll keep moving in the right direction.

Silver Tongue

"You are what your deep driving desire is;

As your desire is, so is your will.

As your will is, so is your deed.

As your deed is, so is your destiny."

—Brihadaranyaka Upanishad, Hindu philosophical treatise

A Word to the Wise

We get what we focus on. If your goal is to get married, your energy and enthusiasm will stop at the wedding. If your goal is to have a happy and loving marriage, it will continue long after the wedding.

Think carefully about your goals. Make sure they are within your control or influence. You don't want to have to depend on the actions of others or external events to reach them.

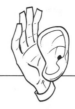

Listen to This

John Naber turned his daydream into medals. His dream was to win an Olympic gold medal. This is how he turned it into a goal and then into reality.

He set his sights on the Olympic gold medal in backstroke in four years time. He calculated he needed to improve his current time over 200 meters by four seconds. That's a lot for a swimmer. So he divided this into smaller improvement goals. He kept making these goals smaller and smaller until this produced a goal he felt was achievable.

What was this goal? To improve his lap speed by $1/1200$ of a second each time he dived into the pool.

By breaking a large and distant goal into a series of smaller, specific, measurable and achievable goals, and then putting in the time and effort required, John Naber won a total of four Olympic medals in 1976.

A word of caution: Don't confuse "simple" and "specific" with "run of the mill" or "simplistic." Go for goals that will stretch you and that fit in with your values, goals you will get a "buzz" from working toward and be proud to achieve. Remember, mediocrity is a choice; so is excellence. Set yourself goals of excellence.

Silver Tongue

"What would you attempt to do if you knew you could not fail?"

—Robert Schuller

Give Yourself Target Dates

A goal isn't a goal until it has a deadline.

Target dates provide a sense of urgency and increase the precision of our aim. They also help us to divide a large goal into smaller subgoals, each with its own target date. This gives us a way to track our progress. Deadlines can keep us on track and propel us toward our goals.

Make Sure the Goals Are Achievable

Make your goals reachable—with effort. They should be challenging but not impossible, realistic but not too easy.

If a goal is too hard, what's the point in putting in a lot of effort? We know we'll never reach it! If it's too easy, we won't even bother trying. We probably won't even achieve the standard of performance we could have reached, had the goal been more demanding.

The best goals are realistic and, at the same time, challenging. They invite us to work at our cutting edge, where we continually strive to improve our performance. This often takes us out of our comfort zone, which means we need high self-esteem. The kind of goals we set for ourselves take us right back to our values and beliefs.

Silver Tongue

"Don't be afraid to take big steps. You can't cross a chasm in two small jumps."

—David Lloyd George

Include Both Results and Activities

Focus on results *and* activities. Effective goals spell out both the end *results* and the *activities* needed to achieve them.

Results Goals (End Result Goals)	Activity Goals (Doing Goals)
Win the Olympic gold medal in in 200 meter backstroke in four years time	Reduce lap speed by $1/1200$ of a second every time I dive into the pool Train twice a day, ten months a year, for the next four years.
Achieve sales budget this financial year	Make three presentations a week to clients
Win this year's sales competition	Cross-sell on 40% of sales
Attain Grade 1 on the club squash ladder by my birthday	Play at least twice a week with a partner slightly better than I am
Be a loving parent	Hug my kids at least once a day Eat at least three meals a week together.

Start planning your future now!

Conceive

Believe

Achieve ...

Results goals point us in the right direction. They often depend partly on outside factors that we can't fully influence or control. So they must be realistic enough to be achievable and challenging enough to be motivating.

Activity goals without results goals are pointless. They'll keep us busy but will scatter our energy. Activity goals need to be pretty much within our control. They provide good feedback on our day-to-day achievements.

Silver Tongue

"It's a funny thing about life. If you refuse to accept anything but the best, you often get it."

—Somerset Maugham

Plan of Action

The first two letters of goal are *GO!* But before we charge off, we need a plan of action. Focused action will achieve results much better than aimless action.

Action plans don't need to be fancy—a list of activities or steps is usually enough. Even just the first three steps will get us moving in the right direction.

If you don't want to make an elaborate action plan, develop a rolling action plan listing three steps at a time. As long as you know clearly where you're headed and what you need to do, you'll make progress.

Three Steps to Success

Follow the three steps to success.

Step 1: Set Your Goals

We've seen how important goals are. Without them, we're in danger of just muddling along. You might find inspiration in the example of Thomas Edison, who set very clear goals for himself.

At age seven, Edison was expelled from school for being "retarded" and "addled." After this, he never received formal schooling again. He had a diverse series of jobs before setting up a scientific village in New Jersey. His goal was to make one minor invention every 10 days and a "big trick" every six months.

Before long, Edison was applying for 400 patents a year, including the phonograph and the electric light bulb. His clear and challenging STAR goals propelled him into action. That's the power of goal setting!

Step 2: Develop Action Plans

A goal without an action plan is just a wish.

Don't just think it—ink it! In a notebook, write down a few challenging result goals. Then break them down into smaller, more readily achievable activity goals. Make them positive and as specific as you can. Set time frames for each one.

Then develop an action plan.

Keep this notebook handy and refer to it often to check your progress. You may not achieve every goal 100 percent. But how much more will you have achieved by writing them down? Much more.

Step 3: Keep At It

Persistence is what makes the impossible possible, the possible likely, and the likely definite.

Winners often experience more failures because they try more often and keep trying. Why is the Model T called the Model *T?* Because Henry Ford had gone through *A* to *S* before being successful in producing and marketing his car.

French scientist Louis Pasteur's tenacity, among other things, linked germs to disease, rescued the French silk industry from ruin, developed inoculations against anthrax and chicken cholera, developed a treatment for rabies in humans and dogs, and founded the discipline of bacteriology.

Silver Tongue

"My strength lies solely in my tenacity."

—Louis Pasteur

What specific and challenging goals are you working toward? What sort of future are you planning and creating for yourself? Your future begins first in your mind, then in the goals you set, then in the actions you take to move toward them. Your future is in your hands.

A Word to the Wise

Commit to your success. Once a year, perhaps on your birthday, give yourself the priceless gift of spending a few hours to create your future. Sit down and think about your life. What have you achieved so far? What are you good at? What do you need to develop to become even better? What do you want to achieve over the next 12 months?

Use these headings or any others that make sense to you: community, marriage, social, family, career, spirituality, self-growth, health.

The Least You Need to Know

➤ The more clear you are about what you want to achieve, the more successful you will be.

➤ Set STAR goals: Keep them **S**imple and specific, include **T**arget dates, make them **A**chievable, and commit to both **R**esults and activity.

➤ A goal without an action plan is just a wish.

➤ Keep at it.

➤ Remember that mediocrity is a choice; so is excellence. Which will you choose?

➤ If you don't create your own future, someone else will.

Chapter 5

Become a Peak Performer!

In This Chapter

➤ The mind-sets of peak performers

➤ The difference between a compliment and flattery

➤ The feel-good power of praise

➤ Improving your performance every day

Have you ever wondered how it is that some people seem to excel with little effort? They glide graciously through life achieving extraordinary results while others toil away but have few achievements to show for all their efforts. Extensive research into peak performers in all walks of life shows that they have very similar ways of thinking about themselves and others. They share other similar mind-sets, too. Because of this, they operate in similar ways.

This chapter explains six important approaches to life that peak performers, whether in business, public service, private life, school, athletics, or team pursuits, share. If you adopt them, you can become a peak performer, too.

Peak Performers Have High Self-Esteem ...

We can do our best only if we have high self-esteem. After all, if we don't think very much of ourselves, how could we possibly do well, never mind excel, at anything? Our self-talk and subconscious would constantly be working to curtail our performance, not perfect it.

High self-esteem does five important things for us.

As we've seen, it leads to positive self-talk. These silent messages continually bombard our conscious and subconscious minds with instructions on how to behave and communicate. Whether they are positive or negative, we follow these instructions. What begin as mere thoughts become reality.

We've also seen that high self-esteem allows us to have an internal locus of control. This gives us the ability to choose our own thoughts, feelings, actions, and communications. If we can't do this, we are at the whim of outside events and other people.

Silver Tongue

"The road uphill and the road downhill are one and the same."

—Heraclitus

Famous Last Words

Are you an **optimist**, a **pessimist,** or a **realist?** It depends on whether you see the glass as half full (you're an optimist), half empty (you're a pessimist), or twice as big as it needs to be (you're a realist).

We also know that the mind-body link is very strong and that our level of self-esteem leads to very telling body language. Body language that reflects high self-esteem not only announces we respect ourselves, but also invites the respect of others.

High and low self-esteem lead to two entirely different styles of communication. The communication style of people with high self-esteem is clear and open. It reflects both our respect for ourselves as well as our respect for others. We explore this communication style further in Chapter 16, "The Ten Deadly Sins of Communication," and Chapter 20, "Speak for Yourself, Not the World."

High self-esteem allows us to take charge of our behavior and communications and direct them toward achieving the challenging goals we set for ourselves. That's why peak performers are positive people with positive outlooks and positive attitudes.

High self-esteem also allows us to learn from our mistakes rather than be devastated by them or give up because of them. We don't tell ourselves, "See, I knew I couldn't do it!" or "I knew it wouldn't work!" We say something like "Well, I guess I need to practice that a bit more! or "That didn't work out as I'd hoped. I'll try a different way."

This means that peak performers are *optimists* who see mistakes as learning opportunities and problems as springboards. They have the confidence to take responsibility and proactively make things happen.

Psychologist Martin Seligman says optimism breeds confidence, faith in our abilities, and the willingness to keep at it until we've reached our goals. This keeps us going when we hit difficult periods and stumble over hurdles. Optimists know that just because they have one bad day it doesn't mean they're losers. They can see setbacks as challenges and obstacles as stepping stones.

Do you need to learn how to be more optimistic? Here's how:

➤ Avoid blaming yourself for failures. Take responsibility, fix them, and see what you can learn. Then move on.

➤ Recognize that mistakes usually have only a temporary effect.

➤ Don't let mishaps or down days in one area of your life influence other areas of your life.

➤ Pat yourself on the back when you succeed at something or achieve a goal. Think of these successes as lasting achievements that will pay off.

Science is only just beginning to help us understand just how powerful the mind is. Richard Lazarus of the University of California at Berkeley found that patients who repressed pre-operation thoughts about the seriousness of their condition and what could go wrong during surgery suffered fewer post-operative complications than patients who dwelt on the dangers of surgery. Martin Seligman of the University of Pennsylvania found that five years after undergoing a mastectomy, 75 percent of women who refused to yield to their illness were still alive and healthy versus 35 percent who had resigned themselves to their fate.

Foot in Mouth

Don't put people down. Get your kicks from things *you* achieve, not others' failures and shortcomings.

... and Build Self-Esteem in Others

Some people need to build themselves up by tearing others down. Others find ways to bring out the best in people, to "polish their gold." They help them learn, they share ideas and experience. They build up the confidence of others and make them feel good about themselves.

Silver Tongue

"Keep away from people who try to belittle your ambitions. Small people always do that but the really great make you feel that you, too, can become great."

—Mark Twain

It's nice to receive a *compliment*, isn't it? People with high self-esteem who build others' self-esteem are liberal with their praise.

Praise stimulates the brain and releases neuropeptides (natural opiates) and endorphins (those euphoria hormones) in both the giver and the receiver. That's right—offering someone a compliment makes the person who paid it feel good, too!

Praise loudly. Blame softly. In lifting others up, not putting them down, we lift ourselves up.

How to Pay Someone a Compliment

Not feeling so confident about your compliment-paying skills? Here are some easy tips to help you out:

Famous Last Words

What's the difference between **flattery** and a **compliment?** A compliment concerns things that are within a person's control and is usually about something they've done; it must be earned and deserved. Flattery is about things people have little or no control over and did nothing to earn.

➤ Make sure it is genuine. Ten percent of the 100 billion neurons in our brains are "deceit detectors"—they'll spot insincere praise in the blink of an eye!

➤ Be specific—mention the time, place, what the person said or did and why you appreciate it. This lets the person know precisely what is worth their time and effort to do again.

➤ Offer your praise as soon as possible after the event, when it is fresh in everyone's mind. If you wait too long, it might seem like it didn't matter or wasn't really important.

➤ Include your feelings. This adds strength to your compliment.

➤ Pay compliments frequently.

The greatest good we can do for others is not to share our riches, but to reveal theirs.

Sunlight for the Spirit

Someone once said that praise is like sunlight to the human spirit; we cannot flower and grow without it. Without the positive regard of others, it's hard to maintain a positive regard for yourself. Do you use the feel-good power of praise to build self-esteem in others?

If you're more in the habit of being fault-finding, here's how to become a coach, not a critic.

➤ Don't criticize—offer improvement suggestions.

➤ Don't find fault—find remedies.

➤ Don't tell—ask.

➤ Don't find ways to tear others down—create opportunities for them to "star."

➤ Don't interrupt people with your own ideas and opinions—hear people out.

➤ Don't discourage others when they are attempting something difficult or unfamiliar—encourage them.

Of course, praise isn't the only way to build self-esteem in others. Have you ever worked for someone who set high goals for you to work toward, made it clear they had every faith that you would achieve them, and gave you every support you needed?

People like this don't mollycoddle others by doing things for them. They know how to bring the best out in others by showing them how to do things for themselves and helping them achieve things they had never thought possible.

Have you ever had a friend who brought out qualities, skills, and abilities you never realized you possessed or who always made you feel good about yourself? People like this bring out the best in others, too.

Do you build self-esteem in others? Ask yourself the following to find out:

➤ When was the last time you paid someone a compliment?

➤ Are you friendly, patient, and approachable?

➤ Do you set high standards and expect the best of others?

➤ Do you offer help when you can see it is needed?

➤ Do you include people in conversations?

➤ Do you focus on the positive in others?

➤ Do you make an effort to say hello?

➤ Are you open-minded to others' thoughts and ideas?

➤ Are you generous with your constructive feedback?

➤ Do you greet people warmly when you see them?

A Word to the Wise

Attitudes are contagious. Are yours worth catching?

Someone once said that some people bring joy *wherever* they go, while others bring joy *whenever* they go. When do you bring the most joy—upon arrival or upon departure?

People like and trust us for how we make them feel. Who do you make feel important?

➤ Do you thank people for their help?

➤ Do you ask their opinions?

➤ Do you acknowledge others' areas of expertise?

➤ Do you build people up to others?

➤ Do you ask after people's health, experiences, and difficulties?

➤ Do you set challenging goals for others to live up to?

➤ Do you share a laugh with others?

Peak Performers Have High Standards

Have you ever noticed that peak performers surround themselves with other peak performers? They have high expectations of those around them—the people they work with, their friends and associates, their family members. Not unrealistically high expectations, of course, but they certainly don't settle for "second best." Why should they?

Silver Tongue

"The shortest distance between two people is a smile."

—Victor Borge

Foot in Mouth

Don't settle for second best—you deserve better.

High standards go hand in hand with high self-esteem. We expect the best of ourselves and for ourselves. When we have high standards, we naturally set challenging goals and work hard to attain them.

Here are six words that will cost you dearly in your personal life: "This is just how I am."

Here are six words that will cost you dearly in your business life: "We've always done it this way."

Take a tip from the peak performers. Because of their high standards, they constantly pursue improvement—in the way they do things, in the systems they work with, in fact, in everything around them. They continually ask themselves two key questions:

How can I do this *better*?

How can I do this *differently*?

The Improvement Cycle

Dr. Peter Honey has worked with thousands of peak performers and has found that they spend time every day reviewing what they've done and how they've done it, thinking about what worked well and what needed to be improved. They then plan what they will do next time so that they will improve their results.

He has put this into an improvement cycle and taught people from all walks of life to use it for 10 minutes a day. The improvements to their results are astounding.

Use the following improvement cycle every day to improve your results explosively.

Improvement Cycle.

Choose excellence over mediocrity every time you do something, and consistently work toward it.

Peak Performers Take Responsibility

Peak performers set goals and work toward them. In this way, the future determines our actions in the present. This is accomplished against a backdrop of the past because our values, thoughts, and beliefs, all made up of past experiences, influence the goals we set and how easy or challenging we make them.

Peak performers don't rely on other people or random events to achieve their goals for them. They know they are the ones who need to act, and they figure out precisely what they need to do to produce the results they're after. Rather than sitting back passively, waiting for things to happen, peak performers are active participants in fashioning their own future.

In the next chapter, we explore three ways to take responsibility and make things happen.

Silver Tongue

"The future creates the present against a backdrop of the past."

—Theoretical physicist Fred Allen Wolf

Peak Performers Stay Focused on Their Goals

One of the first things race car drivers learn is what to do when they lose control of their car and go into a spin. The natural reaction is to look at the wall (or the trees) they are heading toward but, if they do, that's exactly where they'll end up. So they are taught to focus on where they want to end up—the gaps between the trees, their desired destination.

Psychologists Richard Guzzo of New York University, Ellen Langer of Harvard University, Edwin Locke of the University of Maryland, and many other researchers have found that goal setting increases productivity in terms of both quality and quantity more than any other technique studied, including pay increases. If you want to accomplish anything, set clear and challenging goals. Aiming for easy or vague goals will do little for your productivity.

Don't go overboard when focusing on your goals. Keep them in mind and work toward them, but keep your mind open, too. If you stay mindlessly focused on your goals, you'll miss out on opportunities and get into a rut. You'll end up behaving like a hamster on the running wheel, which will put you in danger of burnout. In the next chapter, we explore three mental techniques for mindfully focusing on your goals and tapping into the power of your subconscious mind to turn them into reality.

A Word to the Wise

Focus on your goals, but live in the present. Know that you can't do anything about your past except learn from it.

Silver Tongue

"When spider webs unite, they can tie up a lion."

—Ethiopian proverb

Peak Performers Communicate and Work Effectively with Others

Andrew Carnegie, once the wealthiest man in the United States, at one point had 43 millionaires working for him. ($1 million then would be worth more than $26 million dollars today.) When asked what made these people so valuable to him, he replied that it wasn't their knowledge of steel but of people that made them so valuable. They were, it seems, excellent communicators who worked effectively with others.

Unless their goals are solitary ones that they can achieve entirely on their own, peak performers have learned how to communicate with others and work effectively with them.

We can often achieve far more working with others than by ourselves. To learn more about how to communicate and work effectively with others … read on!

The Least You Need to Know

➤ Build self-esteem in yourself and others.

➤ Set high standards and expect the best—from yourself and others.

➤ Take responsibility for achieving goals you have set.

➤ Make time every day to reflect on what you've done and how you can improve on it.

➤ Focus on your goals if you want to find your way around problems and setbacks.

➤ Hone your skills of working and communicating effectively with others.

Chapter 6

The Mental Techniques of Peak Performers

In This Chapter

➤ Taking responsibility

➤ Embracing mistakes

➤ Using obstacles as stepping stones

➤ Reprogramming your subconscious

➤ Perfecting your performance without lifting a finger

As you read about the mind-sets of peak performers in the last chapter, you probably realized peak performers are not magical individuals, nor are their techniques difficult to apply. Anyone can think the way peak performers do, and that means thinking the way to success!

Research tell us that at least 50 percent of an athlete's performance success, and an even higher percentage of their performance failures and errors, are due to mental factors. We're not talking about how smart they are, but about things like their attitudes and mind-sets, the way they talk to themselves, and the way they see themselves doing things. In short, we're talking about the way they employ the vast power of their subconscious.

What holds true for athletes and sports people holds true in other walks of life. In this chapter, you will discover how to help your subconscious work energetically and forcefully on your behalf. You will find out how to use the power of your mind to tap the vast potential of your subconscious to achieve your goals and live your dreams.

Take Responsibility!

It's been a hard day. You are relaxing in the living room, with your feet up. You're comfortable and beginning to unwind. There are two children in the kitchen. Suddenly, there is a loud crash and the sound of breaking glass in the kitchen. Too tired to get up to investigate you ask: "What happened?"

What's the response? That's right: "Nothing!" That's denial.

So you say: "Don't tell me nothing! I heard something break! What happened?"

What's the response? That's right: "It wasn't my fault, it was his fault!" That's blame.

So you say: "I don't care whose fault it is. What happened?"

Silver Tongue

"No one but a fool worries about things they cannot influence."

—Samuel Johnson

You've guessed it: "The stupid bottle was slippery and it fell out of my hand." That's an excuse.

Wouldn't it be nice to hear instead: "I dropped the juice bottle. I'm just getting the mop to clean it up"? That's taking responsibility.

Many adults have turned denial, blame, and excuses into something of an art form. When we're denying there is a problem, blaming others for it, or making excuses rather than conquering it, we're not taking responsibility. Nothing will change.

Focus Your Efforts Where They'll Count

What's the point of whining and moaning about the weather, the price of tea in China, or global politics? We might care about them but we certainly can't have much of a direct influence on them!

Peak performers focus their attention and efforts on things they can control or influence, where they will count.

Silver Tongue

"Grant me the strength to change the things I can, the courage to accept the things I can't, and the wisdom to know the difference."

—Reinhold Niebuhr

Do you focus your attention, energies, and efforts on things you can control and shape, too? You can control your own behavior, actions, and communications. And with your actions and communications you can influence the people around you.

Instead of blaming the economy, or a budget that's set too high, or not enough money, or other people, or any one of the thousand and one excuses others make, peak performers assess the situation, see what might be preventing them from achieving their goals, and take steps to remove, circumvent, or diminish those obstacles.

Embrace Mistakes!

Naturally, not everything peak performers do is successful. That's okay. As Soichera Honda, founder of Honda Motor Corporation, said, "Success is 99% failure." It takes a lot of strikes to hit a home run!

Because of their high self-esteem, peak performers are comfortable with mistakes. A strike isn't a disaster; rather, it's one step closer to a home run! Mistakes are feedback on performance and opportunities for learning.

Think of it like this: An error doesn't become a mistake until you refuse to correct it.

The high self-esteem of peak performers also allows them to step out of their comfort zones to try new approaches when what they're doing isn't working. In fact, peak performers step out of their comfort zones a lot! When you think about it, that's really the only way to learn and get better.

Successful people make plenty of ~~mistakes~~ learning opportunities if for no other reason than they attempt more and they don't give up—they keep on trying until they get the results they want. They don't blame themselves for failures, and they regard mistakes as temporary setbacks.

Focus on Solutions, Not Problems

Peak performers keep their thoughts, words, and mental pictures consistent with the direction they want to go, the goals they want to achieve, and the people they want to be. They don't dwell on their difficulties; they zero in on ways to overcome them.

Do you see difficulties in every opportunity or opportunities in every difficulty? If we keep our eyes

Foot in Mouth

Don't let mistakes and failures get you down or paralyze you from taking action to make things better or improve your performance.

Treat failures as practice shots. Use the Improvement Cycle discussed in Chapter 5, "Become a Peak Performer!" to learn from your errors.

A Word to the Wise

When you make a mistake ...

Acknowledge it ...

Correct it ...

Learn from it ...

Carry on!

When you stumble, don't get up empty-handed.

firmly set on our goals, it's easier to find our way around problems. Focusing on problems and difficulties only gets us stuck there!

The difference between stepping stones and stumbling blocks is how you use them.

A Visualization Success Story

On May 3, 1994, eleven bullets from a semi-automatic SKK Chinese assault rifle entered Derrick McManus's body, piercing bones, muscles, and organs. It took less than three seconds. Derrick collapsed and crawled out of the line of fire. By the time help reached him three hours later, Derrick had lost 80 percent of his blood—so much blood that the doctor on the scene estimated that Derrick was 30 seconds away from an irrecoverable heart attack.

Silver Tongue

"Obstacles are those frightful things you see when you take your eyes off your goal."

—Henry Ford

Derrick had always enjoyed taking on challenges, setting himself goals, seeing himself achieve them. Because of his profession, he also prepared for the worst.

A member of the elite Australian Police Star Division (the Star Division is responsible for counter-terrorist operations, resolution of hostage and siege situations, high-risk arrests, VIP security, riot control, cliff/cave/mine rescues, underwater search and recovery operations, and searches for missing/lost persons), he had mentally rehearsed the possibility of being shot many times. His action plan specified what he wanted his body to do if he were shot. He frequently visualized himself putting it into action. He wasn't being pessimistic, just realistic.

On that day in Nuriootpa, in South Australia's delightful Barrossa Valley, Derrick was not only shot, he was dying. And he knew it. "I set myself a goal—to stay alive and be able to interact with my children, even if it's from a wheelchair." Lying helpless, pinned down by a gunman, Derrick put his mental plan into action. As he felt his limbs closing down from lack of blood, he took control. He talked himself into staying calm, slowing down his rate of breathing, his pulse rate, and, ultimately, his rate of blood loss. He focused on living "so that when my children hit their trials and tribulations in life, I'll be there for them." Through conscious effort, Derrick talked himself into staying alive and seeing his family again.

Derrick was rushed to the Royal Adelaide Hospital and was given a 50/50 chance of surviving the initial seven-hour operation. Once out of intensive care, he underwent a series of operations, but it looked as though he might not regain the full use of his legs. This was a hard blow for a physically active and fit person.

"I was in a predicament. I knew I couldn't change the past and, to make my future better, I'd have to deal with the situation as it was at the time."

He couldn't give up his dream job, though, so he set himself a dream-goal: to rejoin STAR Division. Others considered this unrealistic, considering the doctors were predicting he'd never walk properly again.

Derrick didn't dwell on his problems and focus on the difficulties lying ahead on his road to recovery. He divided his dream-goal of active duty with Star Division back into a series of smaller goals. "First, it was standing; then it was being able to walk around the bed. I would visualize myself achieving each goal and, as I got closer to achieving each goal, I set my next one." Recovery for Derrick was a series of small challenging goals.

Derrick worked so hard at his full recovery that the Physiotherapists Association of South Australia recognized him with an award for perseverance and dedication to rehabilitation.

In 1997, against all predictions, Derrick McManus rejoined the Star Division on active duty. He has since participated in VIP operations, rescues, and high-risk siege situations.

Visualize for Success

When you see yourself in your mind's eye doing something, do you imagine accomplishments, tributes, and triumphs? Or do you see flops, failures, and fiascoes?

Visualizing can work for you or against you. It depends on what you picture—success or failure.

We've all heard the saying "Practice makes perfect." Actually, only perfect practice makes perfect. And where is the only place we can practice perfection? In our mind's eye.

Reprogram Your Brain

Mental practice alters our brain's and our body's programming. Every time we practice perfection in our mind's eye, we establish and strengthen the neural pathways in our brain. If we visualize correctly, the brain will not distinguish between a physical performance and a mental performance— we can actually build muscles without lifting a finger! This makes mental practice as good as actual physical practice.

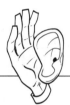

Listen to This

Arnold Schwarzenegger, the well known Austrian-born body builder and actor and the youngest Mr. Universe in history, visualized success.

"Weight lifting is all 'mind over matter'. As long as the mind can envision the fact you can do something, you can ... I visualized myself being there already— having achieved the goal already. Working out *is* just the physical follow-through, a reminder of the vision you're focusing on."

From *Superlearning*, Dell Publishing

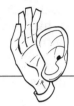

Listen to This

Stephen Kosslyn of Harvard University, researching how visualization actually works, asked people to imagine tensing and relaxing the muscles of their right index finger, but without actually moving it. They did this for several minutes every day. Four weeks later, the strength of their index finger had increased by 20 percent. Making the neural connections mentally was just as effective as making them physically. Visualization causes physical changes in the brain and body in the same way that physical effort does, whether it's strengthening muscles or communicating more effectively.

Visualizing programs our body to do exactly what we mentally rehearse. It works because, if we do something once, even in our mind, we've built a mental pathway. This makes it easier to do a second time.

Famous Last Words

You can improve your performance at golf or keep your cool in a difficult situation without actually practicing everyday through visualization. Intensely imagining yourself swinging that flawless golf swing or keeping your communication cool in a tough situation actually builds neural pathways and muscular responses. Do this often enough, and your body will follow its preprogrammed directions when you're in the actual situation.

In fact, we will improve faster with repeated mental rehearsal because we won't be imprinting our mistakes and the "not quite perfects" that are inevitable with physical practice. The more we practice perfection through mental rehearsals, the stronger the neural pathways will become and the better we will perform when the time comes. This is what neurologist Ian Robertson, of Trinity College, Dublin, calls "sculpting the brain."

Sports people and athletes have been visualizing for years. In fact, one of the world's top golfers, Jack Nicklaus, attributes 50 percent of his success to visualization.

Seeing Your Way to Peak Performance

Do you think visualizing is too hard? Follow these four simple steps:

1. **Verbalize it.** Set yourself a clear and challenging goal, the kind of goal we discussed in

Chapter 4, "Focus for Success." It can be a general goal, such as projecting a positive image at a meeting, or a specific goal—for example, the exact movements of a golf swing or making a fantastic presentation. Be as clear as you can about what you want.

2. **Visualize it.** Relax. This will make your brain more receptive to establishing and strengthening the neural pathways. Now focus all your attention on the task at hand. Imagine your goal in as much detail as you can. See in your mind's eye everything involved: the location, circumstances, other people who will be present, and so on. These serve as mental cues.

3. **Emotionalize it.** Involve your emotions. This strengthens the neural pathways. How does achieving your goal perfectly and excellently feel? Are you thrilled? Filled with energy? Shouting "Yessssss!" inside?

4. **Revise it.** Visualize the same thing over and over, every time you have a spare moment. Rehearse mentally at least three times a day: when you wake up, before going to sleep, and at least once more during the day. Visualize and emotionalize just before the actual event.

> **A Word to the Wise**
>
> Use visualization to alter your brain's programming. Don't see yourself floundering and failing; see yourself striving and succeeding.

The fastest way to improve any performance is to combine regular physical practice with regular mental practice.

To really strengthen those neural circuits and engage your powerful subconscious, make your mental practice powerful and vigorous. Visualize intensely, with focused concentration. Unless you do this, the results will be marginal.

The more intensely you visualize, the more you strengthen your neural pathways; and the more often you visualize, the more likely they are to propel you into the performance you've practiced.

> **A Word to the Wise**
>
> If something is done once, even in the mind, it becomes easier to do a second time. Mentally rehearse excellent performance for every important event in your life.

A Guide to Visualization

Here is a step-by-step guide to visualization:

1. **Pinpoint your goal.**

   Identify a clear goal with a tangible result.

2. **Set up the mental screen.**

   Set up a mental screen and watch yourself achieving your goal as if you were seeing yourself on TV or a movie screen. Watch and listen to what is occurring on the screen.

   Adjust the "controls" for brightness, distance, focus, color, size, volume, tone, and tempo until you can see and hear clearly. (The distance should be such that you can watch yourself objectively.) If you have trouble seeing and hearing yourself achieving the goal, get a "sense" of doing it.

   Relax while you see and hear yourself achieving your goal.

3. **Identify the specific inner resource(s) you need.**

   As you watch yourself achieving your goal, think about what works and what doesn't. Identify the inner, or personal, resources you are drawing on to achieve this peak performance. For example: confidence, a positive attitude, a sense of joyfulness, an awareness of other people's feelings, seeing things from someone else's point of view, or breathing calmly and deeply. Write this down.

   If it's difficult to identify the inner resources you need, here are three other ways:

   (i) Think of a time when you did something similar that worked really well. What inner resources did you use then?

   (ii) Who do you know that does this really well that you can use as a role model? Mentally watch your role model achieve your goal. See exactly how she or he does it. What resources is your role-model using? Now replace your role model with yourself. Use those same resources.

   (iii) Pretend you have the personal qualities you need—act as if you already possess them. What inner resources are you calling on?

   Keep watching the screen as you achieve your goal exactly the way you want to. Draw purposefully on those inner resources you need. See the details—what is happening? Fine-tune anything you need to.

4. **Do the reality check.**

   How do you know you are achieving your goal exactly the way you want to? What could go wrong in real life?

   Run through your mental movie again, this time encountering the problem and fixing it. Do this as many times as you need to until you have

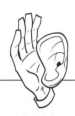

Listen to This

According to Karl Pibram, a neurophysiologist at Stanford University, mental rehearsal stimulates the neurology and results in micro muscle movements. It helps us embrace a level of performance that we may otherwise reject. It establishes in our minds what we see, hear, and feel in practice and so provides a clear target at which to aim.

met and successfully dealt with anything that might realistically go wrong. If you need more inner resources, go back to step 3.

5. Live run.

Run your mental movie again. This time, step into it, so that instead of watching yourself, you are looking out through your own eyes and hearing yourself achieve your goal through your own ears. What are you doing? How are you feeling? What are you saying and how are you saying it? Be yourself in your mind's eye as you achieve your goal and experience it fully.

Make sure it feels right. Make any changes you need to until you are fully satisfied.

It has been said that our brains work in a similar way to computers. The GIGO Principle certainly seems to hold true for both: Garbage In, Garbage Out. Make sure you program your brain with gold not garbage!

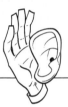

Listen to This

The Canadian Institute of Stress did a study on 32 two-kilometer runners divided into four groups.

The first group continued their normal training and over six weeks improved their time by eight seconds.

The second group used 15 minutes of self-relaxation four times a week and continued their normal training. Their time improved by 1 minute 12 seconds.

The third group used self-relaxation plus five minutes visualization and their normal training. They improved their time by 3 minutes 8 seconds.

The fourth group used self-relaxation plus five minutes visualization plus affirmations with their normal training. Their time improved by 3 minutes 39 seconds.

Advance with Affirmations

Do you know you can consciously program your subconscious to support your efforts to be a better communicator? You can do this with a special type of self-talk called *affirmations.* These are positive thoughts and instructions you deliberately embed into your subconscious. You can use them to reprogram your attitudes, beliefs, and behavior.

Famous Last Words

Affirmations are a performance-enhancing technique of embedding, through repetition, a short, positive, first person, present tense statement asserting a desired characteristic into your subconscious.

Affirmations are short, simple, easy-to-remember instructions phrased as strong, positive present-tense statements that focus our actions and communications to get the results we want and become the person we want to be. The more we repeat them, the more strongly we program our subconscious. We build and strengthen neural pathways so that, eventually, they "fire" automatically.

Keep Them Simple

Make your affirmations easy to remember. so you can carry them around in your head and repeat them every chance you get. The most effective times are just as you wake up and just as you are going to sleep, when your brain is relaxed and in a more receptive state.

Write Them Down

Write down your affirmations to increase their effect. If you repeat, say, six affirmations two or three times a day, you will probably find that in about three weeks, you will begin to see some results.

Alone, affirmations will not change your behavior. But used with other steps you can take, they can help to improve your results dramatically. Many studies have confirmed this.

Guidelines for Affirmations

Here are some easy guidelines you can follow when you create your own affirmations.

- ✔ Use the first person present tense (I am ...).
- ✔ Keep them short and specific.
- ✔ Make them positive. Affirm what you do want, not what you don't want. (I easily remain calm under pressure—*not* I don't panic.)
- ✔ Make them live, real, and dramatic, so you can see, hear, and feel them as you say them.
- ✔ Repeat them often, but at least twice a day.
- ✔ Write them on index cards so you can read them until you get to know them.

To develop a good set of affirmations, look at the descriptions of peak performers listed below. Go through them and change them into the first person—I've completed the first one for you.

➤ Peak performers have high self-esteem and build self-esteem in others.

I have high self-esteem and build self-esteem in others.

➤ Peak performers have high standards.

_____

➤ Peak performers continually look for ways to improve.

_____

➤ Peak performers take responsibility.

_____

➤ Peak performers focus their efforts where they'll count.

_____

➤ Peak performers learn from their mistakes.

_____

➤ Peak performers stay focused on their goals.

_____

➤ Peak performers focus on solutions, not problems.

_____

➤ Peak performers communicate and work effectively with others.

_____

Our conscious mind works only when we're awake. It uses logic and creativity to communicate, make decisions, analyze information, set goals, make plans, and think things through. It can deal with several things at once, provided they are routine and familiar. Concentrating fully on more than one thing at a time overloads it.

Our subconscious can deal with an infinite number of things at the same time. It works constantly, even when we're asleep. It retains everything that happens to us and around us, everything we experience, think, and feel to provide an endless pool of information, insights, and conclusions.

We can program it to help us or hold us back. We can learn to use its vast potential, or tune it out, to our lasting detriment.

A Word to the Wise

Use affirmations to keep focused on your goals and reduce your negative self-talk.

The Least You Need to Know

➤ Don't blame others or make excuses—take responsibility for making things happen.

➤ Don't scatter your energy and efforts—focus them where they'll count.

➤ Don't waste your mistakes—learn from them.

➤ Don't ponder on problems—search for solutions.

➤ Use visualization and affirmation to build neural pathways and program your subconscious.

Part 2

The Dance of Communication

Understand and take charge of your communications.

Communication isn't about us feeding others information or about others pouring their points into our heads. It's about relationships, understanding, and expectations. It is like a chemical reaction in which two elements form an indivisible, interdependent compound.

In short, communication is a dance—something that happens between people. Every dancer is different and every dance is different.

In this part of the book, you'll find out about the dance of communication and its five-part tempo. You'll learn how to lead a smooth and graceful communication dance by recognizing and overcoming the many stumbling blocks that can trip you up, staying in charge of your communications, and putting yourself in your communication partners' shoes.

Chapter 7

Everything We Do Is Communication

In This Chapter

➤ Everything is communication

➤ Communication is a dance

➤ The five-part tempo of the communication dance

➤ The to and fro of communication

➤ Things that trip us up

We can't *not* communicate. Every day, in many ways, we communicate. We communicate our thoughts, our feelings, and our desires. We communicate whether, and how much, we like and respect someone. We communicate happiness, uncertainty, delight, and misery.

Simple or complex, intentional or inadvertent, planned or *ad hoc,* active or passive, communication is one of our key tools for achieving results, satisfying our needs, and fulfilling our ambitions. Whether we do it well or poorly, communication forms the chief part of each of our days.

The way we communicate reflects our innermost selves, our skills, and our confidence. It highlights or hides our talents and accomplishments. It indicates how much appreciation and respect we accord ourselves and expect from others.

Our ability to communicate strongly influences our friendships, promotions, pay raises, responsibilities, and career paths. It directly affects the level of support and help we receive from others and dictates our ability to have our ideas accepted and implemented. How well we gather and give information, ideas, and feelings determines how well we solve problems, make decisions, reach agreements, and resolve disagreements.

In this chapter, we'll explore the five part tempo of the dance of clear communication and examine what gets in the way in the environment as well as within and between the communication dancers.

Why Bother?

Studies tell us that 70 percent of mistakes in the workplace are a direct result of poor communication, yet avoiding mistakes is only one of the many reasons people communicate. As the figure that follows shows, there are many other reasons that people communicate.

If these communications are not done well, problems will result.

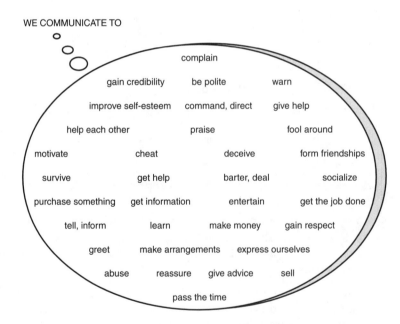

Here's a list of some common causes of communication difficulties:

➤ lack of information or knowledge

➤ not explaining priorities or goals properly

➤ not listening

➤ not understanding fully and failing to ask questions

➤ mind made up, preconceived ideas

➤ not understanding others' needs

➤ not thinking it through clearly, jumping to conclusions

➤ losing patience, allowing discussion to become heated

➤ short of time

➤ bad mood

➤ failure to explore alternatives

If we don't recognize and deal with these difficulties, it stands to reason that the effectiveness of our communication will be severely reduced.

Communication failures can cause …

➤ loss of business.

➤ frustration, hostility, tension.

➤ loss of goodwill.

➤ dissatisfaction with others.

➤ gossip and rumors.

➤ lowered morale.

➤ loss of sleep.

➤ loss of creativity.

➤ loss of enthusiasm.

➤ loss of team spirit.

➤ mistakes, inefficiencies.

➤ high employee turnover.

➤ lowered productivity.

➤ absenteeism.

➤ misunderstandings.

➤ conflict and arguments.

➤ poor cooperation and coordination.

➤ drop in self-esteem and confidence.

➤ damaged personal or company image.

➤ loss of friendships.

These are results we don't want and can't afford!

What could have a more profound impact on the quality of our daily lives and relationships than communication?

The Five-Part Tempo of the Communication Dance

Communication is much more than just giving and receiving a message. It is a reciprocal process. It is something that happens between and among people. We do it together.

For instance, this book itself isn't the communication. The communication lies in the meanings you, the reader, take from it. You are part of its communication. If no one reads this book and therefore takes no meaning from it, no communication will take place. All we would have is symbols on paper.

Communication is a dance. It happens *between* people. We communicate *with* others; we don't talk *at* them. Pet parakeets talk *at* us, not *with* us!

Poor communicators have never learned the dance of good communication. They can't change their rhythm or steps to suit the other person or the circumstances.

Good communicators swing, rock, and roll to the music.

Have you ever discussed something with someone and found that you were able to clarify and develop your ideas as you spoke? You may even have discussed the same thing with someone else, but there was no clarification or development of your ideas. The difference is in the process—what is going on between you. This is the dance of communication.

The First Beat: Everything We Do Is Communication

People are full of verbal and nonverbal, intended, accidental, and involuntary messages. The words we say are only the tip of the iceberg—they make up only between 7 and 30 percent of our messages, depending on the situation.

The volume and tone of voice we use, the degree of eye contact we make, our stance, and the tilt of our head all help the receiver to interpret our words and take meaning from them.

When we choose what to wear in the morning, we choose something that communicates a message about our self-image and self-esteem. The car we drive, the house we live in, the clothing and accessories we choose all communicate how we feel about ourselves and how we wish to be treated by others. When we place personal items on our desk at work, we communicate something else about ourselves: What we believe holds importance and worth.

When we move or change our posture, seating position, or facial expression, we express something about our attitudes and feelings. The words we choose to use or omit and the strength and energy with which we say them also tell a story. Consciously or unconsciously, we use the three *V*s of communication to send messages and receive them.

Silver Tongue

"There are four ways, and only four ways, in which we have contact with the world. We are evaluated and classified by these four contacts: What we do, how we look, what we say, and how we say it."

—Dale Carnegie

➤ Visual: 55 percent of the impact of our communications comes from our body language and symbols.

➤ Voice: 38 percent is from our voice tone, tempo, and volume.

➤ Vords: 7 percent is from the actual vords we use (well, uh, it was either taking a little liberty with the spelling of "words" or changing the "the three *V*s" to "the two *V*s and one *W*" of communication!)

Poor communicators focus on their *own* thoughts, feelings, experiences, and ideas. Their eyes, ears, hearts, and minds aren't receptive to the communications of others whether clear or subtle. Good communicators pay attention to everything the other person is communicating—symbolic, nonverbal, and verbal.

The Second Beat: The Way We Begin Our Message Often Determines the Outcome of the Communication

At one time or another we have all experienced the sensation of being "rubbed the wrong way" when someone first speaks. If we're not careful, our first few words can cause people to tune out or to become defensive—to reject our message.

We don't have much time before the other person has made up his mind whether he likes us, trusts us, wants to do business with us, or wants to get to know us better. Every second counts. It seems we have about 2 minutes when we're face to face, 30 seconds on the telephone, and 10 to 15 seconds on voicemail before the other person has determined what our message really is and whether he is receptive to it.

Poor communicators barge right in. They engage their mouth before their brain.

The more important their message is, the more good communicators think carefully about how, when, and where they will introduce it. They think about how they will frame it: with an analogy, a fact, an anecdote? They think about how they can best help the other person understand the point they want to make and how they can relate it to something that is important to the other person. They think about their overall goal and what they want to achieve from their communication. They think it through first.

Foot in Mouth

Don't just jump into conversations. Part of the success of any communication depends on the way you choose to begin it.

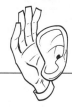

Listen to This

Here's a little experiment. Say the following seven words seven times. The first time, emphasize the first word. The second time, emphasize the second word, and so on. Count how many times the message changes meaning.

I never said he stole our money.

Did you hear seven meanings to these same seven words, depending on which you emphasized?

The Third Beat: The Way We Deliver Our Message Always Affects the Way It Is Received

How we say something is often more important than what we say.

People use a variety of senses to listen to and interpret our messages.

Poor communicators don't think about the way they deliver a message. They just make their point and abdicate responsibility for its accurate reception and interpretation to their unlucky listener. No one ever told them the maxim:

Better to keep your mouth shut and appear a fool than to open your mouth and prove it.

Good communicators think a bit first, especially when the communication is an important one. They manage their body language so that it sends the signals they want to send, they dress appropriately, and they watch their tone of voice. These things are *always* important factors in the way a message is received.

Silver Tongue

"Nothing is so simple it cannot be misunderstood."

—Jr. Teague

A Word to the Wise

Good intentions don't necessarily make for good communications.

The Fourth Beat: The Real Communication Is the Message Received, Not the Message Intended

Have you ever had to backtrack and say something like, "Oh, that's not what I meant at all! What I meant was …"? By then, it's often too late, isn't it? The damage has been done.

It is alarmingly easy for a message to be received in a far different way than we expected. Nevertheless, the real communication is the message others receive regardless of our intentions.

Poor communicators aren't very flexible. They'll say the same thing to 10 different people the same way each time, even though those 10 people all have different levels of understanding, backgrounds, and desires. Then they'll wonder why no one "got it."

Good communicators do their homework. They find out what's important to the other person, how much they already know, and what their previous experience is. That way, they can frame their message so it meshes with the other person's viewpoint. They also monitor the other person's reactions while they're delivering it so they can adjust their delivery as necessary.

A Word to the Wise

What happens between two people trying to communicate with each other? What thoughts run through your mind each time you communicate with a stranger, a friend, a co-worker, a senior executive? When you meet someone for the first time? When you disagree with what they say? What assumptions do you make? What expectations do you hold? How does your past experience affect what you hear?

Listen to the messages you give yourself as you communicate and see what they can teach you.

The Fifth Beat: Communication Is a Two-Way Street—We Have to Give as Well as Gather

We want to state our own point of view clearly, fairly, and persuasively. But if this is all we do, we haven't got communication; we've got a one-way street: a harangue or diatribe! As someone once said, two monologues do not make a dialogue.

Before real communication occurs, we need to hear the other person's point of view clearly. This also helps us state our point of view effectively.

Having both gathered and given good information, we are ready to move on—to reach a decision, solve a problem, negotiate a compromise, win a sale, make a friend, resolve a disagreement, reach an agreement, conclude a deal ….

Poor communicators think the communication is over when they've said their bit.

Good communicators recognize that's usually only the beginning!

Even though we may deliver the same message several times to different people, separately, or in groups, it will be different each time. We will be different (we might have learned something from

Silver Tongue

"For good or ill, your conversation is your advertisement. Every time you open your mouth, you let men look into your mind. Do they see it well clothed, neat, business wise?"

—Bruce Burton

earlier deliveries; we may say it differently because we're thinking it through differently; we may be in a different frame of mind). The next group we deliver it to will be different from the last group. Different people will hear the same message differently because they have different backgrounds, experiences, and mind-sets. The chemistry between the communicators will be different. And so we will dance the communication differently.

A Word to the Wise

These are the three vital components of successful communication: *giving good information, gathering good information,* and *making progress.*

Famous Last Words

Have you ever heard what you wanted to hear or expected to hear? This is because a **communication filter** was operating to eliminate information you didn't expect or didn't want to hear.

Navigating the Obstacle Course

An elegant communication dance also involves nimbly negotiating an obstacle course. We can't remove the hurdles—they're part of communication and there's lots of them. We need to accept them and learn to deal with them as best we can.

There are obstacles within ourselves, called *communication filters,* which screen, delete, distort, and generalize information and messages. They help us interpret events around us while at the same time limit our full and objective understanding of them.

We must recognize and deal with such filters as assumptions, previous experiences, self-image, expectations, and prejudice in both others and ourselves.

There are *communication barriers* in the external environment, such as noise and other distractions, which can frustrate communication. And there are *incompatibilities* between ourselves and the other communicator, such as differences in age, gender, race, background, and interests, that can lead to misunderstandings and even conflict.

The dance of communication is complex.

Be Aware of Communication Filters

Fact #1

In Chapter 2, "Where It All Begins: Your Beliefs," we learned that our parents and other influential people combine with our life experiences to develop within us certain beliefs, mind-sets, paradigms, or ways of looking at the world.

Fact #2

We also learned that the brain strives for order and predictability, accepting ideas, opinions, and information that confirm our beliefs and filtering out those that don't. This helps us to avoid uncomfortable cognitive dissonance.

Fact #3

The brain, in further attempts to create order, automatically interprets our life experiences according to our paradigms and mind-sets. This continually reinforces them as self-fulfilling prophecies.

=

Very strong communication filters!

The need for order and predictability, the tendency to see what we "expect" to see and ignore contradictory information, and the sheer force of habitual thinking blend to form potent and rigid communication filters. They are like psychic protection—they help us make sense of the world and avoid discomfort, unpleasantness, and confusion.

Here's a list of some common communication filters:

➤ premature evaluation

➤ other things on your mind

➤ tendency to jump to conclusions

➤ prejudice

➤ your mind wanders easily

➤ inattention

➤ assumptions

➤ stereotyping

➤ generalizing

➤ thinking we already "know" what the other person's action or message will be

➤ blind spots, which stop us seeing or hearing the other's point

➤ stress

➤ poor listening skills

➤ short attention span

➤ hearing difficulties

➤ "selective hearing" (hearing only what you want to hear)

➤ fixed ideas

➤ preconceptions

➤ ignoring or distorting information contrary to our beliefs

These filters are like well-worn ruts or pathways in our brain. Because our brains work so rapidly, these filters snap into operation in a fraction of an instant. Since most of our filters and paradigms are unconscious, or below our level of awareness, we seldom examine them to see whether they are realistic, up-to-date, helpful, or even valid.

Of course, some of these mind-sets are worthwhile and stop us having to reinvent the wheel. For example, "I should be pleasant and respectful to the boss" and "You get out only what you put in" are two constructive beliefs that you may have.

Other mind-sets, however, are less useful and logical. They hinder communication between people. Ideas about how people "should" behave, assumptions about what "they" are like, and so on all need to be checked against reality from time to time.

Whether or not they are sensible or helpful, we easily confirm and strengthen our mind-sets, paradigms, and fixed ideas. For example, if we have a mind map that says "I'm shy and most people don't like me much," we readily accept signals from others that we can interpret as "They're not interested in what I have to say" and "He dislikes me" and ignore any signals of friendliness or desire to listen to us.

So we receive and interpret only signals of dislike and lack of interest, reinforcing that particular belief. Moreover, because we subconsciously want to be assured that our mind-set is correct, our behavior to others is based on the "fact" that we "know" they don't like us, and so we behave in a way that invites them not to.

A Word to the Wise

When you get the sense that you are not talking to a real person but at you *image* of her or him, stop and ask yourself the following questions: What mind-set is influencing me? What mental image, prejudice, or stereotype am I the victim of? What assumptions have I made that might be unsound? Examine your assumptions and preconceptions and redraft them from logic and the experience you've gained.

On top of this, the other person also has his or her own mind-set. Imagine a young person, who believes old people are silly and grumpy, and a senior citizen who believes that all young people are lazy and slovenly, trying to communicate with each other. They will each "leak" their beliefs about the other in the way they communicate, accept information that confirms their beliefs, and filter out contradictory information.

We now have two people talking, not to each other, but to their images of each other. We can imagine how ineffective communication between them is likely to be!

Once aware of these paradigms and prejudices we can often update or adjust them so that they become more useful and realistic. If this is not possible, acknowledging a prejudice and putting it to one side is our best course of action.

We all have an assortment of filters that serve to obstruct the communication process. Become conscious of the way you communicate with other people. Identify which filters block your communication, acknowledge them, and take steps to remove or reduce them.

Reduce Communication Barriers

There are also barriers in the environment: noise, distractions, too many things happening at once. They can make concentration difficult or cause us to hear only part of a message or a garbled message. They can make us uncomfortable or nervous, reducing our ability to think clearly and communicate well. We've all seen what happens to a conversation among men when an attractive woman walks by them!

Block out noise and distractions and center your attention solely on the other person to overcome communication barriers. Move to a quieter place or one with fewer distractions, or reschedule your meeting to a more convenient time. Ask not to be interrupted. Focus your attention by listening carefully and outlining, mentally or on paper, the key points of what is being said.

Conquer Incompatibilities

Sometimes we are different from, or incompatible with, another person in some way that makes it difficult, awkward, or uncomfortable for us to communicate. Age, gender, and race differences, differences in background, education, personalities, value systems, and lifestyles all fit into this category. Such incompatibilities can kindle communication filters without our realizing it.

Recognize and defeat obstacles in yourself and the environment to achieve successful communication. Ask questions, revise your message, speak more slowly or loudly—whatever it takes to gain understanding.

If our view of the world is totally different from another person's, it can be very difficult to "speak the same language."

Sometimes we express a message poorly; perhaps one of us is hard of hearing or doesn't speak clearly; perhaps one of us is trying to make too many points at once and succeeds only in being confusing. Maybe the other person is sending an ambiguous message that could be interpreted in different ways, or our body language is saying one thing, our words another. Perhaps the message is poorly timed, poorly paced (too fast or too slow) or poorly packaged (too complex, incomplete, poorly worded, or laden with jargon).

In Chapter 8, "Behavior Breeds Behavior," we discuss the meaning and importance of empathy and how this can help to overcome basic differences and incompatibilities.

The main thing to remember about the obstacle course is that it is always there, for everyone. Every dance and every dancer has his or her own unique

Famous Last Words

Incompatibilities between ourselves and another person, such as very different values, beliefs, or past experiences, can also interrupt effective communication.

set of obstacles. Being aware of them and wanting to overcome them, combined with patience and understanding for the other person's obstacles, go a long way towards making our communication more effective.

This, then, is the dance and the five-part tempo of communication. The rest of this book explores how to make the most of them and the least of communication filters, barriers, and incompatibilities.

The Least You Need to Know

➤ Everything you do communicates.

➤ The way you begin and deliver your message affects how it is received.

➤ The real communication is the message others receive, not the message you intend.

➤ Communication is a two-way street—you have to gather, as well as give, good information.

➤ Be aware of, and work to clear or circumvent, the myriad of communication hurdles that are part of every communication situation.

Chapter 8

Behavior Breeds Behavior

In This Chapter

➤ Behavior breeds behavior

➤ Choosing your behavior

➤ Apathy, sympathy, and empathy

➤ The communicator's pledge

➤ Developing empathy

Great communicators have the ability to develop the kind of communications with others that they want. They use their behavior to establish the rhythm of the communication dance. To do this, they need high self-esteem and an internal locus of control.

They also try to see things from the other person's point of view. By putting themselves in the other person's shoes, they can both gather and give good information and make the kind of communication progress they want to make.

That's what we'll explore in this chapter—using your behavior and communications to draw out the sort of behavior and communications you want in others, and seeing things from the other person's point of view without losing your own.

Treat others as you would have them treat you.

You reap what you sow.

These are phrases many of us have heard and maybe even said ourselves, but what do they *really* mean?

The Law of Psychological Reciprocity has a nice ring to it for those who like impressive-sounding jargon. But what does *that* mean?

They all mean the same thing:

Behavior breeds behavior.

We know that people tend to respond to us in the way that we treat them. We reap what we sow.

➤ Be rude to people and they will generally be rude back.

➤ Be polite to people and they will generally be polite in return.

➤ Be considerate to others and they will generally be considerate to you.

➤ Be respectful to people and they will usually be respectful in return.

As a rule, people respond in kind.

Have you ever experienced the delight of unexpectedly excellent service and the "glow" that results? Were you a little "extra pleasant" to others as a consequence? Unfortunately, many of us have also experienced the opposite: discourteous service that made us more short-tempered than usual and perhaps made us less than polite in return.

When we let others influence us, we allow someone else's behavior to breed our behavior. As we saw in Chapter 3, "We Reap What We Sow," this happens when our locus of control is external.

Silver Tongue

"I will praise any man that will praise me."

—William Shakespeare

The opposite occurs when we keep our locus of control internal. Have you ever persuaded someone who was initially uncooperative or unhelpful to smile and become friendly, just by smiling and being friendly to them? This happens all the time. We can see it in restaurants, parking lots, shops and offices every single day if we're on the lookout. This is because people have a natural tendency to respond in tune with the treatment they receive.

That's the *Law of Psychological Reciprocity:* "If you're nice to me, I'll be nice to you; and if you're not, I'll give as good as I get!" This is how behavior breeds behavior.

By keeping our locus of control internal, we can make sure we take charge of our communications and set the tone we want them to take.

Knowing that behavior breeds behavior, you can take charge of the communications you enter into. What tone do you want the conversation to take—relaxed and informal? Be relaxed and informal and the other person will probably follow your lead. Polite and courteous? Be polite and courteous to others to encourage them to be polite and courteous to you. Cooperative and frank? Be cooperative and frank to promote the same in others.

So all we have to do is decide how we want others to treat us. We then treat them that way, and *bingo!* Actually, it isn't *always* that simple, but it's a very good general rule of thumb. And it works far more often than not.

Famous Last Words

The **Law of Psychological Reciprocity** tells us that others tend to treat us as we treat them.

Foot in Mouth

Don't let others influence your behavior. Use your behavior to influence others' behavior.

You Can Choose Your Behavior

Did you ever hear the expression "you catch more flies with honey than with vinegar"? The following anecdote illustrates the reasoning behind that expression.

It was Easter Sunday and the cafés lining Lygon Street were doing a brisk business. Mary went into one to order coffee for the group of friends she was with. The bell clanged as she opened the door. Two voices and the sounds of washing up came from the room at the back. Mary waited, wondering how long it would be before she could join her friends at their table in the sunshine. After a few minutes, she began to lose patience—surely they had heard her come in—they'd have to be deaf not to have heard that door bell!

Clang went the bell again, as a man entered the shop. He and Mary stood waiting, listening to the two voices in the back room. Eventually, a woman came out, drying her hands. Looking at neither of them in particular, she said, "Yeah?"

Fortunately for all of them, it was the man who spoke up. "Gee," he said, "I bet you hate having to work today! I bet there's lots of things you'd rather be doing on this beautiful Easter Sunday!"

"Yeah, I shouldn't be working at all, but someone called in sick. I've got my whole family 'round to my place for a get-together and I'm missing it! Anyway, what can I get for you?" She even smiled as she asked the question.

Silver Tongue

"If you are patient in one moment of anger, you will escape 100 days of sorrow."

—Chinese proverb

Foot in Mouth

Patience is never more important than when you're on the verge of losing it. Don't let other people's anger or bad temper get the better of you. Choose how you want to respond.

A Word to the Wise

Take charge of your communications! Because behavior breeds behavior, use your behavior to take charge and get more of what you want—friendliness, courtesy, respect—more often.

The man pointed to Mary, saying, "Actually, the lady was here first." Mary placed her order and, to her surprise, the woman said, "Go on out, I'll bring the coffee out to you. I'm not supposed to but I will."

Had Mary spoken up first, she wouldn't have been as pleasant as the man who came in after her. Quite the contrary, since she was annoyed by having been kept waiting so long. The way Mary would have communicated wouldn't have prompted the woman to offer to bring out the coffees!

But the man, by being good-humored and friendly, brought this out in the woman, to everyone's benefit.

Some people breed courtesy in the discourteous; pleasantness in the unpleasant; helpfulness in the rude. Their internal locus of control helps them to take charge of their communications and bring out the best in people.

Dealing With Anger

Anger is one letter short of danger.

Have you ever had to deal with an upset, angry person? They might be having a bad hair day, they might be taking out a full week's frustrations on us, they might be trying to communicate in the only way they know. Whatever the reason, when people let their emotions get the better of them, they can be difficult and disagreeable to deal with. And it can be tempting to respond in kind!

When dealing with angry people, do you pull your own strings by retaining your locus of control? Do you take charge of situations and turn them around? By modeling the communication style we want—not by *telling* the other person how to behave—the other person usually gradually calms down, particularly if we show we are listening and understanding their point of view (see Chapter 13, "Draw Out the Full Story," Chapter 15, "Listen, Listen, Listen," and Chapter 27, "Win with Complaints," for more on this).

The Professional Approach

Using the way we communicate to influence others isn't just for social situations. The principle of "behavior breeds behavior" is vital in professional situations, too. (We'll look more at this in Part 4, "Gathering Good Information.")

When we feel good we tend to do good. If you do something nice for someone, they are likely to do something nice for someone else. This is the *ripple effect.* Small kind gestures spread.

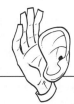

Listen to This

Once upon a time, a social scientist noticed that most people look in the coin return after hanging up a public telephone to see if any coins happen to be there.

Wouldn't it be interesting, he thought, to see what would happen if people actually found coins there?

He devised an experiment where his research team would randomly put coins in return slots so that some public phone users did find some change. They hired a young woman to walk by on cue just as the callers were about to hang up and check the coin slot. She had an armful of books and pretended to stumble. Would the people who had found change behave any differently to those who hadn't?

People who found money in the slot were four times as likely to stop and help the young woman pick up her books.

You Won't Get Anywhere Unless You Walk in the Other Person's Shoes

There's a world of difference between these three words:

Apathy

Empathy

Sympathy

Famous Last Words

Apathy is a lack of feeling, interest, or concern. It is a communication blocker. **Sympathy** is such a close affinity that what affects one person similarly affects the other. What one thinks or feels, so does the other. **Empathy** is the ability to grasp, or participate in, another's experience, feelings, or thoughts without taking them fully on board.

A Word to the Wise

You don't need to agree with someone's position or beliefs in order to understand them.

Apathy is "I couldn't care less!" This is the kiss of death to communication. We can't communicate very long or very well with someone who doesn't care about us or about what we have to say.

Sympathy isn't much better. It involves feeling such a close harmony with someone that whatever affects one similarly affects the other. In most communication situations, this is far more than is necessary or even desirable.

Empathy is quite different. It involves being able to see a situation from the other person's point of view. It doesn't necessarily mean you have to agree with it—in fact, you might totally disagree and still be able to understand it from the other person's perspective.

Empathy brings us closer together so that we can understand and take into account the other person's viewpoint when we communicate with them. It helps us communicate in a way that "oils the wheels," decreases resistance and defensiveness, and helps the other person more readily hear what we have to say.

How do we get closer together? You may have heard the expression …

> *Before we can truly understand another person, we must walk a mile in their moccasins.*

This was originally a Native American saying. The rest of it is …

> *Before we can walk in another person's moccasins, we must first take off our own.*

Some people are so full of their own opinions they have no room for anyone else's. We all need to remove our moccasins from time to time!

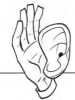

Listen to This

An arrogant man once entered a Buddhist temple and asked the priest to teach him the path to Enlightenment.

"Please join me for a cup of tea," the priest responded.

They sat down and the arrogant man held out his cup for the priest to fill. He watched with some concern as the cup quickly filled and the priest showed no signs of removing the teapot.

The cup began to overflow and scalding tea spilled onto the arrogant man's hands. "This must be a test of some sort," he thought, and said nothing.

Finally, he could stand it no longer. "Stop!" he said. "My cup is over-full. There's no more room!"

"My friend," said the priest, "like your cup, you too are over-full of your own thoughts, opinions, and desires. There is no room for Buddhism. When you can release some of your own thoughts, opinions, and desires and make room for others, come back to me and I will teach you."

Understand the Other's Frame of Reference

Our *frame of reference* is made up of our background and past experiences, our beliefs about ourselves and others, and what we value as important. It is made up of the paradigms and mind-sets through which we view our world.

Our personality type and operating styles also form part of our frame of reference (see Chapter 24, "Tune In to the Same Wavelength"). For example, do you prefer detailed information or are you more interested in just "the bottom line"? Do you need friendly working relations with others in order to

Famous Last Words

Our **frame of reference** is the total of our beliefs, values, experiences, background, personality style, mind-sets, and paradigms. It's where we're coming from.

work well, or do you tend to focus more on simply getting the job done efficiently? Do you prefer to gather information from reading or from talking things through? Different things are important to different people, and everyone functions a little bit differently from everyone else.

A Word to the Wise

Seek out and appreciate the other person's point of view.

Understanding someone else's frame of reference takes empathy. The effort is worth it; because the more we can understand other people's frames of reference—where they're coming from and what is important to them—the easier it is to communicate with them.

If we know what is important to others, we can structure our information to meet their needs. If we have an understanding of some of their background and past experiences, we can provide information in a way they can relate to and recognize. We can find commonalities in our own way of looking at the world and build on them. This helps us to speak the same language and present our message to gain the best results.

Effective communication involves bringing our frames of reference closer together.

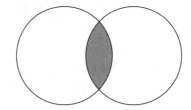

For successful communication, we need to overlap our frames of reference—the way we each see the world—as much as we can. Because we have not had the same experiences as anyone else, a full or complete overlap is not possible. Sometimes, though, we are so similar to another person in terms of upbringing, age, life experiences, beliefs about the world, and so on that our frames of reference overlap considerably and we have an automatic empathy with them.

At other times, only very small overlaps are possible because of the many differences (see Chapter 7, "Everything We Do Is Communication") that exist between us; when this happens, empathy becomes essential to our ability to communicate successfully.

The more overlap we can achieve with another person, whether through the "natural" empathy that results from shared experiences, beliefs, and values or consciously developed empathy, the better our communications with them will be.

This is the real meaning of empathy, and this is why it is central to effective communication.

Develop Empathy

Empathy is a skill. Like any skill, we need to practice it until it comes naturally and automatically to us and we use it habitually.

This means exploring the situation with the other person and asking questions; checking your empathy by stating, in your own words, what you understand the other person's beliefs and thinking to be; and imagining aloud to them what it would be like to be in their position and feel the way they do.

Try this first with people you know and have a good relationship with. As your skills develop, gradually increase the difficulty by practicing empathy with people who are progressively more different from yourself, and finally, with people whose ideas and opinions you find most difficult to understand.

Practice makes perfect!

Clear communicators lead the communication dance by establishing the rhythm they want with their own behavior. They choose the tempo by keeping their locus of control internal so that others don't "pull their strings." Their empathy helps them understand the other person's frame of reference to establish a smooth and graceful dance.

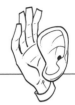

Listen to This

Have you heard the communicator's pledge?

Whether or not I agree or disagree with what you say, I will respect your right to say it and I will try to understand it from your point of view. This, in turn, helps me to communicate my point of view to you more effectively.

The Least You Need to Know

➤ Stay in control of your communications while fully seeing the other person's point of view.

➤ Set the communication tone you want the other person to follow.

➤ Don't react to the tone others set unless you choose to; this way, you're in control.

➤ Learn to walk in the other person's shoes, or you'll get nowhere.

➤ Practice understanding where the other person is coming from.

Part 3
Watch That Body Language!

Improve your communications through your body and your voice.

There's a Cantonese proverb that warns us to watch out for the man whose stomach doesn't move when he laughs. That's good advice.

Does your stomach move when you laugh? Do your talk and your walk say the same thing?

We communicate consciously and subconsciously, and the subconscious often communicates valuable information if we pay attention to it. After all,

Actions speak louder than words.

In this section, you'll discover the importance of first impressions and how to manage them to your advantage. You'll find out how to make sure your body sends the signals you intend and how to make your voice work for you. You'll brush up on reading other people's body language and find out how to make others comfortable in your presence without saying a word.

Chapter 9

First Impressions Count!

In This Chapter

➤ The importance of first impressions

➤ Making your first impressions count

➤ Putting your best foot forward

➤ Putting your best voice forward

Professor Michael Argyle, one of the foremost psychological researchers into body language, calls it "the silent language." Although body language operates mostly outside the focus of our conscious attention, we establish, develop, and maintain relationships primarily through this silent language.

And then there is the wordless verbal language, our voice. Some voices sing, glow, and dance. Others are rich and resonant. Some are vigorous and vibrant, others animated and dynamic. Our words are only a fraction of the message that we send. In fact, how we say those words often matters more than the words themselves.

In this chapter, you will discover how to create a great first impression, with the wordless languages of your body and your voice.

The Body Speaks

Get out of my hair!!

I got cold feet.

She's a pain in the neck.

He's too uptight.

He set the pace.

I'm bored stiff!

He was talking through clenched teeth.

She gets my back up!

It made my skin crawl.

He gave me the cold shoulder.

I've got to hand it to you!

She's on her high horse.

I have itchy palms!

She said that tongue-in-cheek.

Let's stay on our toes!

Don't turn up your nose at me!

Get it off your chest.

I could jump for joy!

Get a hold of yourself!

Let's kick it around.

I'll take a back seat on this.

Bite your tongue!

Which choice are you leaning toward?

Pull yourself together!

These telling expressions show how clearly the body speaks on our behalf. Body language is vital to crystal clear communication. In fact, the way we deliver a message accounts for up to 93 percent of its meaning. Which do you believe when someone's mouth says one thing while his or her body language tells a whole different story? If you're like most people, you'll believe the body language and disregard the words. In the pecking order of meaning, body language is the boss. This makes it a useful language to master!

Silver Tongue

"The eyes are more exact witnesses than the ears."

—Heraclitus

Although some people are better at reading body language than others, we're all rather expert at it. We do it every day, usually unconsciously. Quickly, in the blink of an eye, we sense whether people are friendly or aloof, uneasy or sure of themselves, truthful or deceitful.

This is just as well since body language accounts for such a large part of any spoken message. Ray Birdswhistell, a professor of anthropology at Temple University and author of several books on body language, has found that from 65 to 90 percent of every conversation is interpreted through body language. As you can see from the pie chart below, Professor Albert Mehrabian's research has lead him to place even more emphasis on the importance of body language.

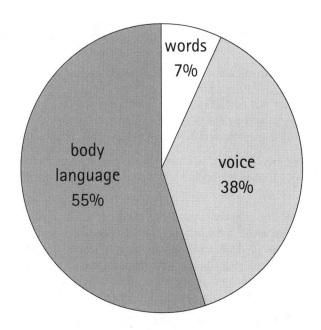

The pie chart illustrates the big role that body language plays in our spoken messages.

Since people react more to what they think we meant rather than to our actual words, it makes sense that we can enhance our communications with others by becoming aware of our body language and the way we say things.

When giving information, we can make sure that the silent signals we send out are transmitting the messages we intend. When gathering information, we can use our body language to encourage others to communicate more with us or to discourage them from communicating further. We can ask questions and make statements without saying a word. We can interpret their feelings and desires, and often, what they *really* mean.

Make Your First Impressions Count

Let's start at the beginning. You have only one chance to make a good first impression.

Rightly or wrongly, first impressions are lasting. They can give us a great start or they can betray us for a long time to come.

Look the Part

Fifty-nine percent of a first impression is made up of how we look: the way we dress, the jewelry we

A Word to the Wise

The body speaks on many levels, often unconsciously. It is often more revealing than verbal language. We can become more effective communicators by managing our own body language and taking other people's into account.

wear, and accessories we carry. Other, less controllable factors, such as age, height, and weight, also form part of the instant image people develop of us.

Let's begin with the symbolic communication of dress. Dress however you want to at home. At work, dress well and follow the unwritten (but real) "uniform code" of your organization. This might be smart but casual clothing, somber suits, or suits with a touch of color in the shirt or tie, scarf or necklace. Men normally avoid brown suits and safari suits for business and women generally avoid fashion extremes.

If you haven't already done so, take a look at the people around you and formulate some guidelines for yourself. The aim is to look professional without making any sartorial statements.

A Word to the Wise

First impressions count. Make sure yours counts in your favor.

If your career aspirations are upward, you may want to dress the same way as the people at the level above you; or dress the way the people in the department, section, or industry you want to move into dress. This will make you more like them and increase your chances of that promotion or transfer.

If you aim to be seen as a capable professional, wear the best quality clothing and accessories your budget allows. Attire may have little to do with actual performance or competence, but symbolically, our personal presentation communicates a strong message and affects how others perceive us.

Body Language—Put Your Best Foot Forward

Most of the remaining 41 percent of the first impression we create, and sustain, comes from our body language.

How is your posture? Are you a Shuffler who continually paces to and fro? A Shifter who constantly moves weight from one foot to the other? A Sprawler who takes up a lot of space? A Sleepyhead who looks as if you hardly have the energy to sit, walk, or stand?

Or does your upright posture show that you are calm, composed, confident, and competent?

Foot in Mouth

The way you sit, stand, and walk conveys a lot about you to others. Don't be a Shuffler, Shifter, Sprawler, or Sleepyhead.

Do you detract from your message and your authority by sucking on a pen; fiddling with a paper clip, your tie, hair, or scarf; scratching; clearing your throat; tapping your foot; or pumping your leg? Empty your mouth and your hands.

People often interpret gestures above the neckline as signs of nervousness. Self-repair and self-grooming gestures, such as adjusting your clothing, also detract from a positive image and look self-conscious and timid while hands on hips can look aggressive, condescending, hostile, or defiant. Putting your hands in your pockets is apt to be interpreted as nervousness.

The kind of body language most likely to make a favorable and professional first impression and earn us attention and respect includes open hand movements that are relaxed yet measured in pace (not extreme, sudden, or quick), an erect posture (not slouching or cowering), and head held up.

Firm eye contact (but not staring), a neutral facial expression or one that accurately reflects our inner feelings, and a relaxed (but not loose) jaw are also important.

Smile (unless it is clearly unsuitable). A sincere smile releases endorphins—"feel-good chemicals"; these cannot help but improve the first impression we make as well as the entire communication process.

When appropriate, and particularly when meeting someone for the first time or after a period of not having seen each other, offer to shake hands. The physical contact establishes a cordial atmosphere and sets the scene for a friendly encounter. Increase this by looking genuinely pleased to meet or see the person again, and the first impressions will be positive ones.

Let Your Voice Ring True!

Our voice influences people's first impressions of us and our message. In fact, about 38 percent of a listener's first impression of us will be based on how we sound.

Your first few words and the way you say them also set the tone of what follows. Your voice should be steady, calm, and strong, without being overly loud (or quiet). Your words should flow fluently, without awkward hesitations, in a steady, even pace, emphasizing key words and phrases.

Put Your Best Voice Forward

When some people speak, we sit up and take notice—their voices might be hearty, powerful, or passionate. When others speak, we switch off—their voices might be flat monotones or condescending, pompous, and pretentious. Some voices are brisk, some severe, others jovial, and others mysterious. We want to hear more of some voices and less—much less—of others!

What do you sound like?

Is your voice **tone** harsh, soft, sharp, or neutral?

A Word to the Wise

How you speak can totally undermine or powerfully strengthen what you intend to say. Think about your delivery and practice improving it.

Is your **pitch** high or low, flat, or sharp?

Is your **volume** loud, quiet, or in between?

Is your **inflection** rising, falling, or sing-song?

Is your voice **speed** fast or slow?

What **emphasis** do you place on words?

Do you **articulate** clearly or do you mumble?

How much **energy** do you speak with?

What **rhythm** do you speak with? Modulated? Staccato?

These details combine to produce the overall impact of our voice and add meaning to (or detract from) our message.

Watch Your Tone—It Can Type You!

Our voice *tone* is the quality of the sound of our voice, its expressiveness and color. It expresses our moods and emotions, and subtle differences in meaning.

What we hear	What we conclude
whining, nasal voice	a complainer
raspy, harsh voice	a crook
high-pitched, quivering voice	a nervous nelly
breathy, lilting, slow voice	a sexy coquette
clear, brisk voice	someone in charge

Famous Last Words

A voice **tone** is the quality of the sound of a voice, its expressiveness and color.

Linguists and psychologists have identified different tones we habitually use when communicating with others. Do any of these apply to you?

➤ accusing and blaming

➤ can-do and matter-of-fact

➤ appeasing and placating

➤ patronizing and haughty

➤ using excessive logic

➤ bored and stuck-up

➤ dogmatic and know-it-all

➤ bossy and bullying

➤ belligerent and quarrelsome

➤ warm and friendly

➤ naive and helpless

➤ positive and cheerful

➤ complaining and whining

➤ thoughtful and quiet

➤ straightforward and clear

➤ dramatic and effusive, over-the-top

➤ dry and dull

A Word to the Wise

Lower your pitch to sound more credible.

Do you recognize your style? Is it the way you intend to come across?

Pitch describes whether we speak with "high notes," "low notes," or an interesting mixture. Too much of one or the other can send people to sleep while constant switching between extremes of pitch can make us sound juvenile or inept. A high-pitched voice can make us sound nervous, overly excited, immature, or unconfident. Deeper voices sound more confident and competent.

Famous Last Words

A voice **pitch** describes how high or low it voice is. The way a voice rises and falls as we speak is it's **inflection.**

Volume can add interest and command attention. Speak more loudly or lower your voice to a whisper to focus attention on an important point.

Breathe deeply and relax your neck muscles and vocal cords to give your voice more volume and richness. This will make it come from deep in your diaphragm rather than high in your throat.

Do your sentences end on a high note, as if you were asking a question? Or do they fall, to show you're making a statement? Upward *inflections* make us sound uncertain and unconfident. Downward inflections sound more authoritative.

Aim for a falling inflection at the end of 80 percent of your sentences. Newsreaders are trained to do this because it sounds more authoritative.

How quickly do you speak? Do your words tumble together, making it difficult to follow them and form a word-picture, or do you hesitate so much that people become impatient or lose the thread of what you're saying?

Vary how quickly you talk depending on …

➤ The subject. How complex is it? How familiar are your listeners with it? With complex or unfamiliar subjects we need to give people more time to assimilate what we're saying.

➤ The listener. How quickly does he or she speak? Try to moderate your speed to be more aligned with the listener's rate of speaking (see also Chapter 12, "Build Rapport," and Chapter 24, "Tune In to the Same Wavelength").

Slow down to sound more thoughtful and serious. This indicates you're choosing your words carefully and can make your message sound more important.

Speak faster to convey excitement, enthusiasm, and energy. Listeners will need to work a bit harder to follow, so a more rapid-fire delivery can also invite attention and make it less likely that minds will wander.

A Word to the Wise

Consciously listen to yourself at least twice a day, or more if you can. How do you sound? How can you improve how you sound? The more often you do this, the more habitual it will become. Eventually, you will check and improve your communications automatically, without even being conscious of doing so.

MOVE IT YA BIG APE!!

Famous Last Words

How much strength, power, and passion do you speak with? That's your vocal **energy.** What sort of cadence, rhythm, and pace do you speak with? That's your vocal **rhythm.**

Speed and pitch make compelling combinations: some people's voices ooze like molasses; others twitter breathlessly; some people force their words out like bullets from an automatic rifle.

The silences or spaces between our words also add interest and emphasis. Pause before a significant point to signal: "Take notice of what I'm about to say."

Emphasize for Clarity

Remember our experiment in Chapter 7, "Everything We Do Is Communication"?

I never said he stole our money.

Reading that sentence seven times, aloud or to yourself, emphasizing each of the seven words in turn, clearly shows that changing the stress on just one word can totally alter the meaning of a message. In fact, the way we emphasize our words can determine the message!

Often, we emphasize words without realizing we're doing so, unconsciously "giving the game away" or "showing our hand."

Perfect Your Vocal Instrument

We will be listened to more if we articulate or enunciate our words clearly. If we mumble or "swallow our words," people will switch off—the effort of listening becomes too great.

Energy and *rhythm* are the intensity, enthusiasm, and tempo with which we speak. With our vocal energy and rhythm, we can send people to sleep or wake them up, excite them, persuade them, and energize them.

We are not born with any particular way of speaking. Rather, we develop characteristic voice tones, pitches, volumes, and speeds through experience and habit, without conscious thought or choice. This is a pity because the human voice is a rich and variable instrument, and with practice, it can enhance and reinforce our messages to ensure that the message received is close to the message intended.

The jury is in. People listen more to your body language and voice than to your words. Do your body language and voice match and enhance what you say?

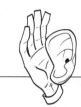

Checking your communications, paying attention to your body language, really listening to what you're saying and how you're saying it, and being conscious of the effect your message is having on others will help you communicate clearly. How you speak and how you look powerfully affect the way others perceive you and receive your messages.

Listen to This

Did you know that the human voice can cover two octaves?

The Least You Need to Know

➤ Make sure peoples' first impressions of you count in your favor.

➤ Create a positive first impression through your stance, actions, expressions, personal presentation, and voice.

➤ The way you sit, stand, and walk conveys a lot about you to others.

➤ Breathe deeply and relax your neck muscles and vocal cords to give your voice richness.

➤ Slow down to sound more thoughtful and serious; lower your pitch to sound more credible.

Chapter 10

Send the Right Signals

In This Chapter

➤ Managing your silent language

➤ Respecting personal space

➤ Applying and reducing pressure

➤ Understanding the cultural context

Have you ever heard the saying, "People don't really care how much you know until they know how much you care?"

We can begin showing how much we care with body language. Without saying a word, we can convey our interest and our understanding, our agreement or disagreement, our comfort or discomfort. We can silently ask questions, assure someone of our honesty, or reassure them of our good will.

Does your body language support your intentions or sabotage them? You'll find out in this chapter.

Sending the Right Signals

The more we attend to our own body language, the more control we have over the nonverbal messages we are sending to others and thus over the communication process itself. The right body language helps us both to gather and give good information.

Do you remember the first three beats of the communication dance from Chapter 7, "Everything We Do Is Communication"?

1. Everything we do is communication.

2. The way we begin our message often determines the outcome of the communication.

3. The way the message is delivered always affects the way the message is received.

Managing our own body language is important. We want to send compatible messages at all levels, including the nonverbal. The better we manage our body language, the stronger our communications become.

Famous Last Words

We can use the letters of a **mnemonic device** as a memory jogger. Each of the letters in the mnemonic is the first letter of other words that you want to remember.

Silver Tongue

"A graceful bearing is to the body what good sense is to the mind."

—Francois Duc De La Rochefoucauld

What do people see in your body language? If you look away or shift away from them, they'll see less than total honesty and commitment. If you clench your fist, they'll probably see frustration or nervousness. If you continually rearrange your tie, scarf, or hair, they'll see tenseness. If you cross your arms and legs, they'll see defensiveness and self-protection.

Here's how to manage your body language so it supports your messages.

Body Language Is SO CLEAR

Here is a *mnemonic device* to help you remember the seven main aspects of managing your body language:

SO CLEAR

As we go through each element, remember that, to some extent, body language is culturally shaped, particularly its more subtle aspects. In today's shrinking world, it pays to be aware of cultural differences, too.

Stand *for Cooperation*

S is for the way you *sit* or *stand* and the way you use *space*.

When you're communicating with someone face-to-face, the way you sit or stand, and use space, can open up or obstruct communication. There are three things to remember.

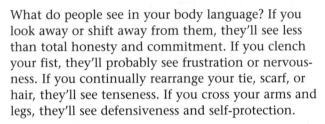

1. **Sitting or standing directly opposite someone, or squaring up to them, is sensed as confrontational.** It puts the communicators into fighting mode. Most of us will automatically sit next to someone we want to cooperate with.

To set the scene for open and cooperative communication, sit or stand more at right angles rather than directly opposite. This sends cooperative messages and gives both parties more gazing space when looking away to think.

Some cultures make a habit of this. Traditional Aboriginal Australians and Native Americans, for example, often stand side by side.

2. **Height communicates.** It lends dignity and authority. Think of where the judge in a courtroom sits, the monarch on the throne, the gold medalist on the dais. We *look up* to people we respect and admire. We place someone *on a pedestal*. The Queen of England *elevates* people to the peerage. People *stand tall and proud*.

A Word to the Wise

If you want to be taken more seriously or express something forcefully, stand up.

Height can place others at a disadvantage, so if you are taller than average, be careful your height doesn't intimidate people. Move slightly away so people don't have to crane their necks looking up at you.

3. **Watch your use of personal space.** We each have an invisible personal space zone around us, and beware anyone who enters it! People are "touchy" about their space generally. Personal space is just that—it's mine! We can trespass in three ways: (1) by getting inside a person's personal space zone; (2) by putting our things in someone else's space (coffee cup, papers, books, shopping bag, briefcase); and (3) by using someone else's equipment, possessions, or space as if they were our own.

Foot in Mouth

It can be threatening when someone towers over you. As far as possible, try to sit or stand on the same level as the person you're talking to.

Trespassing causes resentment. It irritates people and can even make them angry. We feel uncomfortable and "invaded" if people enter our territory uninvited.

Personal Space Zones

Relationship	Personal Space
Intimate: close friends or family	Up to 18 inches, touching range
Personal: friends or close co-workers	1. 5 to 4 feet
Social: co-workers or acquaintances	4 to 5 feet
Public: strangers	5 feet or more, depending on how you perceive their level of friendliness

We need to take cultural differences in personal space zones into account when communicating with people from cultures other than our own. The figures given above are generally applicable to people from most Anglo-Saxon countries. People from Southern Europe and the Middle East have smaller personal space zones than northern Europeans and North Americans. People from rural areas usually have larger personal space zones than people from cities.

A Word to the Wise

Standing too close to people makes them feel uncomfortable and invaded. Stand at arm's length in business and social encounters so they'll feel more relaxed and responsive.

Age and personality make a difference, too: Children, older people, and extroverts sit or stand closer than middle-aged baby boomers and introverts. Attitudes also influence the size of our personal space; generally speaking, we sit or stand closer to people we like.

While touching is infrequent in most business situations, it sometimes occurs—someone might pat another person on the back or place a hand on a shoulder, for instance. Most Asians, however, generally do not touch at all in business situations.

When communicating with people from a different culture, take your cues about personal space zones and physical contact from them. Sensitivity to personal boundaries will save a great deal of embarrassment, discomfort, and misunderstanding.

Open Up

O is for the *openness* of your expression and movements.

Consider two people, one standing with her arms comfortably at her sides, facing towards you, and looking at you; the other with crossed arms and legs, hunched shoulders, feet pointing away from you, chin down. Who looks more approachable? Who would you rather talk to? Who would you open up more with?

Crossed arms, legs, or ankles, face or body turned away, clenched fists, closed or hooded eyes, pinched lips—these convey a clear unspoken message about not wanting to hear, being closed to new ideas and information, defensiveness, self-protection, and even fearfulness. They say "I'm nervous and uncertain, and I'm closed to you and what you are saying."

Body language like this lets us down by giving a negative impression to others. It obstructs communication because it is difficult to give good information to someone sending out such signals. And because of the strong mind-body link that we discussed in Chapter 3, "We Reap What We Sow," negative body language like this makes gathering good information all but impossible: When our body closes up, our ears and mind do, too.

In contrast, openness of gestures and body position and an open and receptive-looking facial expression signal openness of thoughts, mind, and attitudes; openness to communication and to hearing what others have to say; and even of trustworthiness. They signal "I'm confident and I want to hear what you have to say."

Openness shows up in our body language and signals our sincerity, too. It is far easier to give good information to an "open" person than to a "closed" person, just as it is far easier to gather good information when our body language is open.

Center *Your Attention*

C is for how exclusively you *center your attention* on the other person.

Face the person you're speaking with and listen with "focused concentration." Stop doing whatever you're doing, put your pen down, and make the speaker and topic the center of your attention. This means putting other things, including what you will say in reply, out of your mind and listening with your eyes as well as your ears. This builds bridges, helps the speaker get his or her point across, and helps us hear it. It encourages the speaker to continue and reduces the chances that things going on around you will distract you.

The more important a communication is, the more important it is to push any other thoughts from your mind and focus wholly on the speaker and what they are saying.

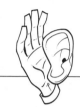

Listen to This

According to the Frank Cole Theory of Beards, almost every second man in the old East German Republic had a full beard. Was it because of the shortage or razor blades? No! The main reason was that they were all so busy spying and informing on each other that beards were a "disguise." No one can clearly see your face to decide whether you're telling the truth or read your lip movements to eavesdrop from a distance!

Silver Tongue

"Sincerity is a certain openness of the heart."

—Francois Duc De La Rochefoucauld

Listen to This

What's the worst body language you've ever seen? Most people describe a person leaning far back in their chair, hands clasped behind their head, elbows out, legs stretched out in front of them. This says: "Hey! I'm so cool! A little worm like you is no threat to me!"

Why is this so offensive? Most of our important organs are protected by our skeletal structure. The exception is "our soft underbelly" which offers little defense. That's why when we feel nervous or under pressure, we instinctively "protect" ourselves by crossing our arms, hunching over, crossing our legs, and so on. Over-exposing the "soft underbelly" is interpreted as arrogance in the extreme by many people.

In short, make the speaker and the topic at hand the center of your attention.

Attention is a silent compliment.

Lean *Slightly Forward*

L is for how you *lean* to show attention, apply pressure, or reduce pressure.

When listening, we can signal that we are paying close attention to the speaker by leaning slightly toward him. This communicates our interest and involvement in the conversation.

Silver Tongue

"Those who are silent, self-effacing, and attentive become the recipients of confidences."

—Thornton Wilder,

If we lean *slightly* more than slightly, but not too far toward the other person, this subtly and silently signals them to provide more information.

Leaning slightly back from the person we're speaking with is a way to take the pressure off. For example, if someone looks nervous or is becoming emotional or talking about a difficult personal matter, lean slightly back to reduce some of the pressure they might be feeling. Again, there is a fine line, because if we lean too far back we could look as if we were not interested.

Make Eye Contact

E is for the way you make *eye contact.*

Tune into the amount of eye contact the other person uses and try to follow their lead.

In Anglo-Saxon cultures, eye contact is very important. Eyes are considered the "windows to the soul." Parents tell their children: "Look at me when I'm speaking to you!" Friends say: "He couldn't even look me in the eye."

Eye contact is a sign of honesty and trustworthiness. It can reassure the other person we're listening, following, and interested, and like the way we incline our body toward or away from someone, it can apply or reduce pressure.

The "right" level of eye contact from a listener encourages the speaker to continue. With too little eye contact, we become lackluster, uninterested listeners.

The "right" level of eye contact from a speaker says, "I'm telling you the truth; you can believe what I say." It also helps to hold the listener's attention. With too much eye contact, we become untrustworthy, intimidating speakers while looking away suggests, "I'm hiding something."

The difficulty here is that the "right" level of eye contact often varies between cultures. The right level of eye contact for Anglo-Saxons is about one-third of the time. More than this causes discomfort.

This isn't the case everywhere, though. In some cultures, such as the Australian Aboriginal culture and some African cultures, this amount of eye contact is considered disrespectful and an invasion of personal space. Averting your eyes is a sign of respect.

Many people from Southeast and North Asian cultures are comfortable with lower levels of eye contact than most Anglo-Saxons, for similar reasons. Especially when someone of a senior rank is speaking to you, it is more polite to gaze downward than to look them directly in the eye.

Foot in Mouth

Don't lean too far or too close, or you'll find yourself invading the other person's space and turning attentiveness into "pressure." This is why we can feel cornered, not complimented, when someone "gets in our face."

Silver Tongue

"The glance is natural magic. The mysterious communication established across a house between two entire strangers, moves all the springs of wonder. The communication by the glance is in the greatest part not subject to the control of the will. It is the bodily symbol of identity with nature. We look into the eyes ... and the eyes will not lie, but make a faithful confession what inhabitant is there."

—Ralph Waldo Emerson

Foot in Mouth

Don't confuse still and balanced with stiff. A person can be comfortably still and relaxed. The effect is quite different.

When listening, Asians often close their eyes. Europeans might panic at this unless they realize that this indicates a highly concentrated level of listening; it is done to block out all distractions in order to listen intently to the speaker. It is, in fact, quite a compliment.

Bearing these important cultural differences in mind, slightly increased levels of eye contact (without staring the other down) can be used to increase pressure in a way that is similar to leaning towards the other person. Conversely, slightly reduced eye contact can reduce pressure, just as leaning slightly away from someone does. Again, sensitivity is the key. Observe the other person's body language to ascertain how you're doing.

At Ease

A is for how *at ease* you are when you communicate.

Are you a fidgeter? People interpret jiggling, tapping, or leaning as inner turmoil, inner confusion, or excitement. Although we may jiggle, tap, or lean purely through habit or to release nervous energy, these actions can distract others and hamper communication. They say "I'm not interested," "I'm bored and want to get out of here," "I'm nervous and uncertain," or "I'm flustered."

You'll look better and you'll be able to communicate better if you're at ease. This means relaxed (comfortably still, not stiff) and balanced (not leaning at any extreme or awkward angles). Sit up straight and no jiggling, tapping feet or pencils, or adjusting clothing or hair. You'll look more self-possessed, self-confident, and authoritative this way, and as a bonus, it's actually healthier.

Reflect *and* Respond

R is for how well we *reflect* and *respond* to what the speaker has said.

Saying something that is unrelated or contradictory to what the speaker has been talking about can bring a discussion to a rapid and resentful halt. Appropriate responses, particularly building on and extending what the speaker has said, and *reflective listening* responses show that we're following the other person's points. This encourages them to continue and adds grace to the dance of communication. In Part 4, "Gathering Good Information," we look at the skill of reflective listening and the importance of restating what the speaker has said to verify our understanding and gather more information. We also look at the importance of repeating the gist of what a person has just said before asking another fact-gathering question, to avoid creating the impression of an "interrogation."

This, essentially, is what responding appropriately consists of. It is the opposite of abruptly leading the conversation onto a different tack.

Make It a Habit

The more we stray from the SO CLEAR standard described above, the more uncomfortable with us other people will feel. Communication will suffer accordingly.

Seven aspects of your body language isn't a lot to remember—unless you're trying to get them "right" all at the same time in an important or difficult communication situation!

The best way to make good body language automatic is to first check your own against the SO CLEAR standard to pinpoint the areas that need work. Then work on them one at a time until each becomes a habit. Keep focusing on perfecting an aspect of your body language until it's automatic, and then move onto the next until you've mastered them all.

If you begin a concerted campaign now, it should take about three weeks to master each component of SO CLEAR body language.

The effort you make at checking your body language and correcting any distracting habits will be well rewarded. Eventually, "doing it all right" will become an unconscious and automatic habit and your body language will automatically and naturally support your spoken communications.

A Word to the Wise

To respond appropriately, build on, extend, or clarify what the speaker has said. This lends smoothness and a natural rhythm to the flow of a conversation.

The Least You Need to Know

➤ Body language may be silent but it speaks volumes.

➤ Respect peoples' personal space.

➤ Stand up if you want to be taken more seriously or express something forcefully.

➤ Open your body language to open your mind.

➤ Focus your attention on the person you are speaking with to gather high quality information.

➤ Summarize or add to what a speaker says for a smooth and naturally flowing conversation.

Chapter 11

Other People's Body Language

In This Chapter

➤ Reading the silent messages of others

➤ Signal clusters

➤ Bad news: negative signals

➤ Good news: positive signals

➤ Practicing your skills

Charles de Talleyrand-Perigord, the eighteenth-century French statesman, said, "Language exists to conceal true thought." Perhaps he wasn't very good at reading body language.

It's true that people don't always say everything that is on their minds. Some people purposely keep things to themselves yet leak their thoughts and opinions through their body language. Others might believe their own words and be surprised that their body language, reflecting their subconscious, is disagreeing with them.

Body language reveals people's true thought. It can forewarn us of problems, such as lack of understanding, disagreement, or budding conflict. It can signal support, agreement, or encouragement. It can show how comfortable a person is with what they're saying or how committed they really are to their words. It can guide our timing and help us judge when to speak up and when not to, when to press for agreement and when to bide our time, when to lighten up and when to apply pressure.

Does people's language conceal their true thought from you, or does their body language reveal it to you? Can you accurately gauge others' reactions and their receptiveness to you and your message? You'll discover how to do this and get some practice in this chapter.

Reading Other People's Body Language

Most of us understand body language intuitively and quickly, and the conclusions we reach often go straight into our subconscious. Sometimes, however, it pays to look out for certain positive and negative signals. Then you'll know whether your communications are succeeding or missing the mark, and you'll be able to adjust the way you are sending your message as necessary.

Reading the Signals

The Signal	What It Says
Nodding the head	This person is listening to me. This person agrees with me.
Scratching the neck or rubbing eyes and looking at the ceiling (if a woman) or the floor (if a man)	This person may not be telling the truth.
Clenched hands	This person is frustrated. (The higher the hands, the higher their frustration.)
Hand on cheek	This person is interested but has some doubts.
Hand on cheek with thumb under chin	This person is interested but has some doubts.
Picking off imaginary lint	This person disagrees with or disapproves of what I've said but isn't willing to say so.
Crossed arms and legs	This person is tuning me out or filtering what I'm saying.

At first, you will probably need to stop and consciously check other people's body language; after a while, noticing and adjusting your communication accordingly becomes automatic.

Many body language signals are self-explanatory when you think about them: a tapping foot can indicate we are anxious to be on our way; rubbing our neck can say:

"You give me a pain in the neck"; a quick intake of breath can signal surprise or sudden understanding.

Foot in Mouth

Be careful how you interpret people's unspoken messages. Crossed arms can say: "I feel threatened by what you're saying and I'm closed to hearing it," but they can also say: "I'm cold!" A tapping foot might mean "I'd like to be on my way"; it might also reflect a lot of nervous energy or a need for the toilet! Scratching our head may mean puzzlement or uncertainty; or it may mean that our head itches. There are no fixed rules, only general principles.

It's important to observe a person's body language in context and establish a "baseline." Crossed arms often indicate defensiveness or disagreement. But some people have been taught in school to fold their arms when they have finished their work. Some people always fold their arms out of habit.

Observe Signal Clusters

Most *body language* signals appear in *clusters,* or groups. Clusters of postures, movements, expressions, or gestures tell us more than isolated, individual signals. They are best considered in the context of a person's entire behavior and the situation.

To continue with the crossed arms example: If our crossed arms were accompanied by rubbing our upper arms with our hands and perhaps stomping our feet and hunching up our shoulders, most people would feel fairly safe in concluding that we were cold, not closed.

If, on the other hand, our crossed arms were accompanied by looking away from the speaker, tapping a foot, and occasionally shaking our head, others could reasonably reach the conclusion that we disagreed with what they were saying.

Let's take this a step further. Our companion's arms are crossed, he's stomping his feet and

Famous Last Words

Body language clusters, or groups of postures, movements, expressions, or gestures, reveal our inner thoughts and impulses.

115

Silver Tongue

"Facial expressions and body gestures are a living language which we all have learned to read as a clue to, and use as a revelation, of character."

—Paul Zucker

A Word to the Wise

Develop the habit of watching people's body language. Try to discover whether anything you have said or done could have triggered particular reactions. Adjust your communication to lead to the best possible result.

hunching his shoulders. Is he tactfully trying to end our conversation? Is he really cold? If so, he can't be concentrating fully on our conversation, so perhaps we should adjourn to another location where he'll be warm, comfortable, and able to give us his full attention?

Perhaps our friend has just come from a particularly difficult meeting or had an argument with someone. Is that still on his mind and his crossed arms, tapping foot, and shaking head have nothing to do with what we are saying and us? If so, should we arrange to meet again later, when he can focus on what we have to say?

Observe Movements

Any movements, particularly sudden movements, can indicate a person's inner state. A sudden shift in position, for example, can be very telling.

If a person suddenly uncrosses their legs, reorients their body toward you and leans slightly forward, you may well have just said something they strongly approve of or want to hear more about. If you noticed this, you would probably want to think about what you just said and what in particular might have been favorably received.

Look Out for Negative Signals

A person's body language can act as an early warning signal that something is amiss in the communication process. Negative signals include …

➤ feet pointed away from you

➤ tapping feet

➤ rapidly nodding head

➤ covering nose

➤ rubbing or scratching neck or nose

➤ looking skyward

➤ avoiding or limiting eye contact

➤ covering mouth

➤ body oriented away from you

➤ tense posture

➤ covering or rubbing ears

➤ "dancing" around

➤ forming a fist, clenching hands

➤ rapidly exhaling breath

➤ fidgeting (e.g., rapidly tapping a pencil)

➤ drumming fingers on the table

➤ buttoning coat or jacket

116

Boredom might look like this:

➤ doodling

➤ drumming fingers

➤ crossed legs with foot swinging or kicking

➤ head in hands

➤ blank stare

➤ taking deep breaths

➤ tapping floor with foot

➤ clicking pen in and out

Frustration might look like this:

➤ short breaths

➤ "tssk" sound

➤ hands tightly clenched

➤ wringing hands

➤ fist-like gestures

➤ pointing index finger

➤ running hand through hair

➤ rubbing back of neck

➤ kicking at the ground or imaginary object

Territorial dominance might look like this:

➤ feet on desk

➤ hands clasped at back of head

➤ back stiffened

➤ thumbs in pockets

➤ hands on lapels of coat

➤ leaning on their "turf" to show possession (equipment, door frame, car)

If you see any of this negative body language, alone or especially in clusters, watch out! What have you just said or done that has put the other person offside? How could you explain things differently? How can you help them see your point of view? Do you need to listen more carefully to their point of view? What action can you take that will put the communication back on track?

Look Out for Positive Signals

Just as body language can alert us to looming problems, it can also herald success. Positive body language signals include …

➤ nodding thoughtfully

➤ relaxed posture

➤ body oriented toward you

➤ open hands

➤ feet pointed toward you

➤ thoughtful "um-hums"

➤ stroking chin

➤ open body position

➤ eye contact, particularly when pupils are dilated (enlarged)

➤ handling the documents or materials you are presenting

Cooperation might look like this:

➤ sprinter's position

➤ open hands

➤ sitting on edge of chair

➤ unbuttoning coat

➤ tilted head

➤ leaning toward you

➤ moving closer to you

Evaluation might look like this:

➤ hand-to-face gestures

➤ tilted head

➤ stroking chin, or chin in palm of hand

➤ taking glasses off and cleaning them

➤ sucking on pen or glasses arm

➤ peering over glasses

When you notice any of these favorable signals, particularly if they appear in clusters, make sure you maintain the positive momentum. What have you been saying, how have you been saying it, and what have you been doing? Keep communicating in the current vein.

Thoughtful awareness of other peoples' body language will help you gauge whether you are succeeding or missing the mark in your communications. See Appendix B, "Body Language Practice," for more information on interpreting body language.

The Least You Need to Know

➤ Body language reveals people's true thoughts.

➤ Most of us interpret body language, often without realizing it.

➤ Tune into negative body language signals.

➤ Be aware of positive body language signals.

➤ Use other people's body language as a guide, but don't read too much into it.

Chapter 12

Build Rapport

In This Chapter

➤ The comfortable harmony of rapport

➤ Building rapport with your voice, body, and energy

➤ Matching and mirroring

➤ Testing for rapport

Have you ever known someone who irritates you? Or met a person whose wavelength you just couldn't seem to tune in to? You lack *rapport* with these people and, because of this, communicating with them is awkward.

Have you ever instantly "clicked" with someone and felt like you'd known them your whole life? Communication flows fully and enjoyably with people like this.

This chapter explores rapport—what it is and how to build it to dramatically enhance all of your communications. You'll also find out how to establish whether you really are on the same wavelength with someone before, for example, asking an important question, trying to reach a joint decision, or trying to persuade them of something.

The Comfortable Harmony of Rapport

Rapport helps build relationships and smooth communication. It reduces conflict and fosters cooperation. It helps achieve results. In short, it is essential to successful communication.

Rapport is based on similarity. When two people are in rapport, the body language and energy level of one is often reflected in the other: They will be sitting in a similar or even identical position, for example, or they will be leaning forward at the same angle or crossing their legs in the same way. They will be using similar gestures and gesturing at similar rates with similar energy.

Famous Last Words

Rapport (pronounced *ra-pore*) is the feeling of being in sync or in harmony with another person. When we have rapport with someone, we feel a sense of affinity and unity. We feel comfortable with them, and communication flows.

Famous Last Words

When people like each other, their body language, energy levels, language, and lots of other things **match.** If you want to build rapport more quickly, you can match another person on purpose.

Their movements often coincide, too. For example, when one person shifts position, so does the other; when one person reaches for a drink, the other does too. Or they might be swinging their legs to the same, silent rhythm.

They might even be speaking at the same speed, with similar intonation or at a similar volume. They might use the same or similar expressions or speak with a similar intensity in their voices.

If we look more closely, we might notice more subtle things they have in common. For instance, they might be breathing in unison. Their comments might be based on shared but unstated values and beliefs about the world. There might be similar degrees of formality or informality in the way they are speaking, the way they are sitting, and the way they are dressed.

This happens instinctively. The more we *like* someone, the more *like them* we will be. This is called *matching*. We naturally and unconsciously match someone we feel rapport with. This matching reinforces and strengthens people's liking for each other and helps their communications flow.

People aren't normally conscious of the fact that they are matching their body language, voice, or energy, but their subconscious notices. They each realize: "This person is really like me in a lot of ways. I like this person and feel comfortable talking to them and sharing my thoughts and ideas." We all like people who are like ourselves.

Build Rapport Through Matching

Rapport develops naturally over time with people we like. We believe and trust people we like. We enjoy being with people we like and find it easy to communicate with them.

We can speed up the process by matching someone verbally and nonverbally on purpose. This establishes a bond allowing communication to flow more easily. It builds cooperative, cordial relationships.

We can match lots of things: a person's beliefs, personal history, vocabulary, style of dress, body language, breathing …. The list goes on and on. Let's look at the three things that are most easily matched.

A Word to the Wise

It's amazing what you can learn when you look. The next time you are in a restaurant or other public place, watch various pairs and groups of people. Who seems to have rapport and who doesn't? Why?

Match Body Language

First, body language. We can match a person's whole body position, the position of the upper or lower half of their body, or the angle of their head and/or shoulders. We can match the type and rate of someone's movements and gestures. We can match these things precisely or partially—the choice is ours.

Test this out. Observe people who are good friends and see in what ways their body language matches. Notice your own body language and the way it matches someone you feel comfortable with. Now purposely match someone's body language and see what happens. (Don't worry about feeling self-conscious, that will fade as matching to build rapport becomes automatic.)

Match Voice

We can match someone's voice—its tone, volume, speed, pitch, rhythm, inflections, intonations, and pauses. We can match the expressions they use, language style, or some of the phrases and words they use. We can match the type of vocabulary and speech patterns (colloquial or correct) they use and their degree of seriousness and formality.

You can test this out, too. Listen to two good friends speaking. Don't they speak at pretty much the same volume and speed? Don't they use similar language and speak with a similar degree of formality or informality? You might even notice two people picking up on each other's accents!

121

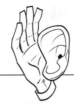

Listen to This

Tall, blonde Cynthia ran a lot of corporate training programs in Southeast Asia. Although she considered her vocal volume to be in the "average" range, she knew that after several days of training, the volume rose automatically because of continually speaking to fairly large numbers.

During breaks, when course participants or their managers came up to speak to her, she made a conscious effort to lower her voice. "Can you imagine," she explained. "First of all, the local people I'm training are much more softly and quietly spoken than I am, so my voice is a bit louder anyway. Secondly, if I speak to them at my accustomed 'training volume', I'd blast them into the stratosphere! We'd have a real communication problem! We're different enough as it is!"

Match Energy

We can match people's energy, too. We can match how rapidly and where they breathe (upper chest, lower chest, stomach) and how they breathe (shallowly or deeply). We can match the energy in their movements and gestures, and in the way they speak.

The next time you're talking to an up-beat person you like a lot, notice whether you also become more animated. The next time you're talking to a restrained person you like, see if you don't become a bit more reserved.

Famous Last Words

Mirroring is cross-over, or back-to-front matching—just like looking in a mirror.

Build Rapport Through Mirroring

Or we can do what is known as cross-over matching, or *mirroring*. For example, if the person's right leg is crossed over the left leg, we cross our left leg over our right leg; if they are rubbing their right forearm with their left hand, we rub our left forearm with our right hand. If they are gently tapping the palm of their hand on their leg, we gently tap our foot to the same silent rhythm.

The idea of building rapport through matching and mirroring is not to copy blindly every movement a person makes or each position they sit in. Rapport is something we do *with* a person not *to* a person.

Match or mirror only when you sincerely want to build rapport and improve communication between yourself and another person and when you feel true respect for that person.

Don't match or mirror if it feels unnatural, uncomfortable, or insincere—this reduces it to an empty technique and does nothing to build rapport.

A Word to the Wise

To build rapport, consciously reduce the differences between yourself and the other person and build on the similarities.

Build Rapport by Identifying Commonalities

Have you ever bumped into someone who once worked for the same company you once did and felt an instant bond? You knew a bit about them and that you shared a similar background and experiences just because of this.

Which stranger would you rather spend time with: someone half your age or someone close to your age? You're more likely to have things in common with the latter.

Silver Tongue

"People with the same sickness sympathize with one another."

—Chinese proverb

Have you ever struck up a conversation with someone to find they went to the same school you did? The quick connection probably helped communication proceed.

Having things in common with others builds rapport because it builds bridges.

When we've been living or traveling away from home for extended periods, most of us perk up at the sound of a familiar accent. This isn't homesickness so much as natural bonds between people.

Rapport is gentle. Match and mirror sensitively and discreetly. *Adjust* your verbal and nonverbal communications to theirs, but don't *copy*.

A Word to the Wise

To help people like you, find and build on commonalities you share: attitudes, likes and dislikes, goals, experiences, backgrounds, values, and hobbies. Emphasise what you share.

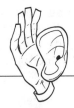

Listen to This

Marie was a typical Bostonian with a typical Boston accent. Irene, from the deep South, moved next door. They became firm friends and spent a lot of time together.

One day, Marie noticed Irene had become distant and asked her if she had done anything to offend her. "Marie," said Irene, "I don't like it that y'all are makin' fun o' mah accent!" Marie was shocked. She certainly hadn't intended to make fun of Irene at all—in fact, she loved listening to her speak. Then she realized that perhaps, although she hadn't intended to, she was pronouncing words in similar ways and using a lot of Irene's inflections.

Without meaning to, Marie had overmatched and offended Irene. It's easy to do this when we like someone a lot.

Test for Rapport

Sometimes we want a clear idea of the strength of rapport between ourselves and another person. If we were about to ask an important question or close a sale, for example, we would probably want to do whatever we could to ensure a positive result by asking our question only when we felt certain that we had built up sufficient rapport.

Famous Last Words

When you shift your position or alter your energy level or voice to see whether the other person follows your lead, you are testing for rapport with a technique called **leading**.

We can test for rapport with a technique known as *leading*. Very simply, we do something differently, for example, shift our position and see whether the other person follows. If the other person follows our lead, matching our new position, this indicates that we have rapport. The more positively and quickly the other person follows our lead, the deeper our rapport is likely to be. Go ahead and pop the question!

You don't always have to shift position: You could talk more quickly or slowly, or more loudly or softly; you could reach for a pen and fiddle with it; you could scratch your shoulder or ankle; you could take a sip of coffee or alter your energy level in some way.

Whatever you alter, if you and the other person have rapport, their subconscious will notice that you are no longer fully in sync and the other person will shift their body language to bring it into line with yours. When this happens, you can be quite certain you have rapport and communication is flowing.

The importance of rapport in communication cannot be overemphasized. The more important a communication situation is, the more you may want to think about matching, mirroring, and identifying commonalities to build rapport quickly and leading to test for rapport.

Foot in Mouth

When you match someone's body language, they should not notice it consciously. You don't want them to think: "Gee, every time I scratch myself, so does he. Every time I move, or sigh, so does he." Or: "I wish she'd stop copying me." Only their *unconscious* minds should notice the similarities. Subtlety is the key.

The Least You Need to Know

➤ Build rapport if you want communication to flow easily.

➤ People like people who are like themselves.

➤ Increase the ways you are like someone through body language, voice, and energy level.

➤ Use the techniques of matching, mirroring, and identifying commonalities gently and discreetly to build rapport and help communication flow.

➤ Watch for signs of matching and mirroring in others to see how much rapport they have.

➤ Test for rapport before asking an important question if you want to increase your chances of a "Yes!"

Part 4

Gathering Good Information

Learn how things are from the other person's point of view.

John Stuart Mill, the nineteenth-century English philosopher and economist, said, "He who knows only his own side of the case, knows little of that." Understanding only our own point of view would not only make us very poor communicators but we wouldn't learn much either! Sadly, hearing the other side does not come automatically.

Linguists estimate there are about 4,500 languages in the world. Actually, there are over six billion! Each of us talks, listens, and thinks in our own special language, called an idiolect. This is our personal dialect, the unique way we each put words together. It is shaped by our culture, experience, background, personality, beliefs, and values. The chances of meeting someone else who speaks our precise language are remote indeed!

We saw in Part 2, "The Dance of Communication," that communication is a process that takes place between people. Good communicators bring their frames of reference together as much as they can to blend their languages and achieve mutual understanding. Just as it takes two to tango, the dance of every communication, even written communication, involves interaction between the communicators.

It entails sharing viewpoints, feelings, thoughts, and ideas to achieve mutual understanding. The ability to gather good information is essential to a graceful, harmonious, and gratifying dance.

The eighteenth-century French author, philosopher, and satirist Françoise Marie Voltaire said, "Judge a man by his questions, not by his answers." In this section, we'll look at how to draw out the full story by asking great questions and listening to the answers and by following four stages of drawing out the full story.

Chapter 13

Draw Out the Full Story

In This Chapter

➤ Listening habits to avoid

➤ Four rudiments of focusing on the speaker

➤ Open questions and closed questions

➤ Affirmative listening

➤ Four steps to drawing out the full story

Are you in the habit of trying to see things from the speaker's point of view? We all need to if we are to truly communicate. This empathic understanding helps us respond appropriately to the speaker and draw out the full story.

Focusing attentively on the speaker and seeing things from his or her point of view is at the core of gathering good information and good communication. In this chapter, we look at how *not* to listen, how to stay focused on the speaker, and a four-step formula for drawing out the full story.

Are You Guilty of Poor Listening Habits?

How often do you tune someone out as disturbing "background noise"? While it might sometimes make sense to tune out a toddler's continuous chatter, tuning out short-circuits any chance of good communication with adults.

Have you ever pretended to listen while continuing what you were doing or thinking? Pretending to give the speaker our attention and occasionally nodding our head and mumbling "uh-huh" is not communication.

Have you ever listened with only half an ear, intending to "tune in" when something of significance is said? Unfortunately, our ability to filter information selectively like this is not very reliable, and we miss a great deal of valuable information as a result.

There are other bad habits that stop people from drawing out the full story. Are any of these yours?

Ask yourself, do I …

➤ formulate my own reply while the other person speaks?

➤ let my mind wander?

➤ "tune out" a point of view that differs from my own preconceived ideas?

➤ interrupt speakers?

➤ finish speakers' sentences for them?

➤ talk while other people are speaking?

➤ jump to conclusions?

➤ hear only what I want to hear, expect to hear, or what I assume the speaker will say?

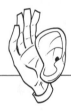

Listen to This

The Chinese character for listen, pronounced *ting*, is made up of four characters: the heart, the mind, the ears, and the eyes.

The truth is, people often need to feel heard before they can hear. We often need to gather good information before we can give it. To gather good information, we need to focus on the speaker. Not pretend to focus, but genuinely attend to and tune into what the speaker is saying, feeling, and meaning. We do this with our eyes, ears, hearts, and minds.

More than that, speakers need to sense that we are trying to understand their point of view and that we won't ignore it, stifle it, criticizes, or condemn it. Only then will they be willing to bother to continue giving us good information.

Don't fake it if you are too busy or preoccupied to focus on what someone is trying to tell you. Gathering good information hinges on being able to focus on the other person. If you really can't, arrange a better time to meet.

Focus on the Speaker

What can we do to improve our ability to focus on the speaker? Here are some ideas, grouped into environmental, physical, mental, and verbal categories.

Get the Environment Right

As we discussed in Chapter 7, "Everything We Do Is Communication," it is important to remove any obstacles that prevent us from focusing on the speaker. Noise and other distractions can break our attention and block the communication process.

Listen to This

Anthropologist Edward Hall, in his book *Beyond Culture,* suggests that we need to see words in the context in which they are spoken. Who says the words? Where are they said? How are they spoken? What is the background? What led to these words being spoken?

European, American, and Australian cultures emphasize the words themselves while most other cultures emphasize, and place more trust in, the context to arrive at an understanding of meaning.

What do you place more faith in: people saying what they mean and meaning what they say, or the "between the lines" of what is not said?

Be Physically Involved

Attend the conversation physically, too. We saw how to manage our body language in Chapter 10, "Send the Right Signals," and how to match and mirror to build rapport in Chapter 12, "Build Rapport."

Attentive body language helps us to focus on the speaker and encourages the speaker to give us more information because it will be clear that he or she has our attention.

Be Mentally Involved

Here are six suggestions to help keep your mind on the speaker:

➤ **Clear your mind.** Do you have something else on your mind? Put it mentally to one side for now, or note it down if you think you might forget it; it will still be there when you've finished listening.

➤ **Take notes.** If the topic is important, take notes to help keep the information straight in your mind and assist you to concentrate.

➤ **Summarize the main points and ideas** mentally as you listen and note any shifts in the speaker's body language, tone of voice, facial expression, and so on.

➤ **Suspend judgment.** If you are weighing up the worth, accuracy, or validity of what is being said as you listen, you'll commit some of the ten deadly communication sins described in the Chapter 16, "The Ten Deadly Sins of Communication."

➤ **Use your free mental time wisely.** Since we think faster than people talk, use some of your free mental time while you're listening to pay attention to the representational system in which the other person is speaking (see Chapter 19, "Speak the Other Person's Language") and to discover their motives and personality type or temperament (see Chapter 24, "Tune In to the Same Wavelength").

A Word to the Wise

Listen first, then assess. Follow the speaker's train of thought, listening to understand not evaluate.

➤ **Listen for the meanings behind the words.** What is she really saying? What does she need from you? Look and listen for clues to how to make your point of view understood when you stop gathering and start giving good information.

Check It Verbally

Here are four ways to check out what the speaker has said.

1. Paraphrase it by putting it in your own words.

2. Clarify it by asking questions to uncover more detail, so you can be sure what the speaker means.

3. Probe it further, with questions that draw out more information.

4. Summarize it to check your understanding.

Foot in Mouth

Don't fake it if you're not sure you've heard or understood something correctly. Check it.

Are you concerned you'll seem pushy or prying? Most people will interpret your attempts to make sure you've understood correctly as thoughtfulness and an indication that you care about what they have said and what you are going to say.

Here are three ways to round out the information you're gathering to build up a full picture:

➤ If someone is giving you facts, ask how they interpret them.

➤ If they're giving you their opinions, we can ask what facts or experiences they base them on.

➤ If feelings are missing, we can ask how they feel about the topic or what their gut reaction is.

A checklist for focusing on the speaker

✔ Ask questions and listen to the answer without adding your own thoughts.

✔ Don't interrupt the speaker.

✔ Give the speaker time to have their say.

✔ Bite your tongue: Resist the temptation to talk about yourself, your opinions, your experiences—just for now.

✔ Manage your body language to show you are listening.

✔ Squash any negative, judgmental, sarcastic, or otherwise critical responses.

✔ Observe the speaker's body language, tone of voice, and facial expressions, so you can "listen between the lines" for what the speaker is actually communicating.

✔ Stick to the point; avoid being side-tracked or distracted.

✔ Mentally summarize and sift what the speaker is saying into key themes.

✔ Build rapport to help the speaker feel comfortable with you.

✔ Keep at it—it takes practice!

A Word to the Wise

Give yourself time to think. Don't feel you need to respond the moment the speaker pauses. Reflect on what he's said and its meaning. Then perhaps restate it to check your understanding.

You cannot gather good information without focusing on the speaker. Once you're able to do that, you can draw out the full story with your EARS, the four steps described below.

Use Your EARS!

Lend me your ears …

E Explore by asking questions.

A Affirm to show you're listening.

R Reflect your understanding.

S Silence. Listen some more!

Explore by Asking Open Questions

The kind of questions you ask can greatly influence the kind of answer you get in return.

A *closed question* is one that can be answered with a "yes," "no," or a short statement of fact. If we ask a closed question, chances are we will receive less than the full story; it's too easy to respond to a closed question with a "yes," a "no," or a fact.

Famous Last Words

A **closed question** is one that can be answered with a "yes," "no," or a short statement of fact.

Closed questions

"What is your favorite animal?" "A dog."

"Do you like your job?" "Yes."

"Did you have any problems?" "No."

"Who do you work for?" "John."

As you'll see in the following section, closed questions can be good for finding out facts and for preventing someone from being longwinded. Generally, though, they are not helpful for drawing out the full story.

Open questions are much better for drawing out the full story because they leave the way open for a range of responses. An open question is any question (or statement, for that matter) that encourages the speaker to provide fuller information and details.

Famous Last Words

An **open question** is one that encourages a full response.

Open questions

"Tell me about your favorite animal."

"What do you like most about your work?"

"What problems did you run into?"

"What's your boss like?"

Open questions usually net us a lot of information. Note that some open "questions" are actually statements. Note also that there is no real rule, such as "Open questions start with who, what, where, when, why, and how." Closed questions can start with these words, too.

Asking open questions needs more skill than most people realize. It takes practice. Rephrase these closed questions to make them open. There are a few ideas in Appendix C, "Turning Closed Questions Into Open Questions."

"When did that happen?"_____

"Was your trip successful?"_____

"Did you like that candidate?"_____

"Did you have a good meeting?'"_____

"Why did that happen?"_____

Try to avoid questions that start with "Why ...," such as "Why did you do that?" "Why" questions can make people defensive and unwilling to give you the information you need.

Affirm to Show You're Listening

When someone is talking, we can use *affirmative listening* to show we're listening and encourage the speaker to continue. In other words, "nod and grunt" and use attentive body language (see Chapter 10, "Send the Right Signals").

Reflect Your Understanding

When the speaker has expressed a full thought, it's time to give a reflective listening response. As we will see in Chapter 15, "Listen, Listen, Listen," this is when we restate, in our own words, the gist of what the speaker has expressed—his feelings or meanings or both, whichever we decide is most appropriate.

This allows us to check our understanding and enables the speaker to clear up any misunderstandings. It also helps us to draw out the full story since a reflective listening response is invariably followed by more information and elaboration.

Silence: Now Listen Some More!

When you have given your reflective listening response, pause; this allows the speaker time to think about what you have said and how to respond.

Famous Last Words

Affirmative listening means using attentive body language and other "minimal encouragers," such as "uh-uhms" to encourage the speaker to continue.

Because reflective listening responses promote well-considered replies, this may take a few seconds—this is where your "silence" is helpful. People can't think things through if we're talking!

A Word to the Wise

After giving a reflective response, pause and count to six. By the time you get to six, nine times out of ten the speaker will have begun speaking again. If nothing has happened once you've reached six, continue to wait expectantly or make another reflective listening response.

Foot in Mouth

If you need to gather a lot of information quickly, you're in danger of asking a string of closed questions. If you're not careful, the recipient will feel as if you're interrogating her or him and communication will grind to a halt.

To avoid this, flag your intention, explain your purpose, and seek permission before asking a lot of closed questions.

Closed Questions Can Be Useful

Closed questions limit a person's thinking and yield less information. Although they aren't as good as open questions for helping draw out the full story, they can be good for helping to "fill in the blanks."

Use closed questions …

➤ to help someone decide quickly: Would you prefer the large size? It's cheaper that way.

➤ when you need a specific piece of information: Would you be able to change your appointment from Tuesday afternoon to Tuesday morning?

➤ to clarify: Was that two o'clock or three o'clock?

➤ when you want to gain agreement: Are you satisfied with that approach?

➤ to bring someone who has digressed back to the main point: Earlier you said …. Is that right?

➤ to complete one aspect of a decision and move on to the next: So that's the seating plan. Is there anything else we need to cover before moving on to discuss the menu?

➤ to summarize and/or check your understanding: So the main issues we need to sort out are …. Is that right?

➤ to help someone be more specific: You mentioned that happens a lot. Can you give me an idea of how many times it has happened this month so that I'll have a better idea of the extent of the problem?

➤ to check agreement: I've decided to …. Is that acceptable to you?

If you need to ask a lot of closed questions, "flag" your intention first. Say something like: "I'd like to ask you a few questions about that if you don't mind," or "So that I can determine whether you qualify, I'll need to ask you some questions; is that okay?"

Flag	Letting them know what we're about to do,
Purpose	and why,
Permission	and checking whether this is all right, increases people's cooperation and readiness to provide the information we need.

Suppose, for example, we go into a tire store to buy a new set of tires. The salesperson will need to know our driving habits in order to recommend the appropriate tire for our needs. She will need to consider such information as how much driving we do over a year, the kind of roads we drive on, and the loads that we normally carry, along with our driving habits and main concerns as a driver. Closed questions will uncover that information.

Imagine a conversation like this:

Salesperson:	*How much driving do you do?*
Customer:	*Oh, mostly just into town and back.*
Salesperson:	*What sort of roads?*
Customer:	*Um, mostly good, paved roads; the odd dirt track at weekends.*
Salesperson:	*Speeds?*
Customer:	*Oh, I'm pretty law-abiding.*
Salesperson:	*What do you carry?*
Customer:	*Just Granny and the kids at the weekend. Otherwise, it's just me.*

Foot in Mouth

To stop a series of fact-finding questions becoming an interrogation, make a short summary of each answer before you ask your next question.

Our salesperson has some information. Now suppose she softens each question by preceding it with a short summary of what the customer has just said. This shows him that he is being listened to, and makes the discussion more like a relaxed, friendly conversation.

Let's begin the conversation with the Flag/Purpose/Permission technique.

Salesperson:	*So that I can determine which tire will best suit your needs, I'd like to ask you some questions about your driving habits, all right?*
Customer:	*Yeah, sure, go right ahead.*
Salesperson:	*How much driving would you say you do?*

Customer:	*Oh, mostly just into town and back.*
Salesperson:	*I see; fairly average mileage there. And what sort of roads do you mostly drive on?*
Customer:	*Um, mostly good, paved roads; the odd dirt track at weekends, though, but not often.*
Salesperson:	*Okay, so pretty good roads, usually.*
Customer:	*Well, actually, I go up and down into the mountains nearly every day.*
Salesperson:	*I see. I hadn't realized you live in the mountains. That actually adds a lot of wear to your tires. I suppose cornering and handling are important to you?*
Customer:	*Oh, absolutely.*
Salesperson:	*And what sort of speeds do you normally drive at?*
Customer:	*Oh, I'm pretty law-abiding. I generally keep to the speed limit.*
Salesperson:	*Okay, so we don't need a super high-performance tire. Do you carry any loads at all?*
Customer:	*Just Granny and the kids at the weekend. Otherwise, it's just me.*

There's a lot more information for the salesperson to work from here. In addition, we have a customer who is feeling much more relaxed and disposed towards making a purchase. The conversational tone set by the salesperson, the use of the Flag/Purpose/Permission technique, which shows respect, and short summaries to show listening, see to this.

A Word to the Wise

When you ask a question, make eye contact while the person is responding and show, by your body language, that you're listening—nod and grunt.

And that's all there is to it. Keep exploring with open questions, filling in the blanks with closed questions, and affirming to show you're listening as often as necessary until you feel able to accurately reflect your understanding and listen some more.

Once you've drawn out the full story, you can present your point of view. When you do, it will be based on good information and a thorough understanding of the speaker's point of view. This means you'll be able to explain your way of seeing things for maximum persuasion and understanding.

Whenever good communication is important, whenever there is a need to gather or to give good information, focus on the speaker. If you sense that someone resists what you're saying, disagrees, or is confused or uncertain, it is even more important really to focus on him and find out what is going on.

Gather some good information. Ask what is worrying, troubling, concerning, or confusing her; what is holding her back from agreeing or giving you her full support? What other information does she need?

The more fully you can focus on people and what they're saying and use your EARS, the more information you will get. The more difficult the communication situation is, the more important it is to do this.

The Least You Need to Know

➤ For people to be willing to talk, you need to show them you're listening.

➤ Get out of the habit of using poor listening habits if you want to be a good communicator.

➤ Clear your mind and focus it on the speaker.

➤ Concentrate and check you have understood before putting in your two cents' worth.

➤ Silence is golden—you'll learn a lot by keeping your mouth shut.

Chapter 14

Ask the Right Questions

In This Chapter

➤ Questions to lose, questions to use

➤ Six types of questions that aren't questions

➤ Questions to cut through the haze and the fog

➤ Questions to find out what's really in a person's head

David Frost, the well-known BBC television interviewer, once said, "You can tell the quality of a question by the quality of the response."

People frequently need our help to give us good information. When this happens, we can ask questions to draw out the full story and fill out the details to form a clear picture. We can ask questions to determine a speaker's frame of reference, their wants and needs, hopes and fears.

In this chapter, you'll find out the questions to stay away from, the questions that will harvest bountiful information, and some important "tricks of the trade" when asking questions to gather good information.

Avoid Unhelpful Questions

You may need to lose a few of these unhelpful questions to make room for the helpful ones.

Famous Last Words

Has anyone ever said something to you like: "That's just plain wrong, don't you think?" or "Shall I pick you up at 10 o'clock?" or "Do you feel like eating out tonight?" These are really **pseudo questions** because they only pretend to be questions; they are really statements" "I think that's wrong." "I'd like to pick you up at 10 o'clock." "I feel like eating out tonight."

Closed and "Why" Questions

Asking questions is a bit of an art. In the last chapter, we saw that closed questions are not helpful for drawing out good information and that "Why ..." questions can make people defensive.

Let's run through three other types of unhelpful questions. To closed questions and "Why ..." questions, we can add *pseudo questions, leading questions,* and *multiple questions* to complete the list of unhelpful kinds of questions.

Pseudo Questions

People often hide their feelings and opinions behind what are called *pseudo questions.* Communications are rife with these, so much so that we can divide pseudo questions into six categories.

Coercive questions are leading questions that narrow or limit the possible answers and trap the other person into giving the answer we want.

> "Don't you think ...?"

> "..., right?"

> "Do you think we should ...?"

> "Wouldn't you think they'd ...?"

> "Wouldn't you rather ... [do this]?"

What we really mean is "I think" or "Let's ... [do this]. "

Hypothetical questions are an indirect, backdoor way of making a statement.

> "If you were in charge here, wouldn't you ...?"

> "If we have time, would you like to ...?"

What we really mean is "If I were in charge here, I'd do it this way ..." or "I'd like to ... if we have time."

Hypothetical questions ask people to place themselves in an imaginary situation and tell you what they would do. This tests both their imagination and their tact because hypothetical questions usually lead people into giving the answer you want.

Imperative questions turn a demand or command into an apparent request for information or action.

"Have you done anything about ...?"

"When will you be finished with ...?"

"When are you going to ...?"

What we really mean is "I think you should have seen to ... by now" or "I need you to have finished ..." or "I think you should have finished ..." or "I think you should do it soon."

Imperative questions soft soap our feelings and dress them up as requests for information or action. They can be tactful, or they can be a way of masking our real feelings or needs.

Rather than stating what you think or want, have you ever asked the other person what they think or want, with your fingers crossed hoping that what he or she wants will be the same as what you want? If so, you asked a *screened question*.

"Where do you want to go?"

"What do you think our first move should be?"

"What do you want to do?"

If what you are thinking is "I'd like to go here" or "I think X should be our first move" or "Let's do this," you have asked a screened question.

Screened questions can be part of the give and take of working or living with someone and save us from appearing too pushy. They can also be a way of hiding behind a polite veneer and make us seem meek and uncertain.

Gotcha! questions indirectly (and seemingly innocently) point out a weakness in the other person or show up mistakes they have made.

"Didn't you say ...? [and look how wrong you were!]."

"Did you have trouble with your car again this morning?" (in front of the boss, knowing the person was late).

"If I remember, weren't you in favor of ... [that failed initiative]?"

Silver Tongue

"Life is not so short but that there is always time enough for courtesy."

—Ralph Waldo Emerson

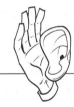

Listen to This

Socratic irony is asking a series of seemingly innocent and innocuous questions that eventually make the other person's false beliefs or assumptions apparent. They are a form of Gotcha! questions used to educate not humiliate.

Gotcha! questions may look innocent, but they end up smearing egg all over the face of their victim.

Set-up questions are double-whammy coercive questions. We set someone up, then cut them down.

> "Wouldn't you agree … [timekeeping is important] …? Then do you think you could manage to be on time from now on?"

Set-up questions can also be double-whammy Gotcha! questions:

> "Don't you think we should boycott French products because of their nuclear bombing in the Pacific?"

> "Oh, yes, that was terrible, wasn't it?"

> "I notice you're wearing French perfume, though."

Double-whammy questions that rebound on the victim and put them in a difficult or embarrassing situation aren't really questions at all; they're set-ups. "Set 'em up, mow 'em down."

Pseudo questions like these make people feel uncomfortable and put them on guard because they intuitively know that there is more behind such questions than meets the eye. They destroy communication and, if used often enough, they destroy relationships, too.

Leading Questions

A leading question implies the answer we are looking for; its recipient would have to be brave, stupid, or reckless to give us the "wrong" answer.

➤ An interviewer might ask a job candidate: "Would you accept this job if it were offered to you?"

➤ A manager might ask a team member: "You won't have problems with that, will you?"

➤ A husband might ask a wife: "How do you like the meal I've prepared, dear?"

Multiple Questions

A *multiple question* is actually several questions asked at the same time. This confuses people because they don't know which one to answer first and usually answer only the last one. Unfortunately, as we add to our string of questions, each one tends to be more trite and meaningless than the last, so we finish up with very little information and a rapidly eroding conversation.

➤ A manager might ask a team member: "How did you get on with that? Did you have any troubles? Anything you'd like to tell me about? Anything at all? Or was everything all right?"

➤ An office worker might ask a colleague: "Do you think I should accept the transfer to your section? What's it like working there? Is everyone friendly? Is the supervisor nice? Are they sticklers for timekeeping or is everything fairly relaxed? Do you think I should transfer?"

➤ A parent might ask a teenager: "I'm worried because you've seemed a bit quiet and despondent lately. I wondered if there was a problem at school, perhaps. Or perhaps you've cleared everything up? Or maybe there's a work problem you'd like to talk to me about? Or have you had a fight with one of your friends? Or is it just that you're feeling a bit quiet lately? Is there anything I can do?"

As you can see, multiple questions won't help us gather much good information.

Neutral Questioning

Question neutrally and allow the person time to think.

If you are uncertain—ask.

If you are certain—ask.

If you are not uncertain,

you may be kidding yourself.

To clear up ambiguities or draw out the full story, find out information, opinions, or even facts, ask your questions in an unprovocative, neutral tone of voice. This will help the other person feel relaxed enough to be willing and able to give you the information you need.

Having asked your question, give the person time to think.

Question—

Pause—

Wait for the response—

Pay attention to the answer.

Famous Last Words

If you've ever asked a string of questions, one right after another, you may have noticed that the last question was the weakest one. Unfortunately, the last question in a chain of **multiple questions** is usually the one that is answered.

Foot in Mouth

Don't ramble on or answer the question you've just asked, or fill a thoughtful silence with nervous chatter.

Silver Tongue

"The question put by a wise man is half the answer."

—Rabbinic scholar Jacob Emden

MOVE IT YA BIG APE!!

Famous Last Words

Probing questions explore a topic while **clarifying questions** get a point or detail straight.

A Word to the Wise

Don't ask questions aimlessly but with a purpose.

Useful Kinds of Questions

Use open, general, probing, and unspoken questions to uncover the information you need.

Open Questions

As we saw in the last chapter, open questions yield lots of information because they allow a person to explain what is most important or interesting to them and encourage elaboration. They're great for gathering good information.

General Questions

A *general question* is good for introducing a topic or highlighting the one we wish to pursue further. They are usually open questions.

"Jan, you just mentioned the difficulties you've had with the ticketing procedure. Can you tell me a bit more about them?"

Probing and Clarifying Questions

People can use ambiguous words deliberately to confuse, gloss over, avoid, put us on the wrong track, or give a false impression. Not if we ask good questions, though!

Probing questions relate to the topic we want to explore further. They encourage the speaker to flesh out the details. They can be either closed or open questions.

Clarifying questions serve much the same purpose. They request information on a specific detail that you may have missed or want included.

Some probing questions

Can you be more specific?

What do you want me to do?

Can you fill me in on the details?

Who is involved?

Do you have a particular situation in mind?

What might cause that, do you think?

Can you give me an example of that?

Where does that happen?

When does that happen?

What happened then?

For instance?

Can you put a percent to it?

How many are you talking about?

How does this affect you?

Who in particular is affected?

How can I help?

What in particular do you like/dislike?

Oh, do tell!

Was anyone else involved?

How did that come about?

Where did you say you were?

What did you make of it?

Unspoken Questions

We ask *unspoken questions* nonverbally by raising an eyebrow, leaning slightly forward, opening your eyes wide, making deliberate eye contact, saying "Hmmm?" with a rising inflection. All say "Tell me more" and encourage people to continue.

The expectant pause, or "six second silence" is also an unspoken question.

You can also echo, or repeat, the last few words or a phrase the person has said, with or without a rising inflection. This, too, is a cue to continue.

Famous Last Words

Unspoken questions are asked nonverbally, for example, by lifting an eyebrow or leaning slightly forward toward the speaker.

Tricks of the Trade

Professional communicators know just how imprecise language can be. They listen intently for vague words, sweeping generalizations, jargon that means something to the speaker but not the listener, and unspoken rules and comparisons. Then they probe and clarify to help their conversational partner make their meaning clear.

Help People to Be Specific

When someone makes a vague statement, such as …

> "That's not good enough."

> "That's not acceptable to me."

> "She's a wonderful employee."

… help him or her to be more specific by asking, in effect, "What [vague word] specifically?" Our goal is to help the other person make their communication clearer and more concrete. Otherwise, we won't ever know for sure what they're talking about.

For example, if someone says: "That's not good enough," you could respond by saying, "I'm not clear about just what you mean by 'not good enough'; what would help to make it good enough?" or "In what way is it not good enough?"

If someone says, "That's not acceptable to me," you could say something like, "What would make it acceptable to you?" or "Can you give me an idea of what in particular isn't acceptable to you?"

To "She's a wonderful employee," you might respond by asking, "What in particular do you appreciate about her?"

Clarify Jargon

According to a Danish proverb, it's better to ask twice than to lose your way once. It's easy to get lost in a maze of jargon that may mean something to a technical expert but leaves us far behind.

Foot in Mouth

"When someone says 'That's a good question,' You can be pretty sure it's a lot better than the answer you're going to get."

—Franklin P. Jones

Whether people use jargon to sound smart, from habit, or because the jargon isn't jargon to them—they use the term all the time—it can lead to confusion. If you don't know what it means, ask or risk getting lost.

Jargon? Use these questions or comments to help speakers speak plain English:

➤ I'm sorry, you lost me.

➤ Could you explain that so someone outside your field could understand it?

➤ Could you explain that without the jargon?

➤ What does that mean?

➤ Why is that number significant?

➤ What does that refer to?

➤ What do those abbreviations/that acronym stand for?

➤ I'm not familiar with that term.

Make Assumptions and "Rules" Explicit

Words like *should, shouldn't, must, have to, can't,* and *ought* imply an underlying assumption or an implicit rule. It can be useful to bring these assumptions and unspoken "rules" into the open and test them against reality. We can do this by asking a question.

Another way is to merely repeat the word or phrase in a questioning tone to encourage the speaker to clarify the statement. "Should?" "Shouldn't?" "You must?" "You feel you ought to?" Or we might say "What would happen if you did/didn't?"

Depending on the situation, you might need to soften these questions with modifiers like: "I wonder what would happen if you didn't ..." or "I'm curious about what you mean by ...."

Build rapport nonverbally (see Chapter 9, "First Impressions Count!"); otherwise, these questions, while bringing assumptions and "rules" to the surface, might also be interpreted as argumentative.

A Word to the Wise

Build rapport verbally and non-verbally when you ask the person to define their "vague word" so they don't feel you're challenging or criticizing them. Flesh out your request for more information with "verbiage": "I was wondering ..." or "What do you mean when you say ...?"

Tie Down Generalizations

As we saw in Part 1, "Communication Begins Inside," an important function of the brain is to make the complicated and often contradictory processes of life neat and tidy. This helps us get through each day without too much trauma and in a reasonably efficient manner.

In the processes of tidying up, people often generalize from one or a few similar situations to all similar situations.

A Word to the Wise

Don't be intimidated by jargon. Keep asking questions if you're interested in understanding what the person is trying to tell you.

For example, if we work for an authoritarian and inconsiderate boss, we might conclude that that is how all bosses are. If we have a run of bad luck with a few team members, we may generalize that all team members are lazy, irresponsible, and undependable. If we have been "dropped in it" once by the production manager, we may conclude that all production managers or even all managers must be watched carefully.

Just as assumptions and implied rules often benefit from exposure and examination, so do generalizations. Clues to generalizations are words such as *always, never, all,* and *every.* Again, questions such as "Always?" or "Never?" or "What would happen if you did?" can be asked. This will provide new information.

Similarly, we can ask questions to find out what's behind ambiguous words, such as "they," as in "*They* won't allow that." Questions such as "Who won't allow that?" or "What would happen if we did it anyway?" will usually provide more good information.

Silver Tongue

"It is harder to ask a sensible question than to supply a sensible answer."

—Persian proverb

Help Analyze Comparisons

People make comparisons every day. Words, such as *better, worse, easier, harder,* and so on, alert us that we need to make the comparison explicit so that we can assess its validity. This can also uncover a lot of useful information.

"Better than what?" or "Worse than what?" or "Easier than what?" will be the theme of the questions we ask here to make the comparisons more explicit and help us to test them.

Has Your Message Hit Home?

Questions can also help us to make sure that the other person has understood our message. We may want to ask someone we have just given instructions to how they plan to proceed; this will show whether we've communicated clearly. Or we may want to ask a person to summarize their understanding of what we've just agreed, to highlight any areas of misunderstanding or concern that we need to clear up.

However we choose to ask, our aim is to be sure that clear communication has taken place before we say our "goodbyes." This will save problems and maybe even embarrassment later on.

If in doubt, check it out.

The Least You Need to Know

➤ Make it a habit to ask questions to draw out good information. It will save you time and frustration.

➤ Avoid closed, "why," pseudo, leading, and multiple questions.

➤ Question tactfully and neutrally so people don't feel challenged or pushed.

➤ Use open, general, probing, clarifying, and unspoken questions to gather good information.

➤ Ask questions to help people be specific, clarify jargon, make rules and assumptions explicit, examine generalizations, and analyze comparisons.

➤ Use questions to check that you made your message clear.

Chapter 15

Listen, Listen, Listen

In This Chapter

➤ Good listening, bad listening, true listening

➤ Reflective listening and its uses

➤ When to use and not use reflective listening

➤ Five reflective listening skills

The words *listen* and *silent* may have the same letters, but listening is more than just keeping quiet and more than just hearing. In other words, it's more than the other half of speaking.

Listening to others encourages them to listen to us. It helps us develop relationships and learn things. It saves us embarrassment and mistakes.

In this chapter, you will discover why and how to *really* listen to gather good information.

True Listening

Sometimes, we're so busy listening to ourselves, we forget to listen to the other person. Yet if we don't listen to people, we can't really communicate with them.

Real listening takes self-discipline and includes the responses we make, the questions we ask, and our body language. With high-quality listening, we can understand people's intentions, aspirations, and fears. True listening is done with our heart, our mind, and our eyes, as well as our ears.

Do you listen with the intent of replying or do you listen to understand? If we listen to reply, we won't understand or learn as much as if we listen to understand.

True listening requires us temporarily to set aside our own thoughts, expectations, worries, biases, and desires. This can be difficult, particularly if we think we have something important to add or if we feel strongly about what the other person is saying. Just as we can't listen and speak at the same time, we can't listen and think about what we will say at the same time.

A Word to the Wise

If a speaker's message or your relationship with the speaker is important, don't just hear what is said—really listen to understand.

Putting our thoughts on hold is the only way we can concentrate fully on what is being said and experience the world from the speaker's point of view.

Here's a pop quiz for you:

Are we equipped with two ears and one mouth ...

1. because we should listen twice as much as we talk.
2. because listening is twice as difficult as talking.
3. as a reminder to use them in that proportion.
4. all of the above.

Silver Tongue

"You cannot truly listen to anyone and do anything else at the same time."

—M. Scott Peck

Listening is hard work. When we really listen, our blood pressure rises, our temperature goes up, and our pulse quickens. These are the same physiological changes that would occur if we jogged down the street.

Most people don't listen—they just wait for their turn to talk.

Listening is a sophisticated skill requiring considerable practice. Most of us, after all, have many bad habits to overcome and, because listening is hard work, it's so much easier not to listen properly.

Why don't we listen better? There are many reasons. Here are some:

➤ We think we have something better to say ourselves.

➤ We're given no reason to listen.

➤ We think we know what they'll say.

➤ There are too many distractions.

➤ We've had a busy day and we're too tired to listen carefully.

➤ We're busy listening to our own thoughts instead.

➤ We don't like the speaker or the message.

➤ Our minds are closed.

➤ We filter the speaker's message, hearing only what we want to hear.

➤ We jump to conclusions.

➤ We'd rather be talking so that we would feel more involved and more in control.

➤ We're thinking about what we'll say when it's our turn to speak.

➤ We put what we hear into the context of our own experiences rather than trying to see things from the speaker's viewpoint.

➤ We mentally criticize the message or the speaker.

Silver Tongue

"One friend, one person who is truly understanding, who takes the trouble to listen to us and consider our problems, can change our whole outlook on the world."

—Elton Mayo

The ability to listen is probably the most underrated skill in communication. Yet listening is essential in gathering and giving good information. It breaks down communication barriers, filters, and incompatibilities. It is important in establishing and maintaining good relationships and avoiding conflict and misunderstandings. Ask anyone who communicates and works well with others what their secret is, and 90 percent of them will give you an answer that involves the ability to listen.

Communication is as much about listening as it is talking.

How Can We Listen? Let Us Count the Ways ...

There are degrees of listening, ranging from tuning someone out and not listening to listening actively and with empathy.

"Half-an-Ear" Listening

Many forms of "listening" are actually unhelpful. Listening with half an ear, for example, shows in our body language and discourages all but the most determined speaker.

Foot in Mouth

Is your door open but your mind closed?

Sometimes we're unaware of how much our body language affects others. Does your manner say "You're an interruption" or "Hurry up, I'm busy"? If someone comes in to speak to you, do you carry on with what you're doing while you try to listen?

If so, ask yourself: "Which is more important—what I'm doing, or hearing what this person has to say?" Since we can focus only on one thing at a time, make a decision and focus on whichever is more important. Remember, though, that what you're doing will probably still be there after you have listened!

"Stunned Mullet" Listening

"Stunned mullet" listening, or listening passively (blank stares, no nonverbal signals, such as head nods, to encourage the speaker) may be fine for watching television, but it discourages a speaker from continuing and actually makes it quite difficult to do so.

Affirmative Listening

We can garner twice as much information from affirmative listening as from "stunned mullet" listening. When we "nod and grunt" while others speak, it shows them we are following their thoughts and encourages them to continue without disrupting their flow. The main drawback with affirmative listening is that there is no feedback to check our understanding.

Reflective Listening

Reflective listening is the highest level of listening. The most difficult in terms of skills and effort required, it also brings us the greatest rewards in terms of information, understanding, and results. Great communication is more likely to occur with *reflective listening* than with any other form of listening.

Famous Last Words

Reflective listening achieves three important things. It helps you listen better; it shows the speaker you are listening and encourages them to continue; and it allows the speaker to clear up anything you have misunderstood. This makes it one of the best ways to gather good information.

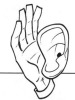

Listen to This

Are the lights are on but no one's at home. Here's how to show you're at home when listening:

➤ Nod.

➤ Say "uh-huh," "I see ...," or "mmmmm."

➤ Repeat a key word or phrase.

➤ Lean slightly forward, toward the speaker.

➤ Orient your body toward the speaker.

➤ Maintain eye contact: if your eyes wander, your mind will, too.

Reflective listening stimulates thought in both the speaker and the listener and keeps both communicators fully involved in the conversation. It requires us to first do some mental work to understand what the speaker is saying. Then we feed our understanding back to the speaker. This shows the speaker we've heard and understood, encouraging her to continue, and gives us feedback on how well we've understood.

A reflective listening response can also help speakers to clarify their thoughts and communicate them more accurately. Words and often thoughts are imprecise, which can make it difficult for people to say what they mean. A reflective listening response helps speakers develop their thoughts and gives them a chance to clarify what they have said or add further information. With reflective listening, we gather more good information than with any other form of listening. It makes the communication dance far more satisfying.

The messages we send with our reflective listening responses are: "You are important to me and your message is important to me. I want to hear and understand what you have to say.

Let's Get Reflective!

With reflective listening, we can feed back our understanding of the meaning of what the speaker has said, their feelings about it, or both, whichever suits the occasion and the context of the conversation.

A reflective listening response doesn't necessarily suggest agreement. We may agree with, feel ambivalent about, or strongly disagree with the speaker. However, even if we disagree, we can still give a reflective listening response to show we have listened to and understood the speaker's point of view.

The speaker may want to modify our reflective listening restatement, which is fine—it just means we haven't understood perfectly.

If what we have said is what the speaker meant, further clarification or more information will probably follow. Either way, we're learning a great deal about the speaker's thoughts and feelings and giving them the gift of listening.

Here are some more tips for listening.

A Word to the Wise

Take what you have seen and heard, mentally summarize it and then restate, in your own words, the speaker's main points or how you understand the speaker to be feeling. Make sure you summarize your understanding in a tentative, not dogmatic, way.

Once you've given your reflective listening response, allow the speaker a moment to consider what you've said before replying.

➤ Develop patience. Practice paying attention to the person speaking to you. Push away any internal dialogue and stay focused on listening.

➤ Listen to understand what the person is really saying.

➤ Listen to, not against.

➤ Observe body language. Listen for what is not said.

➤ Take your lesson from the Chinese *ting:* listen with your eyes, mind, and heart, as well as your ears (see Chapter 13, "Draw Out the Full Story").

➤ "Send back" what you've heard to verify it by restating the speaker's meaning and/or their feelings in your own words.

➤ Match the speaker's tempo and tone in your responses.

➤ Remember, you don't need to agree, just understand things from the speaker's perspective.

How to Listen Reflectively

Reflective listening isn't difficult; it just takes practice. Here are five guidelines to keep in mind as you reflect your understanding of the speaker's message or feelings.

➤ When several points are made, summarize the one that you want to focus on. This will help you keep the conversation pointed in the direction you want to take.

➤ When several emotions are expressed, reflect the final one, as this is usually the most accurate.

➤ Keep your reflective listening restatement short to keep the focus on the speaker.

➤ Only reflect what's there—don't start guessing.

➤ Wait out thoughtful silences.

Summarize your understanding in a tentative way:

➤ "You sound ..."

➤ "You seem ..."

➤ "Your idea is ..."

➤ "To you it must be like ..."

➤ "That must irritate you."

➤ "Let me summarize ..."

➤ "You seem to be saying ..."

➤ "You must feel as though ..."

➤ "If I understand you correctly ..."

➤ "If I were in your shoes, I'd feel ..."

Notice that reflective listening responses are statements, not questions. This is because a question might get only a "yes" or "no" reply, or a reply at a more superficial level. Reflective listening statements encourage a complete and accurate reply.

When to Use Reflective Listening

Because reflective listening requires so much effort, you may not want to do it all the time. Here are some situations that are ideal for your reflective listening skills:

To gather good information

➤ to draw out more information

➤ to show you are listening and to encourage the speaker to continue

➤ when encountering new ideas

➤ when there's a problem to be solved and you need to get all the facts

➤ when you're not sure what the speaker means

When there is conflict

➤ whenever you think you disagree with the speaker

➤ to prevent or minimize misunderstanding

➤ before you disagree

To affirm or support someone

➤ when the speaker wants to talk;

➤ to show your acceptance of the speaker;

➤ to provide feedback of your understanding;

➤ to check your understanding; and

➤ when the speaker is responding with their point of view after you have explained yours

In emotional situations

➤ to defuse emotion

➤ to calm down an upset, angry, or otherwise emotional person

➤ when someone has said something with real emotion in their voice or is talking about their feelings or emotions

➤ to allow a speaker's emotions or feelings to be expressed without becoming emotional yourself

➤ if the speaker is talking about a personal matter or problem

Foot in Mouth

Don't show disapproval when giving a reflective listening response. Remain neutral.

Silver Tongue

"The road to the heart is the ear."

—Françoise Marie Voltaire

When Not to Use Reflective Listening

There are two occasions in particular when we should avoid making reflective listening responses. The first is if we don't like or respect the speaker. In this case, we might use emotive words or phrases and/or a critical tone of voice, which would warn the speaker to stop rather than encourage them to continue.

The second time not to use reflective listening is when it would be a substitute for clearly stating our own side of things or a way of hiding our own thoughts or feelings. Keeping other people talking as a way of not contributing our own thoughts and feelings isn't communication!

Five Reflective Listening Skills

There are five ways to reflect your understanding of a person's feelings and what they have said.

Paraphrasing Meanings

Translate into your own words what the speaker has said. This achieves two useful things: It allows you to check your understanding and it encourages the speaker to continue.

Speaker: *... and I find it so frustrating because I'm really doing my best to get the project finished on time. I'm quite happy to put in the extra hours it takes, but everything and everyone seems against me!*

Reflective listening response: *You sound as if you feel let down and that you're not getting enough support.*

Speaker: *Yes, that's just it, although I know people aren't being difficult on purpose—they're busy too, and ...*

Reflecting Feelings

When someone is expressing emotion or feelings or looks emotional (upset, angry, excited), convey your empathy and encourage the speaker to continue.

Speaker: *I'm so fed up! How do they expect me to manage properly when the budgets come out with so many inaccuracies? I spend most of my time poring over them to spot the mistakes instead of getting on with my real job!*

Reflective listening response: *That certainly sounds annoying.*

Speaker: *You're not kidding! The point is, there's so much to get done and I need to be hampered like this like I need a hole in my head.*

Reflective listening response: *You sound really fed up.*

Speaker: *I suppose I am .... Really, what I'd like is ...*

or

Speaker: *This project is going nowhere except 'round in circles!*

Reflective listening response: *You sound pretty frustrated.*

Speaker: *Yes, I am. It's all talk and no action. We can't even agree on the basic principles. Still, I guess it's early days yet.*

Reflecting Facts

Briefly summarize the content, or factual aspects, of what the speaker has said. This will allow you to check your understanding and gather more information.

Speaker: *There's been a lot of activity while you were away. Angie crashed her car and needed a few days off. Bernie came down with the flu; Kerry sprained her ankle, and we had to get a temp who somehow managed to lose all our main files off the master disk. I'm really glad you're back!*

161

Reflective listening response: *Well! It sounds as though you've had plenty to keep you busy all right!*

Speaker: *I'll say! And if I do say so myself, I think I managed everything quite well. Here's what I've done …*

Synthesizing

Blend several of the speaker's ideas into one theme or idea. This helps you check your understanding and helps the speaker clarify his thinking.

Speaker: *… The first thing that happened was a major policy change, which no one could possibly have predicted. Then one of our best technicians resigned. Then the deadline was brought forward although I suppose we could have seen that coming. But, really, it's been one thing after another.*

Reflective listening response: *So there's been a series of stumbling blocks making things particularly difficult.*

Speaker: *You're not kidding! I think the straw that broke the camel's back was the policy change. If it weren't for that, we'd have a fighting chance.*

Reflective listening response: *You sound as if you feel all is lost.*

Speaker: *Well, not all lost. We're certainly behind the eight ball, though.*

Imagining Out Loud

Imagine what it must be like to be in the speaker's place.

Manager: *… and so I really need those reports to be finished on time in the future.*

Employee: *I just can't seem to satisfy anybody around here! Everyone's my boss; everyone complains. If it isn't one thing it's another.*

Manager: *I guess it must be hard for you, providing administrative support to several people.*

Employee: *It isn't just that …*

or

Speaker: *… and I really don't know which way to jump. There are pros and cons to each action and the repercussions could be quite serious.*

Reflective listening response: *If I were in your place, I think I'd feel rather hesitant to make any decision in case I made the wrong one.*

Speaker: *Yes, that's just it … I guess I really need some more information … Perhaps I'll gather a few opinions, too, from people who have more experience in this area than I do.*

Are you wondering whether reflective listening could lead to a never-ending conversation? It won't. Stop reflective listening when you feel the speaker has said all there is to say—when you've heard the full story. Then move to the obvious next step. This may be, for example, problem solving, saying how you see things from your point of view, or deciding what should happen next.

With practice, your ability to listen accurately will improve. But true listening is never effortless and always requires a degree of willpower. The results are worth the effort. After all, no one is likely to do us the honor of listening to us if we don't do them the honor of listening to them.

The Least You Need to Know

➤ Listening is critical to gathering good information. It is a skill that takes practice and willpower.

➤ To truly listen, you'll need to involve your heart, your mind, and your eyes, as well as your ears.

➤ If you're thinking about what you'll say next or mentally criticizing the speaker or her message, you're not really listening.

➤ Don't fake listening, and don't fail to give nonverbal assurances that you're listening and following the speaker's points.

➤ Reflective listening helps you understand the speaker's point of view and also helps the speaker state that point of view more clearly.

➤ Use reflective listening even if you don't agree with the speaker as long as you can remain neutral.

Chapter 16

The Ten Deadly Sins of Communication

In This Chapter

➤ Why sins hurt

➤ Avoiding being patronizing

➤ Avoiding sending signals

➤ Avoiding avoiding

As we gather good information, thoughts often run through our minds. Even if we're paying full attention to what the other person is saying, we may let these thoughts prevent us from gathering information as well as we could.

For example, we might be thinking, "What a load of old nonsense!" or "Gee, she's about as articulate as a crow" or "He's really wrong to see it like this." Or "Boy, Freud would *love* this!" Or we may be thinking "He's on the wrong track; I'll just set him straight" or "I know *just* what she should do!" or even "This is getting a bit too close to the bone for me—time to change the subject!"

The trouble is, when we're judging or evaluating or being critical in other ways, it usually leaks out through our body language. Even worse, our negative thoughts can come out in what we say. Instead of reflecting our understanding, we reflect our own thoughts through one or more of the ten deadly sins of communication. The speaker picks up that we're not agreeing or open to hearing their thoughts and, not surprisingly, begins to clam up.

In this chapter, you'll learn what the ten deadly sins of communication are and how to avoid them.

The Ten Deadly Sins of Communication

Committing any one of the ten deadly communication sins can quickly destroy any communication. They can be broken into three major categories, patronizing, sending signals, and avoiding, as follows:

Patronizing sins:

1. Evaluating
2. Moralizing
3. Playing psychologist or labeling
4. Making sarcastic remarks

Sending signals sins:

5. Commanding
6. Railroading
7. Threatening
8. Giving unsolicited advice

Avoiding sins:

9. Being vague
10. Diverting

Adapted from People Skills *by Richard Bolton.*

These sins lead to guesswork, misunderstandings, irritation, frustration, and complete communication breakdowns. They put up barriers and create ill will. Unfortunately, these sins are committed around us every day. That makes it easy for us to commit them, too—after all, that's the way people talk to each other, right?

Yet this is not the way to communicate if we want our communication to be successful. As you read about each sin, think about when you have heard it. How did you respond? Do you ever commit it yourself? When and with whom?

Famous Last Words

When we communicate with someone in a condescending way, we're **patronizing** him or her. This happens if we feel superior to them in some way.

Patronizing

If we're feeling superior to someone in some way, it's easy, in fact almost inevitable, that we fall into the trap of *patronizing*. Even if we don't mean to, we look down our noses and speak with an air and a tone of condescension.

Evaluating

When we pass a judgment on someone, it could imply that we think we are in some way better than they are. This is especially so when we judge others in a general rather than specific way.

That's why evaluations, whether positive or negative, can be risky. Sometimes, offering a compliment can come across as patronizing flattery. Sometimes, offering constructive comments can appear as patronizing criticism. It's all in the way we say it.

Evaluating a person's general "worth" or making positive or negative comparisons like "You're a good worker" or "You're hopeless" or "Bob learned that much quicker than you" damage communication because they make the recipient feel he or she is being judged and talked down to.

Avoid general assessments, comparisons, and criticisms by making your points clearly, courteously, and completely, using objective, factual, and neutral words.

Offer sincere praise in a respectful way to avoid sounding superior. Similarly, aim to be a coach and not a critic, and offer improvement suggestions that sound constructive rather than condescending. (Chapter 22, "Ask, Don't Tell" and Chapter 23, "When You Say What You Like, Say Why," examine this in more depth.)

Moralizing

Preaching, blaming, shaming, and dragging up the past are four forms of *moralizing*. They are sure to bring cordial communications to a rapid close.

It's sometimes tempting to become serious and high-minded with someone when we think we know better than they do, that our experience is somehow better or more relevant, or that our values are superior to theirs. So we preach. Since we can never know another person's frame of reference fully, it's likely that from that person's point of view at least, our preaching won't be pertinent or welcome.

Instead of lecturing, try to "walk a mile in their moccasins." The more you do this, the less likely you are to moralize by preaching, blaming, shaming, or dragging up the past and the more likely you are to appreciate, empathize, and accept. Help people explore their situation through reflective listening (see Chapter 15, "Listen, Listen, Listen") and wait for them to ask for our thoughts if they want them.

Famous Last Words

While personal principles and standards are important in leading a good life, when we explain or interpret things from an excessively moralistic point of view, we may end up **moralizing** if we're not careful. Others often see our efforts to "help them live better lives" (and be more like us) as narrow-minded, patronizing, and unwelcome.

Blaming and shaming are two other common forms of moralizing. If someone makes a mistake, should we scold her for it and make her feel bad? Or should we show her what she did wrong and how to do it right next time?

Since people generally don't make mistakes or do things wrong on purpose, focusing on the future and helping them to decide what to do next time is undoubtedly the better option. As we saw in Chapter 5, "Become a Peak Performer!" peak performers don't shame, they find ways to build self-esteem in others.

It can be tempting to point out people's faults, can't it? And once we're on a roll, it's easy to drag up the past, recalling and reliving all the times they've done something wrong or something we disapprove of. Don't do it.

A Word to the Wise

Find solutions, not fault. Build self-esteem in the other person. Focus on the future not the past.

Playing Psychologist, or Labeling

You've probably heard some of the following comments at work or socially:

> "You're just saying that because you've got a problem with authority."

> "You haven't fully understood."

> "Your problem is …"

> "You're lazy."

> "You're not trying hard enough."

Comments like these are examples of labeling—another way of communicating that puts us "up" and the other person "down." It communicates that we think we know something about them that they don't know and aren't we clever.

A Word to the Wise

Resist labeling people or their behavior. If you want them to change something they're saying or doing, describe clearly what you heard or saw, without interpreting or evaluating it. Keep to the facts and, if you want, explain the effect their behavior is having on you. These are legitimate points of discussion. Amateur psychologists' interpretations are not.

There is also a good chance our diagnosis will be wrong and because we have no way of knowing whether we're right or wrong, it's dangerous to diagnose people or their behavior. Once a diagnosis is made, we'll tend to behave towards the other person as if it is correct. This leads to all kinds of difficulties in communication.

Some things are best left unsaid. If you must say something, say it clearly and respectfully, using neutral language and tone of voice. "I" language (see Chapter 20, "Speak for Yourself, Not the World") might also be appropriate.

Making Sarcastic Remarks

Why does *sarcasm* often rub us the wrong way? It's the *meta-message*. This is a term coined by Gerard Nierenberg to describe the message-behind-the-message, or the underlying, real meaning behind the words.

"Hi, good of you to join us" could mean just that. Or, said to someone who is late for a meeting, the meta-message could be "You're late and it's held us up. I'm annoyed."

Although it is not uncommon in some circles, sarcasm is often an aggressive putdown. Even friendly bantering can get out of hand and cause hard feelings. Sarcastic remarks inhibit open communication. Sarcasm, in fact, is in the same league as name-calling, ridiculing, and shaming; and it leads to the same results.

Mother Teresa said, "Kind words can be short and easy to speak, but their echoes are truly endless." Make sure your kind words echo in people's minds not your cruel comments.

Beware of hurting feelings. State your point clearly and considerately rather than resorting to sarcasm. Ask questions rather than dismiss someone's idea or make fun of it.

Silver Tongue

One of the lessons of history is that nothing is often a good thing to do and always a clever thing to say.

—Will Durant

Famous Last Words

The root of **sarcasm** is *sarx* or *sarkos*, from the Greek word meaning "flesh." Sarcasm literally means "to tear flesh." Words might not cut flesh, but they can cut communication and hurt feelings. Callous, contemptuous, and caustic comments hurt. Hostile, disparaging, acrimonious, mocking remarks, and put–downs spoil communication and relationships. **Irony** is a form of sarcasm where we say the opposite of what we mean.

Sending Signals

Most people resent being told what to do. Ninety-nine times out of a hundred, you'll get further with a request than a command or a threat, or by forcing someone into doing your bidding.

Commanding

Commanding is when we tell someone what to do in a way that leaves them no room to discuss, seek

A Word to the Wise

The next time you're tempted to say "You must ..." or "Stop it!" *you* stop! Look for a better way to send your message.

further information, disagree, or even agree. Orders like this make people feel more like a machine than a person. Either an aggressive response or resentful submission will result, depending on our relative status.

Ask, don't tell, is a good principle to follow if you're tempted to bark out a command.

Use your empathy and phrase your message in a way that makes it easy for the other person to understand why you want something done or not done. Make a suggestion or a request. As far as possible, focus on the result you want and let the other person decide what action to take.

Railroading

A more subtle form of commanding is known as railroading, where we politely, often through logical argument, make statements that assume the other person is in agreement, without giving them a genuine opportunity to air their views. By keeping the conversation moving along very rapidly, we "browbeat" the other person into yielding to our point of view.

Slow down. Look for the "nod and grunt" and other verbal and nonverbal signals that indicate the other person's acceptance. If necessary, pause and ask whether they agree with you or what thoughts they can add.

Threatening

"If you don't ..." or "You'd better ...."

Threats can be direct or subtler, implied "or else" messages. Both make people wary and widen the communication gap. Most people look for ways to defend themselves against threats and for ways not to obey.

If there are good reasons why someone should or should not do something, explain them. Clarify the consequences, too, if you want, accurately and fairly. Explain and encourage rather than threaten.

Explain why something needs to happen in a way that doesn't sound as if there's an "or else" attached. "I" language (see Chapter 20) is another useful substitute for sending threats.

Giving Unsolicited Advice

When phrases like "You should ..."; "You ought to ..."; "Have you tried ...?"; and "If you take my advice, you'll ..." pop out of our mouths, we're in danger of forcing our advice or opinions upon people. They'll probably ignore us, making what we say just so much hot air.

If people want our advice or opinion, let them ask for it. Then they'll listen. If you must give some unsolicited advice, ask permission first: "Would you mind if I make a suggestion?" or "Would you be interested in hearing how I'd handle that?"

Avoiding

Have you noticed the aggressive, disrespectful "you" component in these first eight deadly communication sins? The last two sins are more disrespectful to the sinner than the person sinned against. In Chapter 20, we'll talk more about why they obstruct communication.

The keys to avoiding are mutual respect, empathy, and speaking for yourself, or owning" your messages.

Being Vague

When we don't "own" our messages, we might say things like "Everyone knows …" or "Most people agree …." These are ways of avoiding saying what we think.

If we don't make our point openly, people have to guess at what we really mean or want. Unless they're skilled mental telepaths, they usually guess wrong!

We'll look at some effective ways to state requests and opinions later in Chapter 21, "Don't Masquerade Your Thoughts."

Silver Tongue

"Advice is like snow. The softer if falls, the longer it dwells upon and the deeper it sinks into the mind."

—Samuel Taylor Coleridge

Foot in Mouth

Don't be a vague fuddy–duddy! Speak up! Get off the fence and to the point! Be specific! If you have a point to make, make it clearly and cleanly. Don't hint at it in roundabout ways.

Diverting

When a conversation becomes emotional or personal, or when another person begins to reveal something of their true self, some people feel uncomfortable and try to bring the conversation back to trivial matters. This leads to such behaviors as distracting the speaker, changing the subject, or responding in clichés.

Other ways of diverting are reassuring, sympathizing with, or consoling another person using meaningless platitudes. These also keep us uninvolved in the conversation and maintain it at a superficial level.

A Word to the Wise

Come from a position of mutual respect. Don't talk up or down to others or brush their concerns aside with a glib cliché. If you're uncomfortable with the way a conversation is heading, say so.

"You'll feel different tomorrow."

"Don't worry, every cloud has a silver lining, and I just know things will work out."

"I feel so terrible for you."

These are usually unhelpful comments because they tend to miss the mark.

We are not compelled to have a deep and meaningful conversation every time we talk to someone. On the other hand, conversations sometimes offer us more revealing, personal glimpses, and to discourage them automatically is not always desirable. If a friend, team member, or co-worker indicates they want or need to discuss something on a more personal level, shutting them out will not achieve successful communication.

If you catch yourself committing any of these deadly sins—STOP! Take a breath. Center your attention on the other person and reflect your understanding instead of your patronizing thoughts, signals, or discomfort in stating your own opinion.

So banish the sins! Instead, strive for communication that is …

➤ complete, correct and current.

➤ clear, coherent and comprehensible, not confusing, cursory, or cloudy.

➤ credible, consistent, and considered, not coy, counterfeit, or clichéd.

➤ courteous, constructive, and considerate, not crotchety, crude, or cruel.

➤ cooperative, cordial, and complimentary, not curt, cranky, or critical.

➤ comfortable and conversational in tone, not cramped, callous, or cowardly.

➤ candid, not crafty.

➤ crisp, but not curt or cross.

➤ cheerful, calm, and composed, not crazy or crass.

Now *that's* crystal clear communication!

Replace the ten deadly communication sins from your communication repertoire by reflecting your understanding of what the other person has said or saying how things are from your point of view clearly and openly.

The Least You Need to Know

➤ Watch the way you praise and criticize to avoid patronizing.

➤ Request, don't tell or threaten, to avoid sending negative signals.

➤ Resist insulting people by labeling them or their behavior or using pop psychology on them.

➤ Don't offer unwanted advice without checking whether the person is interested in hearing it.

➤ State your point of view clearly and openly to avoid masking it in sarcasm or being vague.

➤ Don't change the subject or respond in clichés if a conversation takes a personal turn.

Part 5

Giving Good Information

Saying how things are from your point of view

Someone once said, "I have often regretted my speech. Never my silence." Calvin Coolidge, the thirtieth President of the United States, said, "You can't know too much, but you can say too much." And while it's certainly true that a closed mouth gathers no feet, that doesn't mean we should never speak!

Sharing our thoughts and joys with others is one of the great pleasures of life. Sharing information and ideas makes the world go 'round.

This part of the book will make sure it is never said of you what the British author George Bernard Shaw said of one unfortunate woman: "The trouble with her is that she lacks the power of conversation but not the power of speech."

Chapter 17

Step Off with the Right Foot

In This Chapter

➤ Preventing "foot-in-mouth" disease

➤ Framing your points

➤ What's in it for me?

➤ Flagging your contributions

Have you ever jumped into a discussion only to end up with both feet planted firmly in your mouth? For most of us, this is a familiar experience, but one we can avoid.

Foot-in-mouth occurs when we give too little thought to the *whats, hows,* and *whys* of a conversation before we begin it. As a result, we fail to achieve the outcome we want. We spend our time poorly and fray our own and other people's tempers unnecessarily.

We'll explore how to avoid foot-in-mouth in this chapter. You'll see how to frame conversations, flag your contributions, and give the other person a reason to listen.

Don't Open Your Mouth Only to Change Feet

The second beat in the communication dance (see Chapter 7, "Everything We Do Is Communication") was: *The way we begin our message often determines the outcome of*

Silver Tongue

"Good and quickly seldom meet."

—George Herbert

Famous Last Words

A **frame** is a short, clear statement to introduce a discussion (what you want to talk about and how) that provides a mental target to aim for.

Foot in Mouth

The next time you're tempted to begin a conversation by barging straight in, pause a moment to collect your thoughts. Think about what you want to say and the best way to introduce it.

the communication. Yet (and you can be honest here), how often do you really plan your first sentence or two before launching into a conversation? If you're like most busy people, the answer is probably: "Not as often as I know I should." And yet, spending a few moments thinking about our opening lines can save us time and frustration not to mention embarrassment.

Before launching into a conversation, it's important to ask yourself what your purpose is. You can easily figure out your purpose by asking yourself the following questions:

➤ Why am I communicating?

➤ What do I want to achieve?

➤ How do I want the discussion to proceed?

➤ How can I best make my point or be most persuasive?

Once we are clear on what we want to achieve, we will be able to state, in our first few sentences, the overall purpose of the conversation and/or how we intend it to proceed. This is called *framing* a conversation: thinking before we speak so that we step off on the right foot.

Frame Your Conversations

Framing helps us in three important ways. First, it helps us guide a conversation toward the desired result. This saves time and tension. Second, it helps us align the other person's expectations of the conversation with our own. Third, it helps us present information in a way that avoids making the other person defensive, bristle at our first few words, or ignore important parts of our message.

Just as a frame encloses a picture, a framing statement encloses the conversation to come: What will be addressed and what won't be; what will be focused on and what won't be. As a frame draws attention to the contents of a picture, a framing statement draws attention to the main aspects of the conversation and sets limits on what will, and won't, be discussed.

Some Types of Framing Statements

Here are some common framing statements.

➤ **Boundaries**   Establish what will and won't be focused on:

Today, we won't be talking about your overall job performance, which is excellent, but only about progress on the Customer Service Project.

➤ **History**   Review the key events that have a bearing on this conversation:

Sal, I'd like to talk about X, which, as you'll recall, we've discussed on three occasions this month. Last time we agreed …

➤ **Purposes**   Present your expectations of the meeting and check whether the other person's expectations are similar or different:

Chris, I'd like to firm up some conclusions and agree on a tentative plan for how best to proceed with this. How does that sound to you?

➤ **Process**   Present an overview of the types of information you would like to present and discuss; or outline how you would like the discussion to proceed:

Kim, I'd like to review our monthly budget and, in particular, the expenditure areas of salaries and wages, rentals, consulting fees, and advertising.

I suggest that we begin with X, then move onto Y, and then discuss C. How does that sound to you?

➤ **Problem**   State the categories of the problem and summarize the data, or facts, as you understand them:

Lee, I'd like to talk about timekeeping. My records show that you've been late to work three times and back late from lunch four times this past month. I have been keeping track of this because timekeeping is important to me. I'd like to discuss with you now any problems or difficulties that could be causing this and decide what we can do about it.

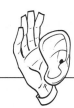

Listen to This

Have you ever watched a dog turn circles on the spot before lying down? Whether there was long grass there or not, she was packing it down to make a comfortable place to lie.

Conversational frames do that for people. They help us get comfortable mentally with what is coming. They help us hear it better, think it through better, and respond to it better.

Use these singly or in combination to frame the discussion to come. Keep your framing statement short, though—one or two sentences. If it's a paragraph, people will become impatient for you to "get down to brass tacks."

Practice Makes Perfect

Developing framing statements is a skill, and the following practice incidents will help you develop it. Read each one, then jot down a short framing statement that you would feel comfortable using to open up a discussion.

1. Peter, a member of a committee that you chair, has a habit of whispering to anyone sitting beside him throughout most of the meetings. It really bugs you, because you need everyone's attention and input, and you think it annoys people trying to hear the others' contributions over Peter's whisperings. You open a discussion (in private) with Peter by saying:

   _____

   _____

2. Carla is a very talented co-worker. Unfortunately, some of your work hinges on Carla completing her work and passing it on to you. She is often late with it, and this means you either have to rush and risk making mistakes or miss your deadlines to your manager. You approach Carla and say:

   _____

   _____

3. Senior management has recently begun talking about achieving more work in less time. Manny is the manager of another department on your floor. His work team and yours work on different aspects of the same process, and you have arranged a meeting with him to discuss how your two teams could work together more smoothly to reduce some of the backlog and move work more quickly. You begin the meeting by saying:

   _____

   _____

4. Sean is your manager. You've put forward a moderate capital expenditure proposal for your section for him to approve, and you've had several meetings with him to go through the details; you know he's quite a slow decision-maker, and you would like to speed up his decision if you can. You've asked for a meeting about it, which you intend to open by saying:

   _____

   _____

5. You supervise the management accounting section. Lately, your customers, that is, managers of other sections, have been suggesting that they would like the

figures to come out more quickly. You've called a team meeting to explore how this might be done. You open the meeting by saying:

_____

_____

6. Ellen is your assistant and, overall, is very able; however, you are concerned that she sometimes fails to meet routine deadlines. When you have discussed this on two occasions (three months ago at her performance appraisal, and again last month), she indicated that she was aware of this and felt that an effort to be more organized would help. She has not shown any improvement and has missed several routine deadlines over the last few weeks. You begin this meeting by saying:

_____

_____

You'll find some model framing statements for these situations in Appendix D, "Some Ideas for Frames;" these are just examples, and your answers will probably be as good—provided they're short and you can imagine yourself saying them.

The What's-In-It-For-Me Factor

A cynic once said, "If you can't get people to listen to you any other way, tell them it's confidential." Fortunately, there are other ways to help people to listen, too.

As early as you can in a conversation, even in the framing statement, include a WIFM: What's In It For Me? (The "Me" refers to the other person: why should the other person listen? What are the benefits to the other person?) If we can give people a reason to listen, they will do so more readily and, usually, more open-mindedly and enthusiastically.

This might mean stating the benefits to them of what we are proposing. Or it might mean appealing to something that interests them or in some other way engaging their desire to cooperate. Our knowledge of the person and the situation will help us provide a tempting WIFM.

More Practice!

Look again at the six practice situations above. In the space below, jot down possible WIFMs that you could bring out early in the discussion. (You might get some ideas from Appendix D.)

A Word to the Wise

When you open a discussion with a framing statement, you could stop there and wait for a reply, or you could continue. Your judgment and observations of the other person's body language will tell you what to do.

1. _____
   _____

2. _____
   _____

3. _____
   _____

4. _____
   _____

5. _____
   _____

6. _____
   _____

Famous Last Words

A **flag** tells people what's coming and helps them hear it, and therefore respond, better. "Let me ask you a question ..." or "The way I see it is ..."or "One final thing we should go over is ...."

Silver Tongue

"Not he is great who can alter matter, but he who can alter my state of mind."

—Ralph Waldo Emerson

Be *subtle* when introducing a WIFM!

Flagging

A *flag* is a type of frame that takes place once the conversation has begun. It lets the person know what is coming next, so they can "orient" themselves to it. It helps people be better listeners. They know to listen for a question, a summary, a different point of view, an example, or whatever it is that you flagged. This reduces the chances of "mis-hearing" and wandering minds.

Flagging is another way of gently helping us to think before we speak because we need to know what we're going to say before we can flag it.

Consider using the following flagging statements the next time you have a conversation with a colleague:

If I've understood correctly ...

In summary, then ...

Let me ask you a question ...

So the main problem seems to be ...

I'd like to return to something you said earlier.

Let me go over that again ...

Flag to make your communication dances flow.

To alter people's states of mind, we need to consider the way we begin our messages. We need to smooth the flow of thoughts by flagging frequently. And we need to provide a benefit to our conversational partner.

We can polish our communication further by carefully choosing our words, speaking openly and honestly, and putting ourselves on the same wavelength as our partner. The following chapters will help you do this.

The Least You Need to Know

➤ Think before you speak.

➤ Don't jump into conversations too quickly—before you do, think about what you want to say.

➤ In a subtle way, give people a reason or some benefit to talk.

➤ Use a short frame to let people know what you want to talk to them about and why.

➤ Frames, WIFMs, and flags help the listener hear and the speaker present information well.

Chapter 18

Choose Your Words for Clarity and Power

In This Chapter

➤ The power of words

➤ Words that influence

➤ Positive, precise, and powerful words

➤ Delivering your words with panache

The content of any message, as we've seen, is made up of far more than the words we use. This is not to say that words are not important—they are. Which of the following would you rather be told?

You look like the first day of spring!

or

You look like the last day of a long hard winter!

Choosing the right word and the right combination of words is, without doubt, an essential step in the dance of communication. In this chapter, we examine the words we use to give good information.

The Power of Words

Yes, our words matter. Words have meaning. Words have power—the power to help or hinder, to instantly irritate or create cooperation, to confuse or to clarify. Depending on our purpose, we can choose words that are aggressive or compliant, neutral or emotive, clear or vague, courteous or challenging. We have a choice.

Suppose we want to explain to someone that we're concerned that their rapid, abrupt manner on the telephone might leave customers with a poor impression of the organization. We could say something like:

> "You're too abrupt on the telephone, Jan; you'll need to be more professional—starting now!"

There are at least three things wrong with this message. First, the overall approach is more likely to upset Jan than to encourage her to soften her telephone manner. Second, the "starting now!" sounds too strong and probably won't achieve the results we want. Commanding, remember, is one of the ten deadly sins of communication. Third, the message is vague: Would Jan think she was being abrupt? What do "abrupt" and "more professional" mean? It's most unlikely that Jan sets out to be either unprofessional or abrupt and, therefore, to ask her to be less of either is pointless.

Let's introduce the conversation with a frame, such as:

> "Jan, I am concerned about the way you speak to customers over the telephone and I'd like to discuss it with you; do you have some time now?"

The frame lets Jan know what the discussion will be about, and asking if she has time now is courteous. So is using Jan's name.

We could make the message itself more specific by saying, for example:

> "I've noticed that you speak quite quickly and I'm worried that this might make it difficult for some of the customers to follow you; after all, you know more about what you're talking about than they do."

> "Also, you're very efficient and tend to give 'the bottom line' only; I think it might be more helpful to customers if you were to round out your discussions with a bit more background."

This approach uses "I" language (see Chapter 20, "Speak for Yourself, Not the World"). It doesn't blame

Silver Tongue

"The ability to express an idea is well nigh as important as the idea itself."

—Bernard Baruch

Silver Tongue

"When the mouth stumbles, it is worse than the foot."

—West African proverb

A Word to the Wise

Choose your words with care; don't use them thoughtlessly or through mere habit.

or criticize; rather, it offers improvement suggestions (see Chapter 22, "Ask, Don't Tell"). Explaining why we're concerned and using neutral language will help to win Jan's cooperation—and we want cooperation not mere compliance. Overall, this second message is more likely to encourage Jan to be cooperative.

The only person who can choose to alter her telephone manner with customers is Jan. Commanding won't do it; all we can do is choose our words carefully and follow through by coaching her and perhaps pointing out the results of altering versus not altering her telephone manner. We'll never get this far, though, without beginning with the right words.

Choose Your Words to Influence

When things are going along smoothly, communication is a lot easier than when the going gets tough. Have you ever wanted to encourage someone to change the way he's saying or doing something?

The words we choose to do this can create defensiveness and lead to arguments, or they can be a positive influence on others.

There is a natural tendency for most of us to send signals or patronize—two of the three types of deadly communication sins—when trying to influence others. It's sometimes easy to feel superior, become domineering, to command or threaten, or to give unsolicited (and therefore unheard or ignored) advice. Sometimes it can be tempting to drag up the past, play psychologist, moralize, or make our point with sarcasm.

This happens even if we attempt (on the surface) to be pleasant and helpful. Underneath, if we feel superior and certain, it will shine through. The more difficult or prolonged the interaction is and the less rapport we feel with the other person, the more pronounced these subconscious motives are likely to become. Communication will begin to break down.

When this happens, energy becomes focused on "winning." Rather than listen, we will mentally prepare a rebuttal while the other person speaks. Frustration will mount. The communicators will become critical of each other; they will take positions, such as: "I am right and you are clearly wrong, unreasonable, stubborn, or downright stupid."

Silver Tongue

"Keep your words soft and sweet in case you have to eat them."

—Anonymous

A Word to the Wise

Stop and think before you speak, especially if you feel annoyed or angry. How can you get your message across in a way that discourages defensiveness and arguments?

The consequences of such a discussion are defensiveness, anger, hostility, eroded mutual respect, and a weak compromise or capitulation by one of the parties; the loser will have lost the battle but not the war.

There are four main ways we can avoid this.

1. Frame your messages carefully.
2. Transmit them factually or descriptively, using neutral (not critical or negative) words.
3. Use a neutral tone of voice.
4. Listen with empathy and understanding so you can see things from the other person's point of view.

This needs a genuine desire to gather as well as give good information, plus some skills—reflective listening skills, the ability to give good information, and skills in problem solving.

Choose Neutral Words

Think about the connotations these pairs of words or phrases have for you:

currently fashionable	receiving a lot of attention
flash in the pan, fad	very popular
abrupt	quick, rapid
undependable	variable
woolly thinking	unclear

Do you agree that the words on the left have negative connotations while those on the right are neutral, factual, or more descriptive?

The same can be true for the sentences we choose. Consider these:

You're lazy and irresponsible.	You've been late three times this week and, although there's a lot of work in your in-basket, you're reading the newspaper.
You're wrong.	I see it differently.
These figures are rubbish!	I need to be more certain about the way figures were arrived at.
Stop interrupting me!	Pat, I'm speaking *or* Just hang on a moment, Pat, I'd like to finish.

How do you respond to loaded, emotion-laden words or phrases with negative connotations? Or to words and phrases, however neutral in themselves, delivered in a hostile voice tone or as a command? Most people respond with defensiveness, resentment, and even hostility; battles often follow.

Do you choose words and phrases that are emotive or imply a negative judgment, or do you choose words and phrases that are objective? Similarly, do you choose a hostile tone of voice or one that is neutral and courteous?

A Word to the Wise

Objective, frank, and factual or descriptive words, phrases, and tones of voice generally encourage listening, fact gathering, and problem solving.

Choose Positive Words

We should also choose positive words and phrases. Negative words and phrases, compared with positive words and phrases, draw quite different responses from people. How do you respond to the words and phrases in the left column below? How do you respond to those in the right column?

Don't be negative!	**Be positive**
You'll have to …	You'll want to …
	I'll need … so that …
I can't do that until Monday.	I'll be able to do that on Monday.
We're all out of that model.	We'll have that model available in just a few days.
I'll try to get someone to phone you back.	I'll ask Kathy to phone you back before four o'clock today.
There shouldn't be any problems with that.	That will be fine.
You never …	How about …?
You should have …	From now on …
	Next time …
You don't understand.	Let me run through that again.
I've told you before not to …	How about trying it this way …
I can't because …	Here's how we can make that happen …

Not bad.	Fantastic!
It's okay.	It's great!
What's the problem?	How can I help?
can't	can
won't	will
problem	solution

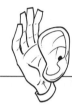

Listen to This

Here are four good reasons to fill your responses with *cans*, not *can'ts*!

1. The way we talk colors the way we think, and the way we think shapes the way we act. Do you want to act negatively or positively?

2. The way we talk sets the tone of a conversation. Do you want your conversations to be negative or positive in tone?

3. The way we talk influences the way others see us. Do you want to be seen in a negative or positive light?

4. Negative words invite gloom and disagreement. If people disagree with what you're saying, they'll only hear about 25 percent of it, much less than if they're in an agreeing, positive frame of mind.

Choose Specific Words

Do you know that the 500 most commonly used words in the English language have an average of 28 meanings each? When we use a word, we know we mean. But do others?

As Humpty Dumpty said to Alice …

A word means just what I want it to mean—

nothing more, nothing less

… (or words to that effect). And that's about the size of it. Oliver Wendell Holmes Jr. put it like this: "A word is not a crystal, transparent, and unchanged; it is the skin of a living thought and may vary greatly in color and content according to the circumstances and the time in which it is used."

Not surprising, then, that what we mean, and what another person understands, can be quite different.

Take the word *order,* for instance. Spend a few seconds and jot down what this word means to you.

Order: _____

_____

You could have written down one of 15 definitions or more than 26 shades of meaning for that one word (some of which are listed in Appendix E, "Some Word Meanings: *Order* and *Strike*"). We so often think we know, don't we?

See how many definitions to the word *strike* you can think of:

Strike: _____

_____

There are 13 definitions of *strike* and over 19 connotations; some of them are listed in Appendix E.

Words can make communication an uncertain business.

Choose words that meet the requirements of the Six *C*s:

CLEAR	COURTEOUS
CONCISE	CORRECT
COMPLETE	CONCRETE

Words must be *clear.* We must be clear in our own minds about what we want or what we intend to convey and say it without jargon or double-speak.

The more *concise* we are, the less likely people are to lose interest and let their attention wander. People can remember only seven (plus or minus two) pieces of information at a time, so we don't want to add to their mental burden with extra words.

At the same time, we need to be as *complete* as our message requires. To find out if we are giving too much or too little information, we can ask questions to check understanding and watch the other person's body language for clues.

Silver Tongue

"I always wanted to be somebody but I see now I should have been more specific."

—Lily Tomlin

A Word to the Wise

If you have any reason to believe that your meaning or intention will be misunderstood, make precisely what you mean, intend, or expect clear. Don't leave it to chance or to guesswork.

Naturally, we always want to be *courteous*. Because behavior breeds behavior, this encourages others to be courteous to us in return.

We also want to be *correct*. Our goal is to avoid confusion not avoid the truth. We don't want to stretch the truth, skirt around it or twist it, color it, exaggerate, or paint a false picture with words.

Abstract words can be used in so many ways that their meaning becomes unclear. People can't raise a mental picture or give quick definition to our meaning. Since abstract words mean different things to different people in different situations, we should replace them with *concrete* words if we want to communicate clearly.

Concrete means specific. *Send* is abstract while *fax, e-mail, courier,* and *express mail* are concrete. *Go* is abstract while verbs like *run, drive,* and *saunter* are concrete.

A clear image is memorable, an abstract one is not. Listen to the difference:

Vague	Concrete, precise, and memorable
Treat the customers nicely.	Make all our customers feel like guests in your home.
Clean the house properly.	I want the house to sparkle.
Do your best.	I'd like it by noon on Wednesday. If it looks as if that won't be possible, please let me know by 3 P.M. on Tuesday.
I'll send it.	I'll fax it to you straight away.

When we use concrete words, we help people form the mental pictures that we want them to. We can paint pictures, create feelings, sensations, and sounds by choosing the right words.

Choose Strong Words

We know weak words when we hear them:

may	possibly	might
could	probably	seems to
if	maybe	soon

We all know feeble phrases, too:

appears to be	I'll do my best, but …
I'll see what I can do	I'll try
weather permitting	If nothing gets in the way
That should be okay	She'll be right

If you're on the receiving end of any of these weak words or phrases, question them. What does the speaker really mean? Assess whether they are taking responsibility to make something happen or brushing it to one side.

If you use weak words, people will usually ignore these escape hatches anyway, and hold you to your word. "I'll try to have it for you by Friday" will probably be heard as "I'll have it for you by Friday." If that's what you mean, why not say so? You might as well be specific and take responsibility with powerful words.

Deliver Your Words with Panache

Using words that are precise and powerful will help the other person to receive the meaning we intend. Choosing words that persuade will help them be heard. Choosing words with punch and power will help them sink in. Choosing words that are neutral or positive, clear, complete, and concrete is the first step.

Then we deliver them.

Foot in Mouth

Don't spoil your messages with wimpy words.

Speak Clearly

Having chosen words that are clear, concise, complete, courteous, correct, and concrete, we need to speak them clearly enough to be understood. Chapter 9, "First Impressions Count!" discusses this in detail.

Use People's Names

A name might be a word, but to paraphrase author and lecturer Dale Carnegie, the sweetest word to anyone's ears is the sound of their own name.

Foot in Mouth

Don't overdo using a person's name. Use it too often and it's just an empty, slick, patronizing, and extremely irritating technique.

Dale Carnegie was right. Using people's names captures their attention. It makes them feel more positive toward our message and us. This is especially true on the telephone, when we should use a person's name more than we would face-to-face.

A Word to the Wise

Bring into play as many senses as you can for precise and memorable communication.

Support Your Words with Visual Aids

Show and tell. If we hear something, chances are that we'll remember 10 to 15 percent of it a day or so later. If we see it, we'll recall 30 to 35 percent of it. Add the two together and we have a fairly memorable communication.

You can literally show a picture, or you can create a mental one with your words.

Give Demonstrations

Show and tell, again. This time so that people can see exactly what happens, precisely how something works, or what exactly is to be done. Demonstrations make communication more memorable.

Provide Examples/Metaphors/Analogies

Story-type examples and specific examples are easy to remember. So are analogies …

She's as cold as ice.

They took to it like ducks to water.

… and metaphors:

Unchain my heart.

I felt like the weight of the world was on my shoulders.

People can relate to examples, metaphors, and analogies and recall them better than straightforward instructions or information.

Format Your Words to Match the Other Person

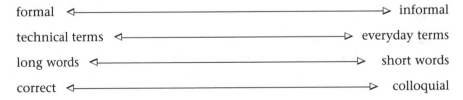

formal ⟵⟶ informal

technical terms ⟵⟶ everyday terms

long words ⟵⟶ short words

correct ⟵⟶ colloquial

People have characteristic ways of speaking, called an *idiolect*. This individual dialect is the unique way they format words and use certain styles of words.

Adapting our own idiolect to incorporate that of our conversational partners by using similar formats and types of words makes it easier for them to understand us. It helps them relate to what we're saying and makes it easier for them to receive our message in the way that we intend. (See also Chapter 12, "Build Rapport," and Chapter 19, "Speak the Other Person's Language.")

Famous Last Words

An **idiolect** is a person's distinctive way of putting words together.

Use the Other Person's "Language"

We know that we can build rapport by matching another person's energy, voice, and body language. We can also build rapport by matching their communication style and choice of words—hat's what the next chapter is all about.

The Least You Need to Know

➤ Especially in difficult communication situations, choose your words carefully.

➤ Use neutral language and a neutral tone of voice if you want to be heard and to be courteous.

➤ Choose positive words if you want a positive response.

➤ Choose specific and strong words for clarity, completeness, concreteness, and correctness.

➤ Make your words memorable with visual aids and demonstrations, metaphors, analogies, and examples.

Chapter 19

Speak the Other Person's Language

> ### In This Chapter
>
> ➤ Neuro-linguistic programming
>
> ➤ Four basic modes, or "languages," of communication
>
> ➤ Recognizing "languages"
>
> ➤ Speaking in four English "languages"

Imagine a wedding photograph taken to capture a wonderful memory, but it's been taken out of focus. Imagine your favorite song, but it's being sung out of tune, with the backbeat not quite right. Imagine a love letter written in legalese. It doesn't quite work, does it?

When two people speak in a different "language," it doesn't quite work, either. This chapter will show you how to bring your communications into focus, tune them to the right key, and set them to the right rhythm. You'll find out how to make your communication crystal clear, ring true, feel right, and make sense.

Neuro-Linguistic Programming

A branch of psychology and psychotherapy, the field of *neuro-linguistic programming* (NLP) was developed in the 1970s by Richard Bandler and John Grinder. It looks at

Famous Last Words

The term **neuro-linguistic pro-gramming** studies the way we take in, deal with, and convey information.

how people perceive and deal with their world and how we can all perceive and deal with it more effectively.

NLP studies how we take in information, process it internally, and "spit it out" again. Neuro-linguists have identified four main "languages" we can use to gather, process, and deliver information, which has important implications for us as communicators.

Understanding the four English languages can help us develop a more genuine understanding of and empathy for others. It can help us build rapport quickly and persuade others more readily. It can help us become far more elegant and eloquent participants in the dance of communication.

Four English Languages

Try this little exercise. Think about a really enjoyable day at the beach. In the space below, write a paragraph about it.

_____

_____

_____

Did you write about the clear blue sky, the sparkling water, and the pure white sand?

Perhaps you wrote about the warmth of the sun on your skin, the gritty sand beneath your feet, the splash of the ocean that cooled you?

Or did you write about the crashing waves, the cry of the sea gulls, and the sounds of children playing?

Possibly, you described the day in clear and objective terms, recounting the weather conditions, the other people who were there, and what you actually did?

The way you described the beach tells us something about the things you notice most about the world around you. Do you most notice what you see, what you hear, or what you feel? Or do you deal with your world objectively and matter-of-factly?

Talking, but Not Communicating

John and Joan have just met and are discussing a movie they have both recently seen.

John: It was one of the most vivid and colorful movies I've ever seen. Did you enjoy it?

Joan: Yes, I felt it was sensational. It really moved me.

John: My favorite scene was where the two heroes had to jump off that 10-mile high cliff into a canyon of nothingness. What amazing camera work! It was like I was right there with them, seeing that vast emptiness come in and out of focus. I actually think my own life flashed before my eyes!

Joan: What I liked most about it was the way it captured the feeling of rough camaraderie and contrasted it with the slipperiness of fate. I felt like warm jelly by the end of it.

Hands up if you think John's next sentence might be something like: "Yeah, well, it's been good to meet you, Joan. I see someone over there I need to catch up with. Bye!" Is your hand in the air? It should be! Joan and John may have been talking about the same movie, but they certainly weren't seeing eye to eye or reading off the same page. They weren't on the same wavelength or in tune with each other's thoughts. They weren't marching to the same drummer or feeling the same vibes from the movie. In short, they were talking but not communicating.

Why not? They were speaking in two different languages. Go back and have a look at John's words. They draw pictures, don't they? He's re-seeing the movie as he talks to Joan.

In contrast, Joan's words are about feelings and textures. She's re-feeling the movie as she talks to John about it.

They saw the same movie, but from two different "worlds." They remember the same movie differently because different things stood out to them, and therefore they recall the same movie differently. It may as well have been two different movies!

A Word to the Wise

Listen to how other people use words and phrase sentences. The field of neuro–linguistic programming teaches us to watch and listen for four basic modes, or representational systems, of communication: visual, auditory, kinaesthetic, and digital.

Visual (Seeing) Language

Pictures are important to visual people. Not surprisingly, the words they use convey lots of visual images:

"Let's look at that in a different way."

"Picture this …"

"I see what you mean."

"He'll take a dim view of that!"

"In my mind's eye, ..."

"She's got tunnel vision."

"That's clear to me."

"That's a bright idea!"

Visual people ...

➤ look up a lot when they think.

➤ speak quickly and in higher tones.

➤ gesture with hands held high.

➤ breathe rapidly, shallowly, or irregularly, high in the chest.

Auditory (Hearing) Language

Sound is important to auditory people, so their words convey lots of sound:

"How does that sound to you?"

"That rings a bell!"

"You're coming through loud and clear."

"Let me rattle that around in my head."

"That idea resonates with me."

Auditory people ...

➤ look to the side a lot when they think.

➤ speak with resonance, more slowly, and in lower tones than visual people.

➤ gesture with hands at mid-torso.

➤ breathe slowly, evenly, in the middle of the chest.

Kinaesthetic (Feeling, Touch) Language

Touch and feelings are important to kinaesthetic people. Their words convey lots of movement, emotions, feelings, and touch sensations:

"How does that sit with you?"

"This concept is hard to grasp."

"Run that by me again."

"Get a grip on yourself!"

"That makes me uncomfortable."

"This is a hassle-free approach."

"Hang in there!"

"My gut reaction ..."

Kinaesthetic people ...

➤ look down and to their right a lot when they think.

➤ speak in deep tones.

➤ gesture a lot, holding their hands low, and they touch themselves a lot.

➤ breathe from the abdomen.

Digital (Logical/Analytical) Language

To digital people, concepts and the words themselves are important. Their language doesn't usually include reference to the five senses; instead, their words convey thought and reflection:

"Have I explained that satisfactorily?"

"All things considered, ..."

"My opinion is ..."

"In the best interests of everyone, I have decided ..."

"What are your thoughts on that?"

Digital people ...

➤ look down and to their left a lot when thinking.

➤ speak in well-modulated, slow-paced, low tones.

➤ gesture minimally.

Visual, auditory, kinaesthetic, and digital do not describe four "types" of people, but the four most common ways that people gather, sift, and convey information—with their eyes, their ears, or their body, or by noticing and thinking about things. Most of us use all these representational systems in varying combinations. Based on habit, though, most of us have an unconscious preference for using one sensory channel, or language, over the others. We have come to excel at it and because of this, we trust it more than the others.

When other people speak our language, communication connections are smooth and rapid.

Visual people easily *view* the world the same way!

Auditory people *click* right away!

Kinaesthetic people *feel* good about each other!

Digital people *consider* each other to be thoughtful, sensible people!

When we don't speak the same language as another person, communication connections can be rough and slow:

➤ A visual person may complain that another person never sees it his way or that the other person always takes such a short-sighted approach.

➤ An auditory person may complain that she can't get on the same wavelength with another person or that the person is too monotonous and drones on and on.

➤ A kinaesthetic person may complain that he can't seem to get through to another person or that the other person is formal, stiff, and out of touch.

➤ A digital person may complain that someone finds difficulty following her thinking on this or state that although the person is charming, she and the other person don't share much in common.

Which are you?

It's easier to speak in our own language and harder to speak in a language we don't use much. Yet the more languages we speak, the more fluent and friendly we can make our communications. To find out which languages you speak well and which you need more practice in, take the short quiz below:

A Word to the Wise

People feel really good when you speak to them in their language.

Which language do you speak? Place a tick next to the statements that best describe you.

___ My stomach churns when I am nervous.

___ I love having my back rubbed.

___ I prefer hands-on involvement with things.

___ I enjoy exercise.

___ I often touch people when I'm talking to them, or touch things to feel their texture.

___ I am aware of my emotions and feelings.

___ I love comfortable chairs.

___ I am sensitive to the vibes of others and sense the mood of a group easily.

___ My intuition often tells me whether I'm right or wrong or whether to trust someone.

___ I fidget a lot.

___ I usually tap out the tempo to music with my hand or foot.

___ I prefer information presented to me with a demonstration, a sample, or a mock-up or model.

___ When I think about something or someone, I see a picture in my mind.

___ When someone is speaking to me, I look at him or her.

___ I like to keep my house neat and tidy.

___ I think fresh flowers really brighten a room.

___ I like to have things explained to me with pictures, diagrams, graphs, and charts.

___ I try to get a mental picture of things.

___ I hate it when people block my view.

___ I prefer to receive work instructions and important information in written form—memo, fax, e-mail, etc.

___ I always have dents and scratches on my car repaired quickly.

___ I'm good at mentally rearranging furniture to see whether it would look good.

___ I enjoy art exhibits and museum displays.

___ I recall people's faces easily.

___ When it comes to games, I enjoy games like Scrabble or Password.

___ When it comes to radio or television, I prefer talk shows and interviews.

___ I make decisions by carefully studying and analyzing the key issues.

___ I am very good at making sense of new data and information.

___ If I'm annoyed or upset, I try to remain composed, although it sometimes shows in the words I use.

___ I think things through, either out loud or silently.

___ I am influenced more by a person's logic than by the way they look or sound.

___ I make purchasing decisions based on overall value.

___ I have my car serviced regularly, so I can depend on it running properly.

___ I sometimes take a while to adapt if the mood of a group of people suddenly changes.

___ My partner often notices that I'm upset before I do.

___ I don't particularly enjoy singing or physical exercise.

___ I prefer information presented to me orally—on voicemail, through discussion, or over the phone.

___ I hum or sing a lot.

___ I often talk things through aloud or to myself, or even to my dog or cat.

___ I can usually hear if someone is singing off-key.

___ I have the best stereo system I can afford, and I enjoy listening to it.

___ I often repeat things to myself so I'll remember them.

___ I can usually hear it if someone is telling the truth.

___ I enjoy conversations with people.

___ I would rather give a talk than write a paper.

___ I pay attention at lectures and speeches.

___ I can tell when my car needs a tune-up from the way it sounds.

___ I pay more attention to what people say than to how they look.

Now turn to Appendix F, "How to Score the Neuro-Linguistic Programming Quiz," to find out how to score your answers.

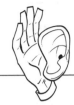

Make Your Communications Glide ...!

We can make our communications crystal clear to someone by identifying their preferred representational mode (visual, auditory, kinaesthetic, or digital) and speaking to them in it. This helps us connect and builds rapport. The other person won't need to translate the material into his or her own language—our words will be meaningful and our information will go straight in.

Words often symbolize the system we use to perceive and represent our world.

Think of English as three foreign languages plus the one you usually communicate in. To speak well in all of them takes a bit of thought, at least initially, until we become familiar with the language.

Here are some words in each of the languages to get you started.

Silver Tongue

"The trouble with a foreign language is you have to think before you speak."

—Swedish proverb

Visual Words

Listen for these visual words used on their own or in phrases, and use them in return.

aim	foresight	overview	appear
frame	pattern	blank	glimpse
glaze	perspective	clarify	blur
hazy	peruse	preview	brilliant

hindsight	picture	clear	illuminate
discern	portray	crystal clear	illusion
reflect	screen	dawn	image
see	spectacle	imagine	sketch
eclipse	graphic	insight	show
distinguish	stare	envision	look
square	enlighten	neat	reveal
delineate	flash	obscure	vague
focus	disillusion	bright	illustrate
survey	clout	outlook	vision
expose	paint	color	view

Auditory Words

Listen for these auditory words used on their own or in phrases, and use them in return.

acclaim	cry	hear	note
ring	aloud	accent	debate
mention	announce	decry	muffle
tone	articulate	shout	describe
growl	attune	sing	dialogue
overtone	babble	discordant	propose
beat	discuss	question	be heard
dissonance	say	rebuff	music
blank out	echo	sound	resounding
clear	boom	exclaim	retort
scream	call	frequency	click
snap	static	chord	rattle
groan	speechless	click	grumble
talk	contact	amplify	harmony
tune	harmonize	key	voice
alarm	sound	ask	loud
speak	explain	listen	tell

Kinaesthetic Words

Listen for these kinaesthetic words, used on their own or in phrases, and use them in return.

activate	throw	complacent	shock
fumble	stir	get hold of	active

connect	grasp	agitate	delightful
hand	anxious	disenchanted	strike
handle	backing	impress	drive
happy	move	balance	embarrassed
hit	hungry	grope	blend
tap	emotional	stroke	impact
bliss	crash	energetic	smash
irritate	sharpen	block	tangible
equilibrium	link	tickle	bond
sore	exasperated	grab	loose
carry	bounce	fall flat	manipulate
calm	fed up	flowing	massage
carry	feel	finger	rub
touch	cemented	sticky	grip
frustrated	crawl	smooth	

Digital Words

Digital words evoke thoughts and concepts more than pictures, sounds, or feelings. Although objective, specific, logical, and accurate, they can be quite "dry" because of their lack of emotion. Use digital words in return.

act	conceive	analyze	know
ambiguous	consider	learn	appreciate
decide	motivate	associate	abstract
discern	perceive	aware	distinct
ponder	be conscious	considered	emphasize
precede	believe	experience	pretend
blend	elaborate	generate	process
calibrate	guess	read	cancel
insensitive	study	recall	choice
integrate	recognize	comprehend	thoughtful
intent			

Use words the way the other person does to build rapport and to smooth and speed communication.

Use terms and language people can understand and adjust your vocabulary to suit the person and the situation. Talk in the other person's "language."

Tune in to, get a picture of, feel your way into, and assess and become aware of which language a person prefers. Use this understanding to build rapport and empathy and communicate with them in their own language.

Foot in Mouth

Don't limit your vocabulary and your communications to only one language. Learn them all to increase your communication flexibility and widen the range of people you communicate well with.

The Least You Need to Know

➤ Neuro-linguistic programming (NLP) is a relatively new branch of psychology and psychotherapy.

➤ People take in, deal with, and convey information in one of four languages.

➤ Listen to people's words and watch their eyes, gestures, and breathing to learn their preferred language.

➤ Learn to speak in other languages to develop your communication flexibility.

➤ Converse with people in their preferred "language" to build rapport and communicate powerfully.

Chapter 20

Speak for Yourself, Not the World

In This Chapter

➤ The fight-flight response

➤ The passive-aggressive cycle

➤ Recognizing assertiveness

➤ Assertive rights *and* obligations

➤ Fact, fantasy, folklore, feelings, and assumptions

We are all born with instincts. We breathe without reminding ourselves to; if something flies through the air towards us, we'll shut our eyes, duck, and protect our heads; if we sense danger, we'll stand our ground and fight, or we'll turn tail and run.

We can override some instincts by developing skills. We can learn to catch a ball without shutting our eyes, ducking, or protecting our heads. Although our instinct for self-preservation is so strong it would be impossible to "learn" to hold our breath until we dropped dead, we can learn to breathe through snorkels or oxygen masks—we can learn to modify even our strongest instincts.

Similarly, we can learn assertiveness skills and use them to override, or at least modify, our instinctive fight-flight response. In this chapter, you'll find out what assertiveness

Famous Last Words

The **limbic system** is buried deep in our central brain. It is involved in basic emotions and feelings, including the fight–flight response, the source of aggressive and passive communication styles.

is and what it isn't, and how to recognize it in yourself and others. You'll find out why it's essential an essential part of effective communication.

The Fight–Flight Response

The seat of our fight-flight response is the *limbic system*, deep inside the second oldest part of our three-part brain. We share this limbic system, and its functions, with the animal realm.

When we sense danger, the limbic system releases adrenaline to energize our muscles to help us fight or flee. It also causes us to breathe more rapidly and shallowly, drawing oxygen from our "thinking brain"—the neocortex or cerebellum—and sending it to the older brain beneath it. This means that when we're in fight-flight mode, our body is ready for action, but our mind isn't. This makes communication, other than through fists or feet, difficult.

Listen to This

Megan was normally quite meek, so meek, in fact, that she seldom stood up for herself. Everyone knew they could rely on Megan to cover for them if they were late back from a break or to help them in their work if they fell behind.

She realized this; it and her resentment of others "taking advantage of her" would build up to the point where she would explode. She would rant and rave about fairly small things, like people borrowing pencils off her desk or not washing up after themselves in the kitchen.

"Megan's letting off steam again," her colleagues would say, and wait for her to calm down. Things would go back to normal for awhile, until Megan's next eruption. Since she never clearly communicated what she was really angry about, nothing ever changed.

Fight-flight was useful for our early ancestors who often faced life-threatening situations. We seldom need it since, thankfully, the potentially deadly situations the instinct was designed for are few and far between for most of us.

The fight instinct mostly shows up as aggressive communication—the win-lose style of force—or as passive communication—the lose-lose run and avoid style—or the lose-win give in and accommodate style of communication.

A lot of people have never developed communication skills beyond the instinctive passive-aggressive styles. Some people seem stuck in one or the other; others swing back and forth between them in what is known as a *passive-aggressive cycle*.

Famous Last Words

Has a normally calm, even placid person ever "blown up" at you over a seeming trifle? That could be the **passive-aggressive cycle:** generally passive communication and behavior with occasional outbursts of aggressive communication and behavior.

Three Styles of Communication

Unlike our inborn passive and aggressive communication styles, assertive communication needs to be learned. To communicate assertively, we need both verbal and nonverbal skills that encourage a win-win outcome. We also need high self-esteem and an internal locus of control, which we covered in Part 1, "Communication Begins Inside."

We also need to prevent the fight-flight response in our more primitive brain from kicking in and access our "thinking brain." Another essential part of assertive communication is respect for others as well as ourselves and a mind-set that says: "I want to be satisfied and I want you to be satisfied, too."

Does that sound like a lot? It isn't, really, especially when you consider that mastering assertiveness is essential for effective communication.

Aggressive Communicators

Do you know anyone who ...

> ➤ talks over you and interrupts you?
> ➤ tells you what to do before finding out what you want to do?
> ➤ treats you as if they're better than you are?
> ➤ makes sarcastic, demeaning, or threatening remarks?
> ➤ doesn't consider what you want, only what they want?
> ➤ always wants to get their way, whatever the cost?

Famous Last Words

Aggressive communicators put their own wants and needs ahead of everyone else's and often ignore or belittle other people's concerns.

Famous Last Words

Passive communicators put other people's wants and needs ahead of their own and often deny or denigrate what they want and need.

Silver Tongue

"Being humble doesn't mean one has to be a mat."

—Maya Angelou

➤ stands too close to you, over you, or in some other way makes you feel physically uncomfortable?

This describes an *aggressive communication* style. Communication like this leads to hostility, anger, and resentment.

Passive Communicators

Do you know anyone who …

➤ hardly ever says what they really think or want?

➤ lets others make decisions for them?

➤ agrees to do things they would rather not do to avoid "making waves"?

➤ speaks hesitantly and quietly?

➤ acts as if they think they are less important than you are?

➤ avoids conflict and disagreement at all costs?

➤ drops hints rather than directly requests that you do something?

This describes *passive communication*. It, too, leads to bad feelings and damages relationships.

Assertive Communicators

Do you know anyone who …

➤ is open and honest about what they're thinking or feeling?

➤ makes a direct request if they would like you to do something, leaving the way open for you to say "no"?

➤ respects themselves and shows respect for you?

➤ finds out what you want, tells you what they want, and looks for ways you can both be happy?

➤ listens to and respects your opinion even if it's different from theirs?

➤ will let you know in a courteous and clear way if you're doing something they would prefer you not to do?

➤ can disagree with you without creating bad feelings?

This describes an *assertive communication* style. Assertive communicators are good at both gathering and giving good information. They can say clearly how things are from their point of view and are willing and able to listen to how things are from other people's points of view.

How to Spot an Assertive Person

Assertive people use a number of important communication skills. They ask questions to gather good information for clarification and to check they have understood correctly. We don't need to guess what they really mean because they give good information in a direct yet courteous way. Assertive people say what's on their minds clearly and carefully: clearly so people don't need to guess at any hidden message, and carefully so that they don't damage the other person's self-esteem.

Assertive people use "I" language. They "own their messages" and "speak for themselves" ("I think," "I feel," "I need," "I'd like," "My opinion is"). Their suggestions are not weighted with advice, commands, *should*s or *ought*s. Their feedback is constructive and free of blame, commands, threats, and demands. They can politely fend off unreasonable requests, deal with criticism, and say "no" graciously. They accept people and points of view different from their own. *Verbally*, assertive people …

➤ make statements that are honest, clear, brief, and to the point.

➤ use "I" statements: "I'd like …" "I appreciate …" "I think …."

➤ distinguish between fact and opinion.

➤ ask, don't tell.

➤ offer improvement suggestions, not advice or commands.

➤ offer constructive criticism, free of blame, assumptions, and *should*s.

➤ ask questions to find out the thoughts and feelings of others.

Famous Last Words

Assertive communication is a learned set of verbal and nonverbal communication skills based on mutual respect that results in clear, open communication. Assertive communicators can say how they see things and hear how others see things. They work toward outcomes that satisfy everyone.

A Word to the Wise

Use assertive people as role models.

213

➤ respect the rights of others as well as their own rights.

➤ communicate mutual respect where the needs of two people conflict and look for mutually acceptable solutions.

Nonverbally, assertive people …

➤ make appropriate eye contact.

➤ sit or stand comfortably erect.

➤ use open gestures to support their comments.

➤ speak in a clear, steady, firm tone of voice.

➤ maintain open, steady, and relaxed facial expressions that accurately reflect their feelings, thoughts, and comments.

➤ speak at a steady, even pace, emphasizing key words, with few awkward hesitations.

The following words are often used to describe assertive people:

honest	considerate	relaxed
flexible	open	tolerant
joyous	confident	accountable
trusting	leaders	mature

A Word to the Wise

Watch people as they communicate. Choose a few people that you believe communicate assertively. Watch what they say and how they say it. Look at their body language If you want to communicate more assertively, use them as role models. Do what they do.

Communicating assertively helps us gather and give good information. It encourages a two-way sharing of ideas, opinions, and beliefs; it helps information flow freely and helps us to avoid sending contradictory messages.

How assertive are you?

Do you take responsibility rather than lay blame?

Do you express your feelings and needs without attacking others?

Do you "pull your own strings"?

Are you self-confident enough to let people see the real you?

Are you comfortable letting others know what you think and feel?

Do you actively pursue your goals without hurting others?

Do you ask for what you want?

Do you set your own priorities?

Can you express pride in your accomplishments without being boastful?

Developing Assertion Skills

The best way to strengthen your assertion skills is to practice them in safe surroundings, with people you trust. Ask them to tell you if you have overstepped the boundary into aggression or if your words and body language don't match.

Don't Trip over the Fine Line Between Assertion and Aggresion!

It can be easy to overstep the boundary of assertion into aggression when first practicing assertive communication. It is as if we are so carried away with our newfound ability to state our own point of view that we forget other people also have a right to state their points of view. This overlooks the empathy and mutual respect aspects of genuine assertion.

Overstepping the mark into aggression is a mistake beginner asserters often make.

Watch Out for Passive Body Language

The other common mistake is to give an assertive message but spoil it with passive body language. People will believe your body language not your words.

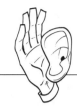

Listen to This

H.G. Wells once asked Mahatma Gandhi for his views on a document Wells had co-authored, titled *Rights of Man*. Gandhi did not agree with the document's emphasis on rights. He responded:

I suggest the right way. Begin with a charter of Duties of Man and I promise the rights will follow as spring follows winter.

A Word to the Wise

When you find yourself in a situation calling for assertive communication, ask yourself how your assertive role models would handle it. Then do it. "Fake it till you make it" is a good motto for practicing assertive communication skills.

Don't Masquerade Your Opinions as Facts

We can categorize information into the Four *F*s: Fact, Fantasy, Folklore, and Feelings.

Facts are facts, and although we like to pretend otherwise, there are not as many facts around as we might think. Opinions are fantasy. We have a bad habit of masquerading our opinions as facts when they're not—they're only opinions, our little fantasies.

Folklore is what we know as hearsay: gossip, the grapevine, the rumor mill. And as we all know, most of this is fiction (although it can be fun)!

We often overlook feelings. There are three kinds of feelings to be aware of in communication. The first is our emotions—are we happy, sad, mad, or glad? We need to tune into them and at the same time, make sure they're not controlling our communications. The second is our intuition, our hunches, our gut feelings. With the world becoming more confusing and complex, our senses are becoming increasingly important, and many of us need to learn to listen to them more often.

Then there are feelings to do with the ego. If you've ever seen someone backed into a corner and forced to "save face or act macho," you've seen ego feelings come to the fore. They don't help communication at all!

Here are five tips to making good use of the Four *F*s of communication:

1. Be sure of your facts and never present anything as a fact that isn't a fact.

2. When you're stating an opinion, let people know that it's your opinion. Own it. Don't masquerade it as a fact.

3. Don't spread folklore (but, by all means, listen to it—it can provide important insights!).

4. Acknowledge and deal with your feelings. Listen to your hunches. Guard against ego-driven communications.

5. When someone is telling you something, listen carefully and ask questions to distinguish between fact, fantasy, folklore, and feelings.

Facts are important. Opinions are valuable—ours and other people's. Just don't masquerade opinions as facts or confuse them with facts!

Fantasy, folklore, and feelings can be important sources of information.

Feelings give us important information, too. If emotions dominate, though, communication will suffer;

A Word to the Wise

As a sender of crystal clear information, distinguish between fact, fantasy, folklore, and feelings.

As a listener, focus carefully to distinguish between these four types of information. If any are missing, ask questions to uncover them. The difference could be important.

Foot in Mouth

Don't let your ego take over communications. Too much emotion pulls us out of our thinking brain and into our older central brain. It can destroy good communication.

people can't concentrate with their emotions running amok. Acknowledge feelings and deal with them carefully. Pay attention to hunches—your own and other people's. Hunches are often our subconscious talking to us.

Be Explicit About Assumptions

While we're distinguishing between orders of information, let's not overlook the ubiquitous assumption.

It's easy to get caught up in assumptions and treat them as facts. Many an expensive and embarrassing decision has been based on incorrect assumptions that no one bothered to check. Many a conflict has flared because of people holding different assumptions about something, which they never checked with each other.

Uncovering assumptions is seldom easy; most are reached almost instantaneously and often unconsciously as the brain tries to make sense of confusing and often contradictory information. We need to be vigilant!

A Word to the Wise

Explicitly state any assumptions you are making. Listen to others carefully to uncover any of their buried assumptions.

The Least You Need to Know

➤ The fight-flight instinct is the root of passive and aggressive communication in which someone always loses.

➤ Mastering assertiveness is essential for effective communication.

➤ If you need to increase your assertiveness, practice with people you trust to give you constructive feedback.

➤ Be careful you don't overstep the bounds of assertion into aggression.

➤ Whether giving or gathering good information, distinguish between fact, fantasy, folklore, and feelings.

➤ Bring any underlying assumptions into the open, so you can test them against reality.

Chapter 21

Don't Masquerade Your Thoughts

In This Chapter

➤ Talking about yourself assertively

➤ Keeping conversations on track

➤ Dealing with criticism

➤ Saying "no" graciously

➤ Dealing with bullies

This chapter explains a range of assertion skills that you can use every day. Some of them help you state what you want, feel, or need clearly and others are particularly useful when you must deal with someone who is behaving aggressively towards you or is in some way ignoring your rights.

If any of these techniques are new to you, practice them in your mind's eye first. Test out what you plan to say with someone whose communication skills you admire. Practice SO CLEAR body language (from Chapter 10, "Send the Right Signals") to support your assertive messages, and keep at it until you're comfortable with these skills. Guard against becoming aggressive in your desire to assert yourself; remember, the other person has rights, too!

Talking About Yourself Assertively

Assertive communication helps us talk about ourselves, our thoughts, and our feelings without sounding arrogant. In this section, you'll find four ways you can speak for yourself with comfort.

Own Your Messages

You've heard the phrases "Everyone knows …" and "Most people —"? These are examples of *not* owning a message.

Foot in Mouth

Don't hide what you think or believe behind what you claim other people think or believe.

Saying "I think …" and "I believe …" are examples of owning our message. Saying "I" or "my" leads to clear communication.

Speak for Yourself

To use "We think …" or "We'd like …," unless we have been elected the official spokesperson for a group, is an example of speaking for everyone. It is hiding what we want to say behind what we are suggesting other people think or want.

Instead of hiding behind some unspecified "we" to state your opinions, say "I think …" or "It seems to me …."

Own Your Feelings

Here are some examples of owning feelings:

I feel that we're going around in circles. Perhaps we need to try a different approach.

I could really do with a break now. How about you?

I'm not following what you're saying.

I'm confused.

I feel pretty angry about this, and I'd like to discuss it with you later.

I feel I'm being pushed into a corner here. I need some time to think about what you're asking.

I feel uncomfortable discussing this right now. Would you mind if we discuss it later?

Sharing what is happening to us personally is often very helpful for getting a discussion "unstuck," strengthening relationships, and accomplishing tasks.

In Chapter 14, "Ask the Right Questions," we saw that pseudo questions and leading questions cause resentment and lead to guessing games and defensiveness. They put people on guard. Inaccurate assumptions and crossed communication wires can also result. The same occurs if we don't own our messages.

Open Up

Do you think the more people know about you, the more vulnerable you are? Think again! It's hard for people to communicate with us unless they know a bit about us. The more we open up, the more they can get to know us. The more they know about us, the more they can trust us, open up to us, like us, and understand us.

Offering information about ourselves, our likes and dislikes, our values and goals, our beliefs, opinions, experiences, failures, and successes, helps people get to know us. It builds understanding, relationships, loyalty, friendships, and a shared frame of reference—"Oh, I understand where you're coming from!"

Listen to This

Elke wore long, flowing dresses and burned a lot of incense. Elke was very tuned into her feelings and whenever people asked for her opinion, she'd look down, put her hand to her mouth, and say "Uhm, how do I feel about that ...?" She continually checked her feelings and shared them with others and talked openly about what was going on in her life.

Elke was an interesting person, but the trouble was, she only seemed to be interested in herself. She never seemed to ask her friends how they were, what was going on in their lives, or how they felt about things. Elke didn't balance her openness about her own feelings with a concern for others. Her friends gradually gave her more and more space for herself.

Being open doesn't mean we should bare our soul to everyone we meet or wear our heart on our sleeve. It certainly doesn't mean talking about ourselves constantly, trying to be the center of attention, or generally acting as if the universe revolves solely around us!

Famous Last Words

Use the **broken record technique** to get through to someone who isn't listening to you. Keep repeating your message until it's heard.

It does mean contributing facts about ourselves to the conversation—our job, our hobbies, our holidays, our thoughts, our plans. The subject doesn't matter—the sharing does.

Don't Be Sidetracked

If someone is ignoring your main message, trying to sidetrack you, or keeps throwing in red herrings, you can use the *broken record technique*. Like a broken record, calmly repeat your main message, as often as necessary, until it is heard.

This doesn't give you permission to brush aside what the other person has to say; equally, don't let them brush aside what you have to say.

Lee: Sam, I'd like to discuss your timekeeping. As you know, because we've discussed it twice before, I need you to be on time in the mornings.

Sam: Oh, I'm sorry about this morning. I had trouble with the car. It's been giving me a lot of bother lately, and …

Lee: I understand that. I still need you here on time in the mornings.

Sam: Well, I always work through lunch hours.

Lee: Yes, and I appreciate that. I need you here on time in the morning, too.

Sam: Well, Jan was late yesterday and you didn't say anything to her!

Lee: Jan had spoken to me before. Sam, what are you going to do about getting here on time in the morning from now on?

This technique helps us make our point without making an enemy.

A Word to the Wise

You may also want to state your understanding of the other person's point as a way of showing that you have heard it. Then repeat your main message.

Deal With Criticism

Sometimes people attack us or criticize us. Constructive criticism is often valuable because it can provide us with important information worthy of consideration. Sometimes we'll want to hear more; sometimes we won't.

Find Out More

To find out more about the criticism, perhaps to decide if it's worth listening to or to help our critic be more specific, we can use the technique of *negative inquiry*. This draws out more specific information.

We keep probing the person's criticisms until they are clear. I've italicized the negative inquiries in the example below.

Chris: Pat, I'd like to see a more thorough job on that Jells report.

Pat: *I'm not sure what you mean by "more thorough," Chris.*

Chris: Well, basically, I'd like to see a lot more detail about how you reached your conclusions.

Pat: Okay, I can easily add that information. *Is there anything else I could do?*

Chris: Maybe a bit more supporting evidence would be good.

Pat: Fine, I can add a couple of tables as an appendix. Would that do it?

Chris: Yes, I think that about covers it. I'd really like to have it by Friday; would that be possible?

Chapter 14 gives additional information on how to ask questions for clarity.

Famous Last Words

Use the **negative inquiry** technique to draw out more information concerning a criticism. Keep asking questions until you understand the person's point.

One Way to Curtail a Discussion

Sometimes, the critic might be correct in what they say, but we don't want to get involved in a discussion, at least not at that moment. We want to avert a discussion swiftly and politely.

Negative assertion is good for this: We actually agree with our critic. As you can imagine, this pretty much stops them in their tracks. We don't have to get involved in discussions we don't want to.

In the example below, let's assume, first, that Pat is a trouble-making colleague and, since Chris needs a reasonably good working relationship with Pat, negative assertion is ideal:

Famous Last Words

Use the **negative assertion** technique to agree with a justified criticism and close off further discussion about it.

Chris:	Pat, this report isn't going to be acceptable.
Pat:	Yes, I realize that and I know exactly what I'll do to improve it.
Chris:	Yes, good, because it really does need a bit of work.
Pat:	You're right.
Chris:	Well, I'm glad you'll be able to fix it up.

Of course, if Chris were Pat's supervisor, Pat would be skating on thin ice here—it would be better to elaborate on how the report was going to be improved. Here's how:

Chris:	Pat, this report isn't going to be acceptable.
Pat:	Yes, I realize that. I thought I'd change the layout to show more white space and add some tables and charts to illustrate my data more clearly. I also thought inserting an executive summary of my conclusions at the beginning would help. What do you think?
Chris:	That sounds good to me. Have you thought about a table of contents, too?
Pat:	That's a good idea. Any other suggestions?
Chris:	No, I think that will give us what we need.

Pat used negative inquiry at the end, too. Use these techniques in any combination that suits your purposes.

Famous Last Words

Use the **fogging** technique to accept the possibility that a criticism may (or may not) be justified without starting an argument or brushing it aside.

Two More Ways to Curtail a Discussion

Sometimes criticism is unfair, unwarranted, or unhelpful. Or we might disagree with it but want to avoid an argument: "Yes, you are." "No, I'm not." "Yes, you are ...." It simply isn't worth discussing.

This is when we can use the *fogging* technique. When we fog a criticism, we acknowledge that perhaps it is true (and perhaps it isn't). For example:

Fred:	Paul, that presentation you gave to the executive committee was chronic!
Paul:	Perhaps it was.

Fred:	I'll say! Boy, was it off!
Paul:	Maybe I could have made a better job of it.
Fred:	Yeah, it sure was boring.
Paul:	I can see you might have found it boring. Maybe next time I'll spruce it up a bit.
Fred:	I hope you do!

With fogging, we neither agree nor disagree with the criticism, nor do we defend ourselves or explain ourselves. It sometimes helps to repeat the gist of the criticism, then fog.

Another way to prevent a discussion is to state assertively that you don't want to discuss the matter right now.

Fred:	Paul, that presentation you gave to the executive committee was chronic!
Paul:	Yes, it was. I don't want to discuss it right now, though.
Fred:	Yeah, I don't blame you. You must be really embarrassed.
Paul:	I really don't want to get into it right now, Fred.
Fred:	Yeah, sure, no worries.

Foot in Mouth

Watch your voice tone—keep it nice and neutral. If a tone of sarcasm creeps in, these techniques become aggressive, not assertive.

Say "No" Graciously

People have a right to ask. And, of course, we have a right to say "no" without feeling guilty.

If a request doesn't mesh with your own priorities, if it would make excessive time or energy demands, or if you'd simply rather not agree, don't beat around the bush. Communicate your "no" in a respectful, clear, and controlled way.

Sometimes it helps to begin with the positives …

Ong:	… and so I really hope you'll be able to join our organizing committee.
James:	I understand what a good cause this is, and I'd love to help out. Unfortunately, I don't have the time right now.

Ong:	James, I understand how busy you are. I hate to impose, but you do have a lot of skills you could bring on board.

... and finish with firm suggestions of alternatives.

James:	I'd really love to help, Ong. It's an important event and I'm sure it would be a rewarding experience. I would help if I could but unfortunately, I can't. Have you thought about asking Margaret? I have worked with her on things like this before and I'm sure she would bring a lot of skills to the committee, too.
Ong:	I understand how busy you are, James. I think that's a great idea about Margaret. I'll speak to her this afternoon.

Did you recognize the broken record technique in the previous example? It's a good way to say "no" without making an enemy. We aren't obliged to suggest alternatives, though:

Tony:	Jan, can you give me a hand compiling this report?
Jan:	I can't; I'm really snowed under myself and I'm rushing to meet a 4 o'clock deadline.
Tony:	But this won't take long.
Jan:	I understand that and I really can't spare the time.
Tony:	Oh, please, Jan, I'd really appreciate it.
Jan:	I really can't help you out just now.

We can also "top and tail" our "no" with positives. For example, James could have said: "I admire and support the cause, Ong. Unfortunately, I don't have the time to help out right now. I wish you well, though."

We can't blame someone for asking. And we have a right to say "no."

We can offer a brief explanation of our "no" if we want to (the more tangible and specific the better), or we can just say "no," politely and firmly.

Caller:	Good morning! How are you today? I would like to invite you to a seminar on how you can save big dollars on a tax-free investment. It's at a wonderful hotel and there will be terrific refreshments. Would you like to attend this Thursday evening or would you prefer Saturday afternoon?
Target:	I'm not interested in attending either.
Caller:	This is a wonderful opportunity to make an investment that will bring you a big return. I'm sure you'll want to take advantage of it or at least hear more about it. We are offering other seminars in

your area next week, too. Can I send you an invitation to one of those? What's your address?

Target: I'm not interested in attending a seminar at all.

Caller: Really? It's a terrific opportunity. Why don't I just mail you an invitation and you can think about it?

Target: No, thanks.

Caller: Are you saying you're perfectly happy with the taxes you're paying and wouldn't like to reduce them?

Target: I'm really not interested.

Caller: Okay, well, thanks for your time.

Use these ideas to speak for yourself; own your messages; deal with criticism; say "no" when you want to; and show respect for the other person. This will dramatically improve your communications.

Don't Be Bullied

Have you ever been bullied? Bullies use extreme aggression to ride roughshod over others. They use whatever power and force they have at their disposal (physical strength, bravado, or status, for example) to get their own way and trample over others. They delight in making people uncomfortable.

Perhaps due to the stresses of modern life or because people are less willing to put up with it and more willing to speak out about it more, bullying seems to be increasing.

Bullying is continual aggressive demeaning remarks and behavior that ignores and undermines the victim's rights to be treated with respect and consideration. Bullies gradually wear their victims down, eroding their self-esteem and self-confidence with a constant stream or ridicule and petty faultfinding. Persistent verbal abuse, humiliation, and undermining a person's worth doesn't leave marks that you can see, but it's just as painful.

People bully because their experience has taught them that bullying behavior gets them what they want. Naturally, if it works, they keep doing it.

A Word to the Wise

If you say "no," don't waver.

Listen to This

Bullies often begin their careers as bullies in childhood and carry the communication pattern into adulthood. They may have low self-esteem and demean others in an attempt to enhance their feelings of self-worth. Their victims are often competent, successful people who make them feel inadequate or threatened in some way.

Often, this means that the habitual bully fails to develop other skills to get their own way, such as assertion skills and other clear communication skills. They become trapped, able to use only those few, largely bullying, skills they have perfected.

If someone tries to bully you verbally, don't stand for it—it will only encourage him to continue. Say the person's name, name what he is doing, and tell him what to do instead. For example:

➤ "Jo, you're interrupting me. Let me finish."

➤ "Jo, it sounds like you're making fun of me. I'm making a serious point and I expect you to listen to it."

➤ "Jo, you're shouting at me. Take a deep breath and we'll talk later."

➤ "Jo, you're shouting at me. I can hear you perfectly well when you speak normally."

It's important to tell bullies what to do instead because often they just don't know any other way to communicate. It might be difficult, but think of yourself as coaching them into better communication.

Assertive communication is more than a set of techniques. It is a set of communication skills based on mutual respect. It involves both gathering and giving good information: the willingness to hear how it is on the other person's side and the ability to say clearly and carefully how it is on our side.

Foot in Mouth

Don't bother to use "I" statements with bullies. They don't work. Be much more direct.

Silver Tongue

"Keep away from angry, sore-tempered men, lest you learn to be like them and endanger your soul."

—Proverbs 15:18

The Least You Need to Know

➤ State your own point of view and the facts as you understand them clearly and calmly.

➤ Use a calm, clear tone of voice supported by SO CLEAR body language when asserting yourself.

➤ If you're new to asserting yourself, practice in your mind's eye until you're comfortable with what you'll say.

➤ Don't let people pressure you into saying "yes" when you want to say "no."

➤ Stand up for yourself (verbally) with bullies.

Chapter 22

Ask, Don't Tell

In This Chapter

➤ Saying how you see things

➤ Using DELWAC to solve problems

➤ The big stick

➤ Persuading without pressuring

We've seen how the deadly communication sins of telling, demanding, commanding, forcing, railroading, and so on draw resistant responses. The spirit of "ask, don't tell" overcomes this.

"Ask, don't tell" is based on mutual respect. It leaves the door open for discussion and increases the possibility of collaborating or reaching a compromise to achieve an outcome that satisfies everyone. It acknowledges that the other person has choices.

In this chapter, you'll find out how to avoid conflict, increase harmony and cooperation, and give good information persuasively. You'll learn an almost sure-fire way to put an end to other people's annoying habits, how to persuade people even when you have no real authority to do so, and how to resolve apparent clashes of needs and wants. You'll also find out how to bring out the "big guns" without resorting to threats, and some ways to build your credibility to increase your persuasiveness.

Telling Asks for Trouble!

Telling is pushy. Since it invites rebellion, why not ask? Choose the option of least resistance. "Ask, don't tell" is an easy habit to form once you see how well it works.

Instead of: "I want that ready by midday!" try: "I really need to have that done by midday; will that be possible for you?" (If the person says "no," you may have to reach a compromise or adjust some priorities.)

Instead of: "Don't do that!" say: "You'll find it easier (or safer) to do it this way."

Instead of: "I hate it when you do that!" try: "Would you mind doing X instead?" or "I'd rather you did X instead."

No demands, no commands, no threats—less resistance.

"I" Statements

Is there anyone who regularly does something that irritates you? It might be a big thing or just a little thing, but it makes your life more difficult. Wouldn't it be great if you could get them to stop! Even so, you might hesitate to raise the issue, not wanting to offend. Perhaps you have raised similar issues and ended up in an argument.

Dr. Thomas Gordon developed *"I" statements* in the late 1970s as a way to explain what we want without forcing people to do things our way. They help us raise things that matter to us and minimize the chances of people taking things the wrong way. They are another assertive communication skill and a powerful way of asking, not telling.

"I" statements specify a person's behavior and state how it affects us or why it is important. Because they are so powerful, a request to someone to alter their behavior, communicated as an "I" statement has a better chance of success than a command, threat, complaint, hint, or other nonassertive form of request.

Famous Last Words

An **"I" statement** is a clear, succinct, and blame-free statement of another's actions and their effect on you, and your preferred outcome.

"I" statements help us to express our point of view calmly without blaming the other person or treading on their toes as would, for example, a demand that they "mend their ways." They help us communicate clearly and cleanly and in a way that won't make the other person wary or defensive. "I" statements pave the way for clear and honest communication and so increase our chances of achieving a positive outcome.

"I" statements contain three parts:

Part 1   What you see or hear or what you think the facts are, stated without blame, using neutral words:

"When you …"

Part 2   How you feel, not what you think:

"I am" or "I get [frustrated, annoyed, angry, thrilled, overjoyed, hurt]"

Part 3   Why it matters, the tangible or intangible consequences of the first part:

"Because ..."

First, you state the facts or the behavior using neutral words. Make your point specifically and briefly, in a way that doesn't sound like a criticism.

Then describe the effect on you. Don't talk about what you think about it ("I think that's totally irresponsible of you") but how you feel about it ("I find it really irritating").

If you can substitute the words "I think" for "I feel," start again. For example, "I feel you are not pulling your weight" = "I think you aren't pulling your weight." Yes, and how do you feel about it? Let down, angry, taken advantage of?

Finally, talk about the consequences or tangible effects of the behavior. Be clear, courteous, and factual. You are not making a demand or a threat—"...and if you don't stop it, I'll ..."—but offering some information—"and that means ..." or "I'm worried that our customers will get the wrong idea, and we'll lose business as a result." This helps the person make an informed decision about whether or not to do something different. It doesn't tell them what to do, but provides them with a reason to consider changing their behavior.

A Word to the Wise

Specify only observable behavior or state the facts as you understand them; don't interpret them.

A Word to the Wise

Saying why it matters evokes the response "Gee, I didn't know it was *that* important!" This increases commitment.

Use "I" Statements for the Small Stuff

If the matter is very clear-cut, you can keep Parts 1 and 2 as they are described above and turn Part 3 into a straightforward request.

Part 1   What you see or hear or what you think the facts are (no blame, neutral words):

"When you ..."

Part 2	How you feel (not what you think):

"I am [frustrated, annoyed, angry, thrilled, overjoyed]."

Part 3	What you would prefer instead:

"I'd prefer that …" or "And what I'd like is …" or "So how about …?"

Foot in Mouth

Take care with "I" statements. There is a fine line between an "I" statement and an attempt to impose your values or wishes on another person. Use them as openers not resolvers.

Foot in Mouth

You can use force and tell someone what to do, but this will probably result, at best, in mere compliance. Try an "I" statement if you want to achieve understanding and commitment. There's a big difference.

In the example below, we explain both why it matters and what we want.

Frame	"Lee, I'd like to discuss this morning's meeting with you.
Part 1	You interjected several times before I had finished speaking and, as a result, I lost my train of thought.
Part 2	I find that really irritating.
Part 3	I'd really like to finish what I'm saying. How about it?"

Constructing "I" statements usually takes practice at first. Think through carefully what you want to say and jot it down. You might not say exactly what you wrote, but the process is very helpful. By writing it down you can clarify your "I" statement to make sure it meets the criteria described above. You can also learn a lot about yourself from composing "I" statements.

Use "I" Statements for the Big Stuff

Not everything is this uncomplicated. When the solution isn't so obvious, we can focus on our overall goal, or the end result we're after, in Part 3 of our statement.

Frame	"Enzo, do you have a couple of minutes? I'd like to talk through the handover procedures from your shift to mine.
Part 1	I know you want to make a quick get-away to get home to your kids. I often have the feeling, though, that this means I'm not getting the full maintenance information and

Part 2   I'm worried this might lead to a machine breakdown or even result in an accident.

Part 3   I'd like to work out a handover system with you that will make me feel comfortable that I have the full maintenance information and that won't hold you back. That would take a big load off my mind during my shift."

Use "I" statements for the Good Stuff

Don't get the impression that "I" statements are just for negative information. They're also effective for offering praise and encouraging more of the behavior we want.

Part 1   "Liz, that presentation was fantastic. You looked relaxed and comfortable and all the key points came across loud and clear. Your visual aids were particularly good because they were easy to read and emphasized your main points.

Part 2   I was really proud to have you on my team.

Part 3   Judging from their enthusiastic response I think the board will approve the proposal."

Part 1 spells out precisely what was good; we've let Liz know what is important to us, which lets her know what to focus on in the future. Part 2 makes her feel great and boosts her confidence. And Part 3 indicates that her effort is worthwhile.

> **A Word to the Wise**
>
> Juggle the order of Parts 1, 2, and 3 of an "I" statement. Say what is most important first. Use all three parts, though, because if you leave one out, you'll weaken your message.

Now Listen!

Make an "I" statement to say what you want clearly and cleanly. Then switch gears to listen: Hear what the other person has to say.

Have you ever taken silence as consent? This can be a mistake. Silence can actually have lots of meanings:

➤ I'm thinking favorably about it.

➤ I'm thinking negatively about it.

➤ I'm considering my options.

➤ I'm considering my response.

➤ I'm counting to 10.

➤ I agree and I'll act on it.

➤ I'm too angry to speak.

➤ I wasn't listening at all, just absent-mindedly nodding.

➤ I'm confused and reluctant to admit it.

➤ I'm confused and don't know how best to ask for clarification.

➤ I feel too powerless to respond meaningfully.

➤ I feel insulted and refuse to respond.

➤ I feel too superior to respond.

For the Really Complicated Stuff, Use DELWAC

DELWAC is an easy-to-remember acronym that helps us turn complaints, criticisms, and accusations into problems to be solved. It prevents us from grumbling, moaning, coercing, or compelling. Because it is in the spirit of "ask, don't tell," it increases cooperation and builds relationships.

D   Describe the situation.

E   Explain your point of view.

L   Listen to theirs.

W   Work out options.

A   Agree a course of action.

C   Check back to see it's working.

And Now for the Big Stick ...

United States President Harry Truman once said of foreign policies, "Walk softly and carry a big stick." Persuading others sometimes requires the same approach. In the beginning, we walk softly with "ask, don't tell." If necessary, we can get a bit more serious with an "I" statement. What if that doesn't work? We move on to the big stick: the Change/Time/Consequence formula:

Change: "If not *this* change,

Time: by *this* time,

Consequence: the consequence will be *this*."

Remember, though, that we can never force someone to do something. People are always free to do as we ask, or not. Options and choices always exist. You don't want to allow options or choice? You really have no choice! The most we can do is point out the consequences to someone of not doing as we ask. It is still up to them to decide whether or not to change their behavior. The Change/Time/Consequence formula helps them make an informed decision.

Do you remember Lee and Sam from Chapter 21, "Don't Masquerade Your Thoughts"? Let's see what Lee can do if Sam continues to arrive late in the mornings.

First, we have the frame and Parts 1 and 2 of the "I" statement. Then Part 3 of the "I" statement becomes the Change/ Time/Consequence formula.

Frame	"Sam, we've talked about your timekeeping three times in the past four weeks.
Part 2	I am very angry that
Part 1	you are continuing to arrive 10 to 20 minutes late in the mornings.
Part 3	This can't continue any longer. You need to know that the next time you arrive late without a very good reason, I will give you a formal warning. Sam, your poor timekeeping could end up costing you your job. I hope it won't come to that."

Lee now switches to reflective listening.

Persuade, Don't Pressure

Persuading is always a gentler option. It's our only option if we have no authority other than our own credibility and communication skills.

For simple things, try this simple formula:

Change:	If …
Reward:	Then …

If you will do *this*, then you'll get *that* reward.

Do what you can to put people into a positive frame of mind and a good mood, so they will respond more positively to your ideas.

Then master three skills to be persuasive: earning credibility, gathering good information, and giving good information.

Silver Tongue

"Of the modes of persuasion furnished by the spoken word, there are three kinds. The first kind depends on the personal character of the speaker; the second on putting the audience into a certain frame of mind; the third on the proof, provided by the words of the speech itself."

—Aristotle

Earn Credibility

Credibility has two ingredients: relationships and expertise. It's easier to persuade people if they see you as ...

➤ likeable.

➤ similar to them.

➤ trustworthy.

➤ flexible.

➤ having demonstrated expertise, knowledge, and experience.

In relationships you can earn credibility by ...

➤ finding things in common.

➤ building rapport.

➤ showing concern and compassion—people appreciate knowing we care.

➤ cooperating whenever you can to help them achieve their goals.

➤ acting in good faith.

➤ being consistent and reliable.

➤ networking and listening.

In your area of expertise you can earn credibility by ...

➤ building your knowledge base.

➤ developing relevant experience.

➤ building a bank of facts, anecdotes, and examples that demonstrate the value of your ideas.

Silver Tongue

"Only dictators and absolute monarchs need never compromise."

—Source unknown

Gather Good Information

Persuading is often more than just tempting someone to accept our point of view. It's also about listening to their point of view and adapting our own accordingly. It's a process of give and take—this is part of the dance of communication.

Find out all that you can about the people you are trying to persuade. Where do they stand on the issue? What related experiences, good or bad, have they had? What is important to them? What are they concerned about? What do they value and hold dear? What are they comfortable with? Are you asking them to give up anything? Or invest their valuable time or energy? Would they prefer other options or scenarios?

Make your ideas fit in with their needs and values, and be willing to compromise so that everyone feels satisfied.

Talking things through and listening to other people's points of view helps us to test and revise our thinking, provided we are open-minded and willing to compromise. It allows us to incorporate other viewpoints, ideas and concerns into our plans, which, in all likelihood, will strengthen them.

This in itself is persuasive. It builds trust and lowers people's fears of being pressured. It increases their willingness to work with us.

Give Good Information

Find ways to explain your point of view that reflects your listeners' perspectives, concerns, and desires. Describe your position so that it highlights its advantages to others. Benefits persuade.

Emotions persuade, too. To really persuade people, capture their emotions and feelings. As we saw in Chapter 18, "Choose Your Words for Clarity and Power," it's important to choose powerful, positive, and memorable words that are clear, concise, and compelling and then support them with visual aids, demonstrations, stories, examples, and analogies. Cold hard facts alone probably won't be enough.

Believe in your position in your heart as well as your mind. Slow down and explain your ideas clearly and patiently; the other person probably won't understand your idea as well as you do (yet).

Match the emotional level of those you are trying to persuade. This strengthens your credibility and ensures you don't become too emotional on the one hand or too cold on the other.

How to Persuade People

Now that you know the importance of credibility and of gathering and giving good information, here are a few more tips for helping people to see things your way without pressuring them:

Silver Tongue

"One of the best ways to persuade others is with your ears—listen to them."

—Dean Rusk

Foot in Mouth

Persuading people is not the right time to use the broken record technique from Chapter 21! Repeating yourself over and over won't convince anyone.

Instead, prepare three or four ways, perhaps in different English "languages" to make your case. (See Chapter 19, "Speak the Other Person's Language.")

➤ Make sure you have their attention.

➤ Collect your thoughts. Don't just start chatting and hope for the best—make sure you know what you want to say and how you want to say it.

➤ Forget the hard sell. It's pushy and invites resistance. Easy does it.

➤ Be willing to compromise. Genuine compromise is essential to effective persuasion. Flexibility often leads to better results anyway.

➤ Paint clear and vivid pictures. Be specific about what you want and what it means for the other person.

➤ See persuasion as a process not a one-off event. Listen, explain, test, revise, over and over again.

➤ Present your ideas as a modification of the *status quo*—not a radical change—if you can. People often accept adjustments more readily than complete changes.

➤ Soften the *you*s or change them into *I*s to avoid sounding pushy.

➤ Focus on the outcome you want and avoid blaming, which gets peoples' hackles up, and negativity, which puts everyone into a negative frame of mind, making agreement more difficult to attain.

➤ Turn complaints into requests.

➤ Adopt a mind-set of sharing information. This will prevent you from arguing or accusing, which lead nowhere.

➤ Explain the *why*s and *wherefore*s. Help the person see things from your point of view and understand things as you understand them. Fill them in on any background in formation they may not have realized.

We can't achieve anything of significance without the help of others. We're more likely to earn this help by following the "ask, don't tell" principle. As John Donne, the sixteenth-century English poet said, "No man is an island."

The Least You Need to Know

➤ Always ask; never demand.

➤ Be a coach not a critic.

➤ Write and practice "I" statements before delivering them until you are comfortable with them.

➤ Use all three parts of an "I" statement, in any order.

➤ Make listening an essential part of persuading.

➤ Don't mistake silence for agreement.

Chapter 23

When You Say What You Like, Say Why

In This Chapter

➤ Three kinds of feedback

➤ Offering feedback

➤ Asking for feedback

➤ Dealing with criticism

➤ Accepting praise

People need feedback. No matter how old we are or how long we have done something, we all need to know that others see and appreciate our contributions. We also benefit from other people's perspectives on what we're good at and how we can improve.

Open communications and good relationships depend on being willing and able to comment on another's approach and receive comments about our own. This helps everyone get better and get along better.

In this chapter, we look at the three types of feedback, the effects of each, and how to ask for, offer, and receive feedback.

Three Types of Feedback

There are three types of *feedback*: positive, negative, and none at all.

Positive Feedback

There are two kinds of positive feedback: general and specific.

When we say something like "You're terrific to work with" or "It's always nice to see you!" this is *general positive feedback*. It makes people feel good—about us and about themselves. If we're sincere and have credibility with the other person, general positive feedback builds relationships and self-esteem.

As Blaise Pascal, the seventeenth-century French mathematician, theologian, and physicist said, "Kind words do not cost much … yet they accomplish much." Don't assume that people who always do the right thing don't need to hear it from you. Most people don't equate silence with approval.

Famous Last Words

In engineering, **feedback** is when the result or effect of something (an output) returns to its source (the input). It's not that different in communication. When people give us feedback, we find out the effect of our actions; when we offer others feedback, we explain the effect of their actions.

Use *specific positive feedback* to get more of the same. When we say something like "You're terrific to work with—you always do what you say you'll do" or "I really admire the way you can calm an irate customer without getting upset yourself," we are practically guaranteeing that the receiver will repeat the specific behavior we referred to.

William James noted that "The deepest principle in human nature is the craving to be appreciated." Take notice of praiseworthy effort, performance, or results. Get into the habit of offering specific positive feedback as soon as possible, so the behavior is repeated.

Negative Feedback

While all positive feedback is uplifting (providing it's deserved and we don't overdo it), it will come as no surprise that we need to be very careful with negative feedback. It can be a great way to build trust, performance, and relationships. Or it can do the opposite.

A Word to the Wise

The absence of praise is often taken as criticism.

There are three kinds of negative feedback: general and specific (which are destructive), and constructive.

Saying something like "Boy, are you dumb!" or "Leave me alone!" or "You're not trying hard enough!" makes people feel bad. *General negative feedback* like this lowers self-esteem and erodes relationships. Don't use it—ever.

There are seven "don'ts" to remember if someone has done something wrong or is doing something you don't want them to do. Don't attack them, just their behavior. Don't launch straight in; find out what happened and why. Don't lose sight of people's good points in the midst of negative feedback. You can't make people better by making them feel bad.

Don't use judgmental language or call people nasty names. Don't dredge up old mistakes or incidents. Don't offer negative feedback in public. Don't lay blame; instead, see what can be learned.

Saying something like "You're not doing it the way I showed you" or "You were late again this morning" is *specific negative feedback*. It merely tells people what *not* to do. This often fails to eliminate the undesired behavior and can easily result in people "playing it safe" because they don't know what to do instead. All they know is "I'm in trouble!"

People make mistakes, often inadvertently. Hopefully, they learn from them. When you need to offer negative feedback, offer it in a way that will help people learn. Keep the focus on improving.

This will turn destructive negative feedback into constructive, or helpful, negative feedback. Follow these four rules to make sure your negative feedback is constructive:

1. Be a coach not a critic—offer improvement suggestions.
2. Say what you do want, not what you don't want.
3. Focus on the future.
4. Maintain or enhance the person's self-esteem.

Silver Tongue

"When a man spends his time giving his wife criticism and advice instead of compliments, he forgets that it was not his good judgement, but his charming manners, that won her heart."

—Helen Rowland

Suggest specific things people can start doing or stop doing to improve. Use neutral words, stay objective, and keep your voice steady. Help people learn from their mistakes or your experience.

Use "I" statements and the other suggestions from Chapter 22, "Ask, Don't Tell," and the general guidelines outlined below, to turn negative feedback into constructive feedback.

If your feedback is positive, don't delay it. If you ignore success, good work, and good deeds, people will either stop trying or avoid you.

If it's negative, delay it only enough to "cool down" and be objective if the situation has upset you—Don't wait too long, though.

Beware: People tend to hear negative information the loudest even when you balance it with positive comments. If you need to offer a constructive comment, move straight into what you want or improvement suggestions. Use phrases like "From now on ..." or "In future ..." or "You might want to try ..." This is a way of saying, "Let's not dwell on the past; it's done. Let's get it right from now on." It is also a way to make performance improvement more likely.

Lessen the sting by making sure you don't imply you're criticizing the person. Focus on objective behaviors not character or abilities. Show how what you're commenting on will help others as well as the person you're giving the feedback to.

No Feedback at All

When there is no feedback at all, people wither up and die psychologically. No feedback sends the message that "You're not important and neither is what you do." If people think they don't matter and what they do doesn't matter, they'll lose interest and motivation.

The bottom line is: Don't ignore people or fail to appreciate them and what they do.

Foot in Mouth

If you fail to offer specific positive feedback when the person shows some improvement, they will think their efforts don't matter after all and return to "the bad old ways."

Silver Tongue

"Do not use a hatchet to remove a fly from your friend's forehead."

—Chinese proverb

Offering Feedback So It Will Be Heard

It's much easier for most of us to offer positive feedback. Yet, because constructive feedback is potentially so valuable, good communicators need to know how to present it.

Here's the bad news: No matter how tactfully we word it, it can still sting. Here are some guidelines to follow to soften the sting and make your constructive negative feedback clear (so it can be understood) and careful (so that it will be helpful enough to be heard).

Think of feedback as a mirror, a way you can offer your observations about another person's behavior. Hold it out in a way that the receiver can "see" it and accept it.

Be Clear and Considerate

If you put yourself briefly in the other person's shoes before giving feedback, you'll probably be able to time it and word it a little bit better.

Stay away from vague and general words that are open to interpretation, and value-laden, judgmental words that easily lead to hurt feelings and arguments.

Using an example from an earlier chapter, "discourteous and abrupt" might mean something to the speaker but probably means something quite different to the person being accused of "discourtesy" and "abruptness." How would you feel if someone accused *you* of being "discourteous and abrupt?!"

Words that are clear and considerate have a better chance of being heard. "Speaking rapidly," "not making much eye contact," and "continuing to do other things while speaking to someone" are more neutral, clear, and considerate. Words like these help people understand what we are talking about and take in on board.

Address Behavior, Not Interpretations or Labels

Instead of using vague and hurtful labels, such as "lazy" or "having a bad attitude," when giving negative feedback, focus on what the person says or does that causes you to conclude he is lazy or she has a bad attitude:

➤ "I never see you helping the others when you've finished your work; what I do see is that you seem to take a break."

➤ "You are walking slowly and shuffling your feet along the floor."

➤ "You allow the phone to ring more than four times before answering it."

It's easier for the recipient of the feedback to hear information given like this because it describes behaviors factually, without interpreting or labeling them.

Feedback should address something the person can change or do something about—in other words, their behavior not their personality. If someone is so shy that they have great difficulty dealing with customers, no feedback, no matter how well intentioned ("You'll really need to learn to relax and speak to customers better") will help.

This also keeps the feedback nonpersonal. Make it quite clear that you are not criticizing the person, just something they are saying or doing.

A Word to the Wise

Don't try to remake people in your own image.

Foot in Mouth

If you say "you" more than "I," you'll sound patronizing or pushy. "You" statements tend to create defensiveness and lead to arguments. Remember your "I" language! It comes across as less domineering and controlling and will meet with less resistance. Instead of "You must" or "you should," say "I need."

Support, Don't Force

Some people give feedback as if they're trying to unload all their hassles at once; that might make them feel better, but it is unhelpful to the receiver. "You do this, and this, and that, and you also do this and you never do that, and while we're at it ...." Such "dumping" creates defensive and resentful responses.

Others tear people down when they give them feedback, as if tearing down the receiver will build up the sender.

It's better to address one issue at a time, providing just enough feedback for the person to assimilate and act upon. They should feel free to accept or reject your feedback.

See yourself as a coach, not a critic. If you care and want to help, not hurt, your feedback will be constructive. Aim to empower and motivate people with your feedback.

A Word to the Wise

To be helpful, the receiver must sense that you are offering feedback constructively, in a spirit of support and encouragement. One good way to show this is to offer improvement suggestions.

Try formulating your feedback along the lines of "I think you would be more effective if ..." or "You might consider trying ...".

By Invitation

The best feedback is feedback that is asked for: "How did I do?" or "What do you think I should do to improve?"

If you are asked, give honest, supportive feedback, both positive specific and constructive.

Share the Effect

If it feels right, mention your feelings or reactions to the person's behavior or share its effects. This might spark a new way of thinking about or looking at a situation.

A Word to the Wise

Keep your feedback short and sincere.

Balance It

Be balanced—give positive as well as constructive feedback. This shows your objectivity, and it helps people to see a truer picture of themselves.

Asking for Useful Feedback

Letting people know we want feedback makes it easier for them to offer it. Letting them know the areas in which we want feedback helps us get information we're interested in.

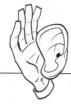

Here are two ways to make sure your feedback is balanced:

➤ **The Keep-Stop-Start approach:** *Keep* doing these effective things; *stop* doing these ineffective things; *start* doing these things that will make you more effective.

➤ **The More-Less-Same approach:** Do *more* of these particular things; do *less* of these ineffective things; *continue* doing these effective things.

Have you ever asked for advice, opinions, or feedback when what you really wanted was corroboration? Here are four tips to follow when you genuinely want some feedback:

➤ **Ask the right people.** Ask a tennis pro for feedback on your serve and a financial advisor for feedback on your investments.

➤ **Say what kind of advice or feedback you want.** Facts? Opinions? Their personal experience? To listen for gaps in your reasoning? To help you reach a decision? To support or encourage what you've already decided? To tell you how great you were? To suggest some ways you could improve?

➤ **Stay focused on what you need to know.**

➤ **Be open to their comments.** If you find yourself saying "Yes, but ..." or "No, that won't work because ..." you probably didn't want their feedback after all.

Watch for nonverbal feedback, too. This is harder to control than verbal responses and often transmits messages that are more accurate. If we are alert to it, we can ask questions to find out more.

Receiving Feedback

Think of feedback as a wheel that moves relationships forward. It can provide us with information to improve our skills, our image, and our relationships. It can help us reach decisions, make plans, find willpower and lift our self-confidence. It can act as a kind of early warning system about potential problems and looming calamities. Best of all, it generates a positive climate of trust, support, and improvement.

Can you accept feedback without feeling angry towards the person who offers it? Or do you "shoot the messenger"? If we brush someone's feedback away, ignore it, argue with it, or offer long-winded excuses or explanations, it may be the last time they offer us any.

Openly accepting feedback can be difficult, especially if it is given in anger, in haste, or by someone we don't much like or respect. Our pride can ache and our ego can be dented. Yet if we have no feedback, it's hard to know what to keep repeating or doing similarly and where to focus our improvement efforts.

When receiving feedback …

A Word to the Wise

See feedback as a gift. Think about it and see how you can best use it. Thank people for their feedback.

➤ Listen, don't resist.

➤ Keep calm and keep breathing! Know that people are trying to help you and that offering you feedback can be difficult or awkward for them, too.

➤ Use the SO CLEAR body language described in Chapter 10, "Send the Right Signals," to show you are receptive.

➤ Explain yourself if appropriate but don't make excuses, blame someone else, or deny there is a problem if there is one.

➤ Don't butt the feedback away with "Yes, but …" or "Yes, however …" Replace them with "I appreciate and …" or "I respect and …" or "I agree and …."

➤ Don't be overly sensitive, self-protective, or cavalier.

➤ Explore the feedback using the EARS formula described in Chapter 13, "Draw Out the Full Story." Ask questions to make sure you've understood.

➤ Summarize the feedback to make sure you understand it.

➤ If you've been caught off-guard or want to do some fact-finding, ask for time to consider the feedback and arrange to meet later.

➤ Don't just say "it won't happen again." Explain what you'll do to prevent it or what you've learned from this.

➤ Thank people for their feedback.

Now think about the feedback, and ask yourself the following questions.

➤ Does the person offering it know what they're talking about?

➤ What other information do you have that supports it?

➤ If you're tempted to ignore it, do you have evidence that contradicts it?

Dealing With Criticism

Not all feedback is kind, so think it through. Some people intend only to hurt; others genuinely hope to help. Some opinions are valid; others aren't.

Until the whole world learns to offer constructive feedback, here are seven tips for receiving criticism:

1. Keep your self-talk positive.

2. Mentally examine your critic's intentions, so you'll know how best to deal with the information. Is the criticism intended to help you grow? To let off steam? To hurt you?

3. Filter the criticism. Strain out the emotion and find the facts. Then you can respond to the useful information and not get caught up in the emotions.

4. Ask questions until you understand what the speaker is trying to tell you.

5. Don't make excuses. Listen to understand. Ask for specifics. Accept responsibility when appropriate.

6. Focus on the future: What can you do to improve? Help your critic become a coach.

7. If the critic's intentions are hurtful, use the fogging or negative assertion techniques discussed in Chapter 21, "Don't Masquerade Your Thoughts."

Silver Tongue

"Well meant are the wounds a friend inflicts, but deceitful are the kisses of an enemy."

—Proverbs 27:6

Don't react to feedback defensively. Self-protection is a natural instinct, and it can be difficult to listen openly to what we perceive as a criticism. Even if it's well meant, constructive feedback can be hard to take!

A defensive reaction will either cut off communication or create arguments and conflict. Others will take it as a sign that we're annoyed, our mind is closed, and that we're feeling threatened. "Yes, the truth hurts" is what they may well be thinking.

Here are some other tips to lower your defenses and perk up your responsiveness:

A Word to the Wise

If you get similar feedback from several sources—listen!

➤ Monitor your reactions. We usually know when we're becoming defensive—maybe our neck or shoulders stiffen, our breathing may shallow and quicken, or we thrust our chin out.

➤ When you feel defensiveness coming on, take a deep breath and focus on what the other person is trying to say. Listen with all your might.

➤ If the defensive responses continue, stall for time. Suggest a short break, pour a glass of water.

➤ Ask questions to find out what the speaker is getting at and to test your understanding.

➤ Know that they're probably not trying to hurt you but to offer you information that they think is important.

Accepting Praise

When someone praises you, smile and say "Thank you!" Brushing it aside with an "Oh, it's nothing!" has two consequences we don't want. First, it is tantamount to saying "You're wrong!" Second, it decreases our chances of receiving more praise. Not only will we miss out on the endorphin and neuropeptide hit and deny it to the person offering the compliment (see Chapter 5, "Become a Peak Performer,"), not knowing what other people like means we may not "keep up the good work." In the end, relationships and open communication can suffer.

Feedback is essential to good communication and effective relationships. Giving and receiving it is a sophisticated skill that takes practice and needs mutual respect and trust in the other person.

The Least You Need to Know

➤ Let people know you notice and care with positive feedback; it strengthens relationships and makes everyone feel good.

➤ Be considerate, specific, realistic, and supportive when offering constructive feedback.

➤ Turn negative feedback into constructive feedback by being a coach, not a critic, and by focusing on the future.

➤ When you want to know how you're doing and how to improve, ask a credible person for some specific feedback.

➤ If you're the recipient of criticism, check the source and their intentions; filter out emotions, and listen closely.

➤ Say "Thank you!" when you receive a compliment.

Chapter 24

Tune In to the Same Wavelength

In This Chapter

➤ What motivates people

➤ How people operate

➤ How people deal with information

➤ Four types of people

➤ Four temperaments

British author George Bernard Shaw once said, "In the right key, one can say anything. In the wrong key, nothing. The only delicate part is the establishment of the key." Do you know someone you just can't seem to get through to? Someone who manages to annoy you or misunderstand you? Perhaps you are speaking in the wrong key. When we're in the wrong key, the message doesn't come through clearly.

What is the right key? It's different for each of us.

This chapter examines how an understanding of personality types and temperaments can help you communicate with people in ways that will accelerate understanding and inspire harmony and cooperation. You will also learn how to become a master of giving good information by learning to identify and link with people's underlying motivations, thinking processes, and ways of looking at the world. In short, you will learn how to establish and speak in the *right key*.

Find Out People's Main Needs

Industrial psychologists John W. Atkinson and David McClelland have shown that we can divide people's main psychological needs into three groups: need for achievement, need for affiliation, and need for power.

People Who Need to Achieve

People with a high *need for achievement* are those who set specific, measurable goals and standards and who keep working until they've accomplished them. They always want to do it better—perhaps better than they've done it before, perhaps better than anyone else has ever done it, perhaps to push the current standard further out. "Never say die" and "Where's the next challenge?" seem to be the achievers' mottoes. Their satisfaction comes from accomplishing goals efficiently.

If you know any achievers, don't hover over or ignore them. Let them take responsibility for their own performance and give them plenty of feedback on how well they're doing.

People Who Need Relationships

Other people are more interested in friendly, cordial relationships. What pleases them is working and spending time with others whose company they enjoy in an easy, give-and-take, relaxed atmosphere. Their high *need for affiliation* drives them, for example, to write more letters, spend more time with their co-workers and friends, and talk on the phone more.

Don't be too matter-of-fact and task-focused with people who have a high need for affiliation. Establish friendly relationships with them, ask about their family, their weekends, their interests, how they think and feel about things.

People Who Need Power

Others thrive on taking charge. They have a high *need for power*. They aim for authority so that they can decide what should be done and make it happen. They surround themselves with prestigious possessions as symbols of their power, they communicate assertively, and are able to influence others in most communication situations.

When dealing with people who need power, allow them to feel in charge and recognize their need to be treated as powerful and important.

Since we're each unique, we each have a different "need recipe": We each have varying mixes and strengths of the needs for achievement, affiliation, and power. These needs are revealed in the way we communicate and behave with others, just as they are revealed in the way others communicate and behave with us.

A Word to the Wise

Listen to the main themes underlying what people say. What pleases them? *Achievement*—completing things efficiently, beating their own records, accomplishing goals? *Affiliation*—genial working and social relationships, making friends with people, helping them? *Power*—being consulted and listened to, taking charge, making things happen?

When you know what drives people, you'll know how to tailor your communications to motivate them.

Work With People's Metaprograms

We looked at some of the lessons of neuro-linguistics in Chapters 12, "Build Rapport," and Chapter 19, "Speak the Other Person's Language." This rich field has more to offer.

People operate internally—make decisions, set goals, take action, find proof, categorize and sort information—in characteristic and identifiable ways. They focus on different things, are convinced in different ways, and have different working styles. If we listen and watch for these, we can connect with and address a person's basic psychological programming. Our communications with them will be crystal clear.

As you read through the descriptions of four important metaprograms below, think of them as two ends of a spectrum. Most people don't fall at one end or the other, but somewhere in between, *toward* one end or toward the other.

Avoiders and Seekers

Avoiders move *away* from things, usually from harmful or threatening things or pain. Their world is a perilous place, so they look for security and protection. If avoiders exercise, it's because they want to avoid being fat and unhealthy. If they read books, it's because they don't want people to think they're uneducated or stupid.

Seekers move *toward* things, usually pleasurable or exciting things. Their world is an exhilarating place. They are often energetic, curious people who are willing to take risks. If they exercise, it's because they love the exercise. If they read books, it's because they enjoy the stories, ideas, and insights they provide.

We all move toward some things and away from others. However, we all have general tendencies to be avoiders or seekers.

How can you find out if someone is an avoider or a seeker? Ask them a question and listen to their answer. Do they pursue positives or avoid negatives? For example, ask what they want from a job; some people will describe their dream job in terms of what they *don't* want, others by talking about what they *do* want. An avoider might want a job that *isn't* in a harsh or unsafe environment, where she *won't* be fired at a moment's notice, *won't* be bored, and *won't* be working for a monster. Seekers focus on the positives; a seeker might want a job that offers reasonable security, fair pay, interesting work, or the opportunity for travel.

If you choose the wrong strategy when trying to influence someone, you'll be speaking at cross-purposes. To persuade an avoider, stress the unpleasant, risky things they will avoid. To convince a seeker, stress the benefits they will gain. That way, you'll be speaking in the right key.

A Word to the Wise

If you want to persuade someone whose proof comes from inside, appeal to what they know to be true. To appeal to those who need external proof, tell them what others say.

Some People "Just Know," Others Need to Be Told

Where does your proof come from? How do you know, for example, if you've done a good job?

Foot in Mouth

If you fail to adjust your natural inclinations to your communication partner, you'll be singing in the wrong key and won't get through.

If you're a mismatcher communicating with a matcher, try to moderate your natural inclination to look for differences. Try to spot a few similarities and acknowledge them.

If you're a matcher communicating with a mismatcher, acknowledge and work with differences and exceptions as well as similarities. Pay attention to mismatchers' ability to spot potential difficulties. And beware of your own tendency to generalize, sometimes to overgeneralize.

Some people "just know" they've done a good job; they find their proof inside themselves. Others need their boss, colleagues, or customers to tell them; their proof comes from outside sources—other people, awards, or certificates.

Matchers and Mismatchers

What do you focus on first—the *similarities* between things or the *differences* between them?

Matchers look for similarities, for sameness. They see and focus on what things have in common. Mismatchers look for differences, for the exceptions, and focus on those.

It's easy to see how mismatchers and matchers would find it difficult to develop rapport—their communication dance would be rather stilted and awkward.

Lone Rangers and Musketeers

Which would you prefer ...

❏ to work independently with the responsibility for results being yours alone?

❏ to work cooperatively as part of a team, achieving results together?

❏ to have others around you but still be responsible for your own results?

The first box describes an *independent* work style. Independent people prefer not to be closely supervised and to "run their own show."

The second box describes a *cooperative* work style. Cooperators function best as part of a group and like to share responsibility.

A Word to the Wise

It pays to know the preferred working style of the people you communicate with, so you know how to assign tasks and present information to them in the right key.

The third box describes the in-between work style called *proximity*. It's nice to have others around for the company but to have sole responsibility at the same time.

Take Personality into Account

People are infinitely complex. Yet wouldn't it be nice if we could learn to spot fundamental personality differences? This would help us dance more gracefully and graciously with our communication partners.

Dr. Carl Jung, building on the work of Sigmund Freud, distinguished between *introverts*, who make up 25 percent of the population and are most interested in the inner world of concepts and ideas; and *extroverts*, the other 75 percent who relate best to the external world of people and things. Introverts are reflective—they think more while extroverts are action-oriented—they're doers. It is often said that introverts think before they speak and extroverts speak before they think.

Then there is a *task focus* or a *people focus*. Some people focus first and foremost on the task at hand while others focus on the people: Does everyone understand and agree with our objectives? Is everyone satisfied, comfortable, happy? Here are four tips for using Jung's work to communicate more effectively with others:

➤ Find out what ideas are important to introverts and try to fit your communications into their idea framework.

➤ Show extroverts how what you are saying fits in with other people's thinking and what the rest of the world is doing.

➤ Focus on the task at hand when holding discussions with task-oriented people.

➤ Include discussion on people issues when talking with people-oriented people.

Famous Last Words

Introverts are thinkers who live their world primarily inside their heads while **extroverts** are doers who use the outside world as a reference point.

A Word to the Wise

Help thinkers by stating the overall theory or concept of what you are presenting. Give them information in a logically built-up sequence. Deal with facts impersonally and consistently.

Four Preferences for Dealing With Information

Jung also described important differences in the way we perceive and process information and what we do with it. He found that we receive and process information in four ways: thinking, feeling, intuiting, and sensing.

Most of us tend to use one or two of these methods more than the others, and so we've become reasonably adept at them. We may use a third method as backup and are often underdeveloped in a fourth; that is, we don't use it much so we've never learned to use it well.

Thinkers

Thinkers, as you might guess, are strong on clear, logical thinking. They are methodical and adept at analyzing problems. They are good with facts and figures, research, and systems analysis.

Feelers

Feelers see things through their personal values and base their judgments on these rather than on an objective weighing up of pros and cons. They are warm and outgoing and enjoy being with people. They excel in cementing team relationships, counseling, arbitrating, and public relations.

Make your values explicit with feelers, so they sense "where you're coming from." Take care to make them feel supported and accepted.

Intuitors

Intuitors have fertile and creative imaginations. They work from intuition and hunches and are good at seeing overall and long-range possibilities. They're also good at long-term planning, creative writing, and generating ideas.

Give intuitors an idea of where you're headed, of what your visions and ultimate goals are. Then let their creative minds work out how to help you achieve those ends.

Sensors

Sensors are down-to-earth, practical, and energetic people. They prefer action to words and ideas and like to "get on with it." They deal in the here-and-now. They're best at initiating projects, setting up deals, negotiating, troubleshooting, and converting ideas into action.

Don't embellish things with too much detail or fancy theory for sensors. Communicate clearly and in practical terms and results and get to the point quickly.

Since Jung's pioneering work in the field of personality types, psychologists have expanded greatly on his findings. We'll look at the two ways personalities are usually grouped in the two sections below, first as four types of people, then as four temperaments.

Four Types of People

This way of understanding people combines the introversion–extroversion and task–people continuums discussed above. This gives us the first of our two main groups of four different personality types: dominant directors, interacting socializers, steady relaters, and conscientious thinkers.

Dominant Directors

These people are extroverts who focus on the task. They are outgoing, direct, competitive, and results-oriented and are often motivated by power. They use their initiative,

are willing to confront people, make decisions easily, and are often ambitious. Strong-willed and practical, they often have a strong need for power. They enjoy taking charge and resist authority from others.

You'll notice that dominant directors get to the point quickly, so quickly that they sometimes seem blunt, pushy, and impatient with others. They're fast-paced, want things done *now*, and dislike sloppy results.

Communicate accurately, clearly, and to the point with the dominant directors and present good work to them. Don't try their patience with abstract theories and concepts, which they would see as lacking substance, or a lot of focus on people issues, which they would see as "fluffy" and unbusinesslike. Stay focused on results.

Interacting Socializers

Also extroverts, interacting socializers focus on people issues. They like people, and their motivations revolve around affiliation. They are enthusiastic, optimistic, sociable, talkative, persuasive, and impulsive. Often disorganized and inattentive to detail, they are good at influencing others. They are fun-loving and energetic, creative and open with their feelings. They thrive on change, new trends and ideas, and recognition of their achievements. They can also be vain, excitable, manipulative, and undisciplined.

Keep details and detailed work well away from interacting socializers, or they feel confined. Let them talk, participate, motivate, and create an enjoyable atmosphere. Treat them as friends.

Steady Relaters

Steady relaters are people-oriented introverts. They focus on people and affiliation in order to achieve the task. They dislike conflict and prefer a known and stable routine to the untried and untested. Quiet and often unassertive, they are loyal, stable, consistent, valuable, and easy-going team players, helpful and eager to please. Good thinkers and patient listeners, steady relaters are good at calming down upset people. They are the glue that holds work teams together. Others sometimes see them as unsure, wishy-washy, awkward, possessive, and insecure conformists.

To discover a steady relater's thoughts or opinions, you may have to ask many open questions and listen carefully; it will be worth it. Make sure you don't overlook them or take their loyalty and contributions for granted.

Conscientious Thinkers

Conscientious thinkers are orderly and systematic. They are introverts who have a strong need for achievement and who focus on the task. They enjoy study and analysis and approach projects and tasks in a diligent, objective fashion. They are serious, accurate, and well-organized perfectionists who produce high-quality work. They can also be stuffy, picky, judgmental, critical, and slow at making decisions.

Don't ask conscientious thinkers to turn in rushed "close enough is good enough" jobs and don't ever present any sloppy work to them! If you need to criticize, do so gently. Explain things fully and carefully and include the details that they crave. If changes are required, don't rush it; spell them out clearly and give them time to ask questions and adjust to the changes.

Four Temperaments

The next set of four personality groupings is made up of analysts, legalists, realists, and empathists. The names highlight important differences between them and help us find the right key to communicate with them.

Analysts

Analysts make up only 12 percent of the population. Their ability to think intuitively makes them valuable for their creativity and good ideas. They're serious, competent, and competitive self-starters who often seem to be married to their job. They are conceptual, theoretical, and logical thinkers who work best on their own.

Keep detail, routine, and practical matters away from analysts. Tell them what you want and then give them the space to develop a plan. Give them ways of keeping score and ask for their thoughts, especially when you are short on good ideas. Don't over-supervise them.

Legalists

Legalists are conservative, serious, loyal, responsible, steady, accurate, and practical. They tend also to be cautious security-seekers and change-avoiders. They make up 40 percent of the population and are good at working with details. They work best in structured, predictable situations where they will reliably apply rules and procedures.

Provide them with the detail they need to complete their work and with formal tokens of recognition for their contributions and efforts. Be punctual and thorough when dealing with legalists and don't spring any surprises on them. They will resist change, so explain any required changes fully and carefully. Count on them to follow the regulations and keep to the routines.

Realists

Realists make up about 35 percent of the population. They're the technical, hands-on, practical people—the action-oriented trouble shooters. Often flamboyant, spontaneous, impulsive, and fun loving, they thrive on excitement. They're open-minded, tolerant, flexible, and good at coping with change.

Give realists well-planned, hands-on training and help with their self-organization and time management. Give them plenty of freedom and enough variety, so they don't get bored and "muck around." Help them to practice and perfect their skills. Count on them to rise to the challenge in a crisis. Enjoy their company.

Empathists

Empathists are natural coaches, helpers, supporters, and encouragers. They are the warm, spiritual, and communicative 13 percent of the population. They are intuitive feelers who work for meaning and harmony.

Give empathists personal instruction and encouragement. Make sure they know the importance of the job they're doing. Appreciate their contributions and, if you find it necessary to offer negative feedback, do it carefully and constructively so they don't interpret it as a personal attack. Give them autonomy and a chance to learn, and don't burden them with detail.

As with the metaprograms, none of these personality types and temperaments are any better or worse than any other—each are different and valuable in its own way.

There is no doubt that recognizing key differences between people helps us to communicate better. Crystal clear communicators use these groupings to recognize and work with people's strengths. We're all different, and it is these differences that make life interesting and help us achieve results. After all, if both of us thought the same, one of us would be unnecessary.

The Least You Need to Know

➤ Find out what motivates people, so you know how to appeal to them.

➤ Work with peoples' metaprograms to communicate in the right key.

➤ Appeal to introverts with ideas and to extroverts with other people's opinions.

➤ Find out how people prefer to deal with information, so you can present it for rapid absorption.

➤ Work with, not against, peoples' personality types for a smooth communication dance.

Part 6
Making Progress

The master principles for successfully dealing with difficult people, resolving conflict, problems, and complaints, and producing decisions that work.

We've seen how giving good information and gathering good information are mutually dependent aspects of effective communication. To paraphrase Benjamin Disraeli, the nineteenth-century British author and Prime Minister:

> *The art of communication consists of the exercise of two fine qualities: You must originate [give good information] and you must empathize [gather good information].*
>
> *You must possess at the same time the habit of communicating and the habit of listening. The union is rare, but irresistible.*

Is that all there is to communication, though? As my father used to say, "Talk is great; but it doesn't pay the bills." What is to be the result of the union Disraeli spoke of?

According to the Irish dramatist, essayist, and critic George Bernard Shaw, "The greatest problem in communicating is the illusion that it has been accomplished." How do we know when and whether we have accomplished communication?

To decide whether the union bore fruit we must look at its results. Did the communication achieve its aims? Did it solve a problem, reach a decision, settle a dispute, or win a friend?

In this section, we explore the ins and outs of accomplishing something with our communication. We explore how to handle and resolve conflict, deal with difficult people and complaints, and solve problems and make decision. These are all skills needed by good communicators everywhere.

Chapter 25

Manage Conflicts with Aplomb

In This Chapter

➤ Five ways to deal with conflict

➤ The win–win payoff

➤ Needs, wants, and worries

➤ Twenty ideas for resolving conflicts

"You have to give and take."

"It's important that everyone wins."

"Listen to the other guy and find out what he really wants."

"People will get you back if you walk all over them."

In their own way, the people above are really saying the same thing:

No one really wins an argument if someone loses.

Nikita Khrushchev, the Soviet premier during the Cold War, once said, "If one cannot catch a bird of paradise, better take a wet hen."

Do we really have to settle for wet hens? We'll learn how to catch that bird of paradise in this chapter.

Bring Problems Into the Open

We can't escape every problem, no matter how much we'd like to. Differences of opinion, crossed swords, locked horns, discord, rivalry, disharmony—in short, conflict in various forms—is part of life. Conflicts aren't the problem—the problem is how we deal with them.

Will we allow conflicts to become a source of stress, drawn-out battles, long-term friction, and ruptured relationships? Or will we deal with them openly and honestly and try to resolve them fairly and to everyone's satisfaction?

According to a Chinese proverb, "When the sandpiper and the clam grapple, it is the fisherman that profits." Do you grapple like the sandpiper and the clam, or do you have a mind-set that says, "I can resolve conflict satisfactorily"? As we saw in Part 1, "Communication Begins Inside," a positive mind-set ensures that the self-fulfilling prophecy, or attaining what you expect, works for you and not against you.

Silver Tongue

"Honest disagreement is often a good sign of progress."

—Gandhi

A positive mind-set means we can bring problems and difficulties out into the open in a cooperative, non-adversarial way. We can talk them through, explore, and discuss them. Once we've explored each other's standpoints, we will be in a position to work together to resolve our differences. This is much better than settling for wet hens, don't you think?

Five Approaches to Conflict

There are five ways we can approach conflict: collaboration, force, avoidance, accommodation, and compromise. Which is your preferred style?

Collaboration

If your chief concern is finding a solution that satisfies everyone, you will talk things over and spend time listening to the other person's point of view. Then you'll spend some more time looking for a mutually acceptable solution, one that you can both live with and support. This is the collaborative, win–win approach.

When it is important that our own, as well as the other person's, wishes are taken into account, we will want to work together to find a solution. The win–win approach leads us to a double win in another way: Not only is it good for developing workable solutions, it's also great for improving relationships.

Collaborate ...

➤ when you need to build long-term relationships.

➤ when the situation is likely to recur.

➤ when your goals are too important to compromise.

➤ when you need support and cooperation to make an agreement work.

Force

Do you ever force your solution on others? How about when the tables are turned and someone forces his solution on you? Are you resentful and angry? Do you resist or want some form of revenge or retaliation? Will he have "won a battle, but not the war" as far as you're concerned? This is how most people respond when something is forced on them and their needs are ignored.

The win–lose approach of force (I win, you lose) might secure the outcome we want, but at a price. Sometimes the price is worth it: The issue may be so important or time so tight that considering the wishes and needs of the other person is not feasible.

If you usually make sure you get your way, take some time to find out first what others want and why they want it. Gather some good information. Try taking what others want and need into account as well as what you want.

Only use force ...

➤ in an emergency.

➤ when the stakes are high and the relationship is irrelevant.

➤ when you need to act quickly.

➤ when you need to enforce an unpopular course of action or an important principle.

Foot in Mouth

Don't impose solutions on others unless it is absolutely necessary. If it is, be aware of the likely consequences. As Confucius said, "You may be able to conquer a person's tongue, but not his heart."

Avoidance

Do you often avoid conflict by sweeping it under the carpet and pretending it doesn't exist or letting it continue and "hoping for the best," leaving a solution to fate or chance? Pretending everything is fine and smoothing things over treats your own wishes and those of the other person as trivial. Neither person "wins."

By letting the conflict continue, there may be hidden benefits to one or both of the parties concerned. Continued conflict can be exciting; it can be an excuse for not getting on with the real work; it can give us something to talk about with others or bring us attention.

Ultimately, if we don't deal with problems, for whatever reason, they fester and worsen over time and relationships suffer.

Avoid conflict only …

➤ when the situation is unlikely to recur.

➤ when the issue is inconsequential in the scheme of things and just not worth discussing.

Five ways to deal with conflict.

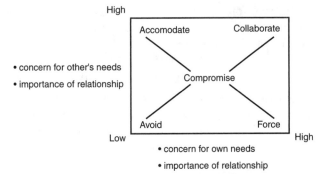

Accommodation

Perhaps you tend to give in to conflict and let the other person have his or her way. This is a lose–win approach if you allow the other person's needs to be met at the expense of your own. Accommodation makes sense only if the issue is not important to us or if the relationship is a lot more important than the issue.

Foot in Mouth

Don't accommodate out of habit. If you often let others have their way even if it inconveniences you, upsets you, or makes you feel uncomfortable, practice saying what's on your mind and letting people know what you would prefer.

Concede to other people …

➤ when harmony is more important than the issue.

➤ when the issue is important to the other person and much less so to you.

➤ when you cannot win.

➤ when you are wrong.

Compromise

The fifth and final way to approach conflict is to split the difference. Poet James Russell Lowell said that compromise "makes a good umbrella but a poor roof."

Although neither person has their wishes or needs met entirely, settling for a compromise is sometimes the best we can do. Compromise might be the approach that will damage a relationship the least while still achieving a reasonably quick, acceptable, and workable solution.

Settle for the wet hen over the bird of paradise ...

> ➤ when the issue is important to both of you but not worth a time-consuming search for a resolution.

> ➤ when the issue is temporary and a quick fix is fine.

> ➤ when you haven't got time for a lengthy discussion but want some of your goals met quickly.

> ➤ when you don't need or want a bird of paradise or it's out of reach and a wet hen will do!

Think It Through First

What is the conflict about? Recognizing the source of the conflict points us in the right direction for resolving it.

Sometimes it's *personalities*. Someone's little quirks, traits, habits, or mannerisms, or the other person's general personality style or approach can sometimes irritate us. Since people are unlikely to change their personality to accommodate us, it is usually best to overlook or learn to live with them.

Clashes over *goals,* on the other hand, often benefit from compromise or collaboration. To try to find common goals, we could look at the bigger picture or at a more detailed picture. The main question you need to ask is "How can we meet the needs of both of us?"

Conflicts over *facts* are easily sorted out. Suspend the discussion until you can find out the facts.

Conflicts over *values,* on the other hand, are difficult to resolve. Probably the best thing to do is to recognize that we are all different, and we can't change another person's values—they are too deep-seated. Often the best thing to do is respectfully agree to disagree.

Famous Last Words

"**Compromise:** Such an adjustment of conflicting interests as gives each adversary the satisfaction of thinking he has got what he ought not to have, and is deprived of nothing except what was justly his due."

—Ambrose Bierce, *The Devil's Dictionary.*

Silver Tongue

"Better half an egg than an empty eggshell."

—Estonian proverb

Foot in Mouth

Don't avoid or accommodate just to avoid confronting the problem lest you take your anger, hurt, or resentment out in other less constructive ways, leading to damaged or even lost relationships.

If you decide to avoid or accommodate, do so having considered your other options. You'll feel better about your decision that way.

Unclear *expectations or standards* are another common source of disputes. We can save face by acknowledging this is the source of the problem: "I know I didn't tell you clearly to do X, so I can understand how you must feel taken by surprise"; "I can understand your confusion because we never made this completely clear."

Force might be quick and avoidance easy, but in the long run, collaboration tends to be more satisfactory. It makes revenge, resistance, and resentment less likely and helps relationships grow and strengthen.

Go for Win–Win

The search for win–win is central to successful communication. How can we put it into practice?

Here are some particular behaviors that successful communicators have identified as helpful and unhelpful during difficult communication situations.

How to Find the Win–Win

Skills to Apply	Traps to Avoid
gathering good information	treating the discussion and outcome like a competition
focusing on one thing at a time	sticking to your own opinion
being patient	not admitting the other has a point
making it clear what is being discussed and why	unclear aims
listening in order to be listened to	everyone talking at once
respecting the other's opinion	interrupting
airing grievances and problems	shouting, losing tempers
wanting to reach agreement	jumping to conclusions
focusing on what you agree on	forcing your 'solution' on the other
focusing on what you both want	focusing only on your own needs and wants

Twenty Ideas for Resolving Conflicts

Here are 20 ideas to help you resolve conflicts gracefully. Use them singly or in combination, and watch your agreements multiply.

1. Attain mutual respect. Mutual respect is a cornerstone of crystal clear communication. When we respect ourselves, we naturally want to solve any problems or difficulties we run into and make sure the solution meets our own wants and needs. Respecting the other person encourages us to make sure that the solution meets their wants and needs, too. Mutual respect leads to win–win solutions.

2. Look for the common ground. Rarely do two people have entirely opposing views with absolutely nothing in common. If we look hard enough, we are bound to find points of agreement or shared goals on which to build. This subtly shifts us from being "opponents" to being on the "same side."

3. Establish needs, wants, and worries. In any situation we have needs (nonnegotiable things that must happen) and wants (negotiable things that we would like to happen) if we are to be content with the solution. We also have worries or concerns—things we really don't want to see happen because they would, in some way, be detrimental to us or those we represent. State yours clearly and take time to find out the other person's needs, wants and worries, by asking questions, listening, and using empathy.

4. Redefine the problem or point of disagreement if necessary. The fresh approach we gain by using different words to describe the problem and looking at it from a different perspective can sometimes break us out of a deadlock.

Step back and see the dispute from a bigger picture, step closer and see the details, or "step to one side" to view the predicament from a different angle. The more we keep "moving around the problem" to explore it and view it from all perspectives, the more likely we are to increase our understanding of it and find an answer.

5. Set a goal, then work backward. What end result do both parties want? What needs to happen first? What needs to happen before that? And before that?

6. Focus on your goals. Staying focused on our points of disagreement will only keep us there. Focus on how to attain the goals you both share, so you can find paths around your problems. Clear goals also give you something to assess your options against.

A Word to the Wise

When you are faced with a situation of conflicting wishes or solutions, or when you identify a problem that must be resolved, be clear about what you want. What is important to you—the issue, the relationship, or both? How hard are you willing to work so that both parties are satisfied?

Silver Tongue

"The only people who listen to both sides of an argument are the neighbors."

—Anonymous

267

A Word to the Wise

When you spell out your own and the other person's needs, wants, and worries, it usually becomes clear that you share a number of them. They are fertile common ground on which to build.

7. Create options. Are you searching for the single best answer? There probably isn't one—the complexity of modern life sees to that! Have several options in mind that would be acceptable to you, the more the better. Know also what would not be acceptable to you. Then the only decision you need to make is "which will work best for me, in this situation, right now."

8. Keep an open mind. No doubt you've heard the saying *Your mind is like a parachute; it only works when it's open.* Rigid thinking, "wearing blinders," and holding onto preconceived ideas destroy attempts at conflict resolution. They lead to treating a problem in terms of competing solutions, or in terms of "only one possible solution—mine." This makes it difficult, if not impossible, to settle differences satisfactorily.

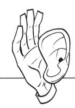

Listen to This

Here are some tips to try to turn disputes into dialogues:

➤ Ask for or give an example.

➤ Ask for or give an analogy.

➤ Explore it further: "Can you tell me more about why you feel so strongly about this?" or "Can I tell you a bit more about ...?"

➤ Summarize: "If I've understood you correctly ..."

➤ Make an assertive request: "Could you express your ideas less personally?"

➤ Stick to the main issues: "I think we're getting off the track here ..."

➤ Keep calm. Watch your temper and your words.

➤ Take a break if things become tense. Get up for a glass of water, call a time out for thinking.

➤ Stop and summarize each of your views.

➤ Get another point of view.

➤ Keep referring to your common ground and shared objectives.

9. Follow the Law of Psychological Reciprocity. In Chapter 8, we learned that "behavior breeds behavior." This principle reminds us to make sure that the way we communicate, both verbally and nonverbally, can calm conflict or create it.

10. Be positive, not negative. Yes, behavior breeds behavior and negativity is catching. A negative approach is depressing and destructive. Statements like "That will never work," "We'll never get anywhere on this," or "You're absolutely wrong" invite a harmful spiral of attacks, counter-attacks, and arguments. A positive approach is catching, too. It is uplifting and encouraging. Shifting our thinking and our words from negative to positive might require some thought, but the results are well worth the effort. Don't set a pattern of always disagreeing or seeing the negative side; offer solutions and encouragement, too.

A Word to the Wise

Forget win–lose. That's for sports. Conflict is not a sport.

11. Be on the same side. It's easy to argue with someone sitting opposite us and difficult to argue with someone sitting next to us. Sitting next to someone literally puts us on the same side. It encourages an attitude of cooperation and allows a collaborative mind-set to surface: "You and I are working together on a shared problem." This might be subtle, but it's effective.

12. Sit down. Problems are usually best discussed sitting down since body language can more easily become aggressive and intimidating, or be interpreted that way, if we're standing.

13. Work together to solve the problems. We are all more committed to the success of a path that we have had a part in planning and that takes us at least some of the way to achieving our goals. Sharing information, pooling ideas, discussing our needs, wants, and worries, and searching for a solution that meets as many of them as possible increases commitment to the solution and, as a bonus, helps understand each other better.

A Word to the Wise

Before you disagree, outline your reasoning and finish up with something like: "And that *is* why I look at it differently." Or summarize your understanding of the other person's views, then say "And here's how I see it ...."

14. Substitute *and* for *but*. *But* butts away the other person's point. It's a verbal hammer that negates what went before it and signals disagreement. It harms relationships. "I take your point but ..." "The report was fine but ..." "You did a good job but ..." "But" signals "bad news."

But blocks; *and* builds. *And* shows we've listened and heard. It acknowledges and extends on what the other person has said. With *and,* we're working with the other's comments; with *but,* we're dismissing them. *And* helps to prevent arguments because it allows two points of view to stand.

269

Sometimes, a straight substitution of *and* for *but* works. Sometimes, we'll need to reconstruct the sentence and make our point quite differently in order to say *and* instead of *but*. If this happens, the reworded statement is invariably stronger, more cooperative, and more effective than the original version.

15. If your approach isn't working, change something. "I've told you a million times!" Well, if it didn't work the first few hundred times, why would we expect it to work this time? Try something different! Change the environment, your approach, your tactics, or your communication style. It doesn't matter that much what you change since what you're doing now isn't working anyway.

16. Take a deep breath. Stress and tension stop the brain from working as efficiently as it can. When we become emotional or feel threatened in some way, the emotional center of our brain drains oxygen from the neocortex, our "thinking brain," and sets off the adrenal reflex. When this happens, we can't think clearly. Our bodies gear up for fight or flight and arguments are the predictable outcome.

17. Share your feelings. Sometimes it helps to let others know how we are faring in the discussion process. For example, if you feel a discussion is going in circles and want a break, we can say so: "I think we've been over this ground a few times; perhaps it's time we had a break." (Chances are the other person feels the same way, too.) Making statements about what we think or feel can open up the discussion again.

18. Use humor. Humor (not the deadly sin of sarcasm!) can relieve tension and keep discussions on a friendly note. It protects us from stress and can defuse threatening situations. Humor helps to make a discussion collaborative not competitive. It increases the chances of finding an unexpected breakthrough.

19. Don't interrupt or be interrupted. It's just as rude to step on a person's thoughts as on their toes.

Take turns speaking and paraphrase the other person's point of view before adding your own.

20. Pick your time. Cato the Younger said, "The first virtue is to restrain the tongue; he approaches nearest to the gods who knows how to be silent, even though he is in the right." Cato probably didn't mean we should hold our tongues forever. He probably meant

A Word to the Wise

To make your point without making an enemy, lose the word *but* and use the word *and*. The word *but* is responsible for a great deal of tension and disagreement. The same is true of *however*, which is just a longer version of the word *but*.

A Word to the Wise

Instead of breathing shallowly, breathe deeply. Three deep breaths will help you relax, reduce your anxiety, and clear your mind. The increased flow of oxygen to your brain and heart will calm you and help you think more clearly and creatively.

to point out the wisdom of biding our time to open a discussion until the moment is right. A quiet place, a private place, a nonthreatening place, a time when there will be enough time to discuss the matter fully.

As we saw in Chapter 18, "Choose Your Words for Clarity and Power," words are powerful and can direct our communication. The next time you're faced with a conflict, try seeing it not as "conflict management" but as "agreement management."

Think over the 20 ideas for resolving conflicts and imagine when or how you could put them to use in your day-to-day life. Be alert to how other successful communicators use them. Have a go at using them yourself—you'll be pleased with the results.

The Least You Need to Know

➤ Remember that no one really wins an argument if someone loses.

➤ Discuss disagreements before they become brawls.

➤ Use the importance of the issue and the relationship to choose the appropriate way to deal with disputes.

➤ Be clear about your goals.

➤ Listen to understand the other person's goals.

➤ Make sure you respect—and show that you respect—both your own and the other person's position.

Chapter 26

How to Deal With Difficult People

In This Chapter

➤ Double checking your psychic mirror

➤ Ten principles for dealing with difficult people

➤ The general strategy

➤ Eight specific strategies

Every time I see him, I long to be lonesome.

Do you know anyone who makes you feel like this? Someone you dread bumping into or will go out of your way to avoid? Few of us make it through life without encountering a *difficult person:* Someone who gets under our skin so much that we find it not just unpleasant, but strenuous, arduous, and grueling, to communicate properly with them.

We end up talking to ourselves, saying what a pain in the neck they are, and wishing they would go away! Worse, we become angry and say or do things we later regret. In bad situations, where we regularly fail to deal well with difficult people, we can become so stressed that our health suffers.

In this chapter, we'll look at some ways to deal with these difficult people.

Ten Principles to Bear in Mind

Let's begin with 10 principles to bear in mind in any difficult communication situation.

1. Let Difficult People Know You've Heard Them and Understood Their Point

People often become difficult if they feel their message isn't getting through. To capture our attention, they may resort to strong language, shouting, exaggerating, or getting "in our face."

If we attend to them, really listen and show we're listening with our body language and our responses, people are less likely to become difficult in the first place. If they have already become difficult, they will usually lower their voice and become more rational—we've noticed them and heard their point, so there is no need to create a fuss.

2. Don't Take It Personally

Difficult behavior is generally not aimed at us personally. It may be aimed at the world in general, at "people like us" in general, (e.g., everyone in our occupation is "tarred with the same brush") or at the organization we represent.

Famous Last Words

A **difficult person** is someone who not just you, but others too, find trying and tiresome. If you're the only one finding someone difficult, have a look in your psychic mirror to see whether the person is really reflecting something about yourself that you don't like very much.

3. They're Probably Doing the Best They Can

Most of us have a range of communication methods and behaviors. We use them because they work. They've worked in the past, and we expect them to continue working. If they don't, we might be flexible enough in our communications to try an alternative approach. Or we might not be.

The habitually difficult person's range of communication methods and behaviors is more limited than most people's. They're probably just doing what they've always done and don't know any other ways to get what they want. Rise one level above the difficult person and accept they are doing their best.

4. Keep Your Cool

Easier said than done? Of course! We can all do it, though.

Brain cells have a higher rate of metabolism than other parts of the body and need relatively more oxygen. Stress drains the brain of oxygen, which causes us to lose our mental balance, our concentration, and our control of emotions. This is why it's important to breathe during times of stress—it supplies the brain with oxygen and helps us think clearly.

Taking a deep breath (or two or three) gives us time to think and catch angry words before they fly out of our mouth.

5. Filter What You're Hearing

As soon as you're faced with an angry or difficult person, erect an imaginary filter. Place it between the two of you, so it can strain out what you don't want—negative emotions, personal jibes, and bad vibes—and let in what you do want—facts and other useful information.

Difficult and angry people often present their feelings as facts, and confuse facts, fantasy, and folklore. Stay alert so that you can gather useful information and, at the same time, filter out any hurtful emotion and personal attacks.

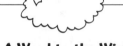

A Word to the Wise

If you're tempted to dig in your heels and "give as good as you're getting," read through Chapter 3, "We Reap What We Sow," and remind yourself how to pull your own strings.

6. Remember Your ABCs

Always Be Courteous

Being courteous can be difficult if we disagree with what the person is saying or if they are saying it in a harsh or hurtful way. Keep breathing and bite your tongue if you have to!

7. Don't Lose Sleep over Chronically Difficult People

A Word to the Wise

Breathe deeply and use positive self-talk to help you keep calm. "I'll work this through." "I'll handle this calmly and well." "I've dealt with people like this before and I know what to do."

Some people are just plain difficult, and there's nothing we can do about it. When faced with a persistently difficult person, think of this little ditty:

Some people bring joy wherever they go.

Others bring joy whenever they go.

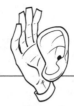

Listen to This

Here's how to disagree without being disagreeable:

➤ Show you've heard and understood by paraphrasing the other's point of view and using neutral language; then express your reservations, concerns, or confusion in a way that shows you are open to hearing the answer.

➤ If you want to disagree with an idea or proposal, offer an alternative or a way to make it work better.

➤ Don't always disagree or see the negative side. Offer solutions and encouragement, too.

➤ Before disagreeing, ask yourself whether correcting the other person will serve any purpose. Often, the facts are beside the point. If they aren't, don't say "I disagree" or "That's not how it happened." Say "I see it differently" or "I remember it like this."

8. We Can't Change Someone's Personality

Work with the behavior, not the person. Bear in mind, though, that we can't force a person to change. As the saying goes, *they gotta wanta.*

A Word to the Wise

Don't let your ego get in the way of dealing effectively with difficult people. Exchange information not emotions.

See the difficult behavior as a problem to be resolved, not a personality to be changed. The "I" statements we discussed in Chapter 22, "Ask, Don't Tell," help people to want to change their behavior because we've explained how it affects us and how we feel about it.

9. Focus on a Good Outcome

The clear communicator's approach is to work toward a satisfactory outcome, not to get "one up" on the difficult person. Our kudos come from dealing effectively with the difficult person.

10. Fix It

You may have heard the following advice:

Fix it. If you can't fix it, learn to live with it. If you can't live with it, leave it.

If the difficult person's behavior is infringing our rights—for example, our right to be treated seriously and with respect—we may decide to try to do something about it, knowing that we may or may not be successful. At other times, we may decide to ignore the difficult behavior or to live with it. Occasionally, we will decide to reduce or remove our contact with the person so that we don't have to put up with their difficult behavior.

It's important to determine what outcome is best for us. If others, for example, a work team or a group of friends, are involved, what outcome is best for everyone concerned? If we must deal with the difficult person in the workplace, what outcome is best for the organization?

The General Strategy

Here's a general approach for dealing with difficult people. Then we'll move on to dealing with specific types of difficult people.

Name That Behavior

Are you thinking that in Chapter 16, "The Ten Deadly Sins of Communication," we learned that labeling is a deadly communication sin? You're right. With difficult people, though, it actually helps to name what it is the person is doing that annoys us so. We won't be saying it to the person, just to ourselves.

Oddly, this can make it less irritating. Rather than let it get under your skin, you can notice it, acknowledge it, and carry on communicating. "Oh, he's looking down his nose at me again. How predictable!" "Oh, there she goes—becoming officious again!"

Step Into Their Moccasins

Try to see things from the difficult person's point of view. Maybe you'll be able to understand it better. We're not talking about playing amateur psychologist here (that deadly sin again) but just to try and get a feel from where this difficult person might be coming from.

People are difficult because they believe it gets them what they want. What might the difficult person be after?

respect

attention

to let off some steam

to have a problem or complaint fixed properly

to have their problem or complaint, or the difficulty it has caused them, acknowledged

to get their way quickly

to be understood

to feel interesting

to feel important

to feel "one-up"

Sometimes, once they've achieved what they're after, the difficult behavior stops. Sometimes, it escalates.

Generally speaking, if the person is genuinely trying to communicate, give them what they want. This holds true, for example, for a customer with a genuine complaint or a person who is angry for a good reason.

On the other hand, if the difficult person is a complainer, back-stabber, gossip, sarcastic person, or bully, we're probably better advised to remove the pay-off or follow the behavior with a consequence they don't like. If we do this often enough, the difficult behavior will begin to diminish.

If the difficult person's communication skills are limited, you may need to coach them on what to do instead. In other words, suggest a replacement behavior.

A Word to the Wise

Figure out what the difficult person is after. Provide it or remove it.

Silver Tongue

"A diplomat is one who thinks twice before saying nothing"

—Anonymous

Pre-Call the Problem

Another tactic is to pre-call the problem. Ask the person for a specific behavior before they begin their usual, difficult one. "Elizabeth, before you jump in here, let me briefly explain why I think this way."

Will Speaking Hurt or Help?

Franklin D. Roosevelt, the thirty-second President of the United States, was right when he said, "It is better to swallow words than to eat them later."

If you decide to address the difficult behavior, here are some tips.

Do

➤ separate the emotions from the issues.

➤ ask yourself: "Am I doing anything to encourage this difficult behavior?"

➤ focus on the outcome you want.

➤ think through what you want to say.

➤ take a deep breath to engage your thinking brain.

➤ make sure your self-talk supports you.

➤ be flexible in how you respond.

➤ stay cool, calm, and collected.

➤ realize that what you say and how you say it can make all the difference.

And don't

➤ take it personally. The difficult person is communicating in the best way they know how.

➤ put yourself down or let yourself be put down.

➤ let the difficult person get to you or give them the power to make you feel bad, upset, or angry.

Choose your battles. If you choose to try to "fix" the problem behavior, "solve" one issue at a time.

A Word to the Wise

Don't discuss the problem when it isn't occurring. Wait for the "teachable moment."

Recognize Anyone?

Here are eight common types of difficult people. If you know any of them, the suggestions below may help you deal with them.

Complainers

Some people are chronic whiners and complainers. They just can't seem to help themselves. Whether it's wilted lettuce at the salad bar, the weather, or the price of gas, they're never satisfied. Nothing suits them. They've never learned the Positivity Principle: *If you can't say something nice, don't say anything at all.*

If you want to try to prevent continual complaining when you're around, try an "I" statement or make a direct request for something positive. Say something like: "Jo, you've said what you don't like about this proposal. I'd like to hear what you do like about it."

Silver Tongue

"I destroy my enemy by making him my friend."

—Abraham Lincoln

A Word to the Wise

Don't ignore, agree with, roll with, laugh at, or in any way treat back-stabbing or jibes as acceptable. If you do, you'll remain a target.

Silver Tongue

"Gossipers talk to us about others. Dull people talk to us about themselves. Interesting people talk to us about ourselves."

—Source unknown

If the person is such a chronic complainer that no amount of coaching will change it, can you ignore their fault-finding with equanimity? If you can't learn to live with it, perhaps it's time to move outside their complaining zone.

In a professional situation when the chronic complainer is the customer, we don't have the option to try to change it, ignore it, or leave it. So here's what to do:

➤ Thank the customer for telling you.

➤ If there is something you can do to placate them, do it.

➤ Use the fogging technique. Say something like, "Yes, thank you. I understand what you're saying, and I'll bear that in mind for next time."

Make sure you do this only with someone who you're sure is complaining just for the sake of complaining. If they've got a genuine gripe, fix it. Repeat the facts as you have understood them (to show you've heard) and switch to problem solving.

Back-Stabbers and Gossips

Back-stabbers and gossips haven't learned to zip their lips if they can't say something nice, either.

If someone is saying things about you behind your back, ask them about it, preferably in private. "I heard you said X; is that true?"

They'll probably deny it. That's fine. "No problem! I thought I'd check it out." You've caught them, and they'll probably think twice before trying it again. If they don't deny it, switch gears to gathering good information; ask questions to find out what's going on (see Chapter 23, "When You Say What You Like, Say Why").

A bit of folklore is interesting, but some people don't know where to draw the line. All they can talk about is other people. Change the subject.

Showoffs

Think of showoffs as frustrated entertainers who want to be noticed and appreciated. Think how grateful they'd be if you spent a bit of time paying attention to them. They'll often calm down once they've been noticed.

If pandering to their ego is too much to bear, you could ignore their grandstanding, try an assertive "I" statement, or avoid their company altogether.

Sarcastic People

If their sarcastic comments are directed at you, address them quickly, as described above under back-stabbers. If they are generally negative, treat them as you would a chronic complainer.

If their sarcasm contains a mixed message, listen and respond to the meta-message, (see Chapter 20, "Speak for Yourself, Not the World") or the real meaning behind the words. That's what is being communicated.

Unreliable People

Some people over promise and under deliver. We probably can't change them, so we might need to learn to live with them. If we don't want to learn to live with them, we should probably learn to live without them!

How prepared are you to remind them to do things? To live with the fact that they might "forget" to do something? This all depends on how much you like their other qualities.

Sometimes, we can arrange to remind them. Sometimes that isn't appropriate. Perhaps an "I" statement would help them understand the effects their failure to stick to their promises is having. That at least might give them an incentive to change their ways.

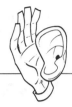

Listen to This

Have you ever been late for a meeting and someone says to you, glancing pointedly at his or her watch, "Good of you to join us" or "Well, good afternoon"? Chances are they don't mean either of those comments. What they're really saying is: "You're late!" Respond to that message with something like: "Yes, I'm sorry I'm late. I hope I haven't held you up." (Of course, if you're always late, you might fall into the category of unreliable people.)

Silver Tongue

"Part of the happiness of life consists not in fighting battles but in avoiding them. A masterly retreat is in itself, a victory."

—Norman Vincent Peale

The bottom line is: if you know someone is unreliable, don't trust them with anything important—you don't want to end up with egg on your face for someone else's errors.

Those Who Must Be Obeyed

Who do you know who wants to be in charge and call all the shots? In Chapter 24, "Tune In to the Same Wavelength," we learned that some people have a high need for power. They can't be content until they're in control.

They may be no more important than we are but, if we are to communicate effectively and make progress with them, we'll need to let them feel important, provided they don't walk all over us. If they are aggressive and ignore our wishes, rights, or needs, we'll need to respond assertively (see Chapter 21, "Don't Masquerade Your Thoughts"). If they're really bad, we might be dealing with a bully.

Bullies

The bully is the exception to what we've been saying so far.

Although the tactics of aggression dominate all the bully's communications, the bully is more than just an aggressive person. Their communications repertoire is very limited. They habitually put others down with their words and body language. It isn't just the need to get their way that's important; they also need to make others feel bad.

Research into bullies and how to deal with them has mushroomed in the last few years. Here's what communication professionals have learned about how to handle them:

➤ Hold your ground. Plant your feet and look the bully in the eye. Don't retreat from their bullying tactics.

➤ Don't attack back or argue; you can't win—bullies have had more practice.

➤ Let them sound off.

➤ Once the worst is over, get their attention. Try saying their name or standing up, for example.

➤ Repeat your understanding of their main point.

➤ Deal with them privately, not in public. Let them save face.

➤ If their behavior is totally unacceptable (shouting, cursing, constantly interrupting you), remember that they probably lack the communication skills to behave in other ways. That's

Foot in Mouth

Don't tell the bully to stop it. Tell them what to do instead.

why telling them not to do it is a waste of time—they probably don't have an alternative behavior to replace the bullying behavior with. Instead, tell the bully what to do. "John, speak to me in a normal tone of voice." Or "Fred, I'm talking. I want to finish."

➤ Don't give in too easily. Don't cry or act hurt. Bullies recognize victim behavior and take full advantage of it.

Will Rogers, the turn-of-the-century cowboy philosopher, said, "I never met a man I didn't like." It's a fair bet he hasn't met some of the difficult people you and I have come across! So here's one last thing to remember:

You can't win 'em all.

Silver Tongue

"Nothing gives one person so great advantage over another as to remain always cool and unruffled under all circumstances."

—Thomas Jefferson

The Least You Need to Know

➤ It's probably not personal.

➤ Difficult people are probably doing the best they can.

➤ Try to see things from their point of view.

➤ Filter out the emotions.

➤ Suggest a different behavior (they probably don't know one).

➤ If you can't provide or remove the pay-off they want, provide a pay-off that they don't like.

Win with Complaints

It's easy to be helpful and courteous when things are going well. It's when they go wrong that our professionalism is tested. This is when it counts most, too.

If you deal with people in a professional or voluntary capacity, you will no doubt be familiar with complaints. After all, it's a rare undertaking that runs smoothly all the time.

We're not talking here about the chronic complainers who are never satisfied no matter how good the product or service or how wonderful the occasion. We saw how to deal with people like that in the last chapter.

In this chapter, we're looking at how to handle a genuine complaint or grievance. It may be from a customer in a restaurant or in a shop or from a customer who thinks we've made a mistake on an invoice. It may be from someone who wants to alert us that something has gone wrong so we can put things right for the next customer or for them the next time they deal with us. Or it may be someone just needing to "let off a little steam."

Welcome Complaints

It takes time and effort to complain. Why should people bother when it's easier just to walk away? Unfortunately, that's just what most people do. We never have a chance to hear what went wrong or have the opportunity to fix it. We lose them, and quite possibly, lose others as well, for the same reasons.

Here are three great reasons to welcome complaints.

Complaints Are Feedback

Whether a complaint is made in person, in writing, or over the telephone, the first thing to do is to recognize that most complaints are feedback. According to PIMS (Profit Impact of Marketing Strategy) research, only 4.3 percent of our unhappy customers ever bother to complain. The other 95.7 percent just vote with their feet. It's often our best and most loyal customers who care enough to complain. After all, they've got a vested interest in us "getting our act together."

Here's an example of how *not* to handle a complaint …

Checking in early at the airport one evening, Karin was told she might catch an earlier flight if she went on stand-by. Getting home earlier than she'd planned sounded great, so she agreed. As she watched the attendant label her suitcase, she spotted a potential problem. Her years of materials handling and systems management experience had given her a "nose" for these things, and she sensed a distinct possibility that her suitcase would not find its way onto her plane.

She mentioned her concern to the attendant. "Don't worry, everything will be fine," came the response. "We know what we're doing."

Sure enough, when Karin arrived at her home airport, her suitcase wasn't there. Since she was pretty sure she knew why, she rang the flight center the next day. She explained that she was put on stand-by the evening before and her suitcase didn't arrive with her. She said she thought she'd spotted a flaw in the system that she'd like to report.

"You'll have to put your complaint in writing," she was told.

"This isn't a complaint. It's some information for you so you can fix the system."

"We don't handle complaints here. You'll really have to put it in writing."

"I haven't got time to put it in writing and I'm not complaining. I've got my suitcase back now and I'm just trying to let you know about a problem in your luggage-handling system for stand-by flights so it can be rectified."

"Well, I can't help you. You'll have to call the airport manager."

"Okay, what's the number?"

"Actually, we don't give out that information."

Will Karin ever bother to pass on information to the airline again?

Does the airline need information from customers like Karin?

Complaints Are Warnings

Since most customers don't bother to complain, we should view each complaint not as an isolated incident but as symptomatic of the way our organization habitually operates.

Complaints Are Opportunities

Do you know that if you handle a complaint well, your customer will be more loyal to you than if everything had gone smoothly all along? PIMS research also shows us that 95 percent of customers will remain loyal to us if we fix their complaint quickly and well.

Dealing With a Complaint

So how do we handle a complaint "well"? It's the way we go about dealing with it that is important. In fact, most customers would rather be dealt with respectfully than have the problem fixed in their favor. Yes, most customers would rather we treat them with respect than resolve the problem in their favor.

It's the process, not the outcome, that matters most. The process is L-L-A-R-A-A.

L-L-A-R-A-A

L-L-A-R-A-A is an acronym we can easily remember.

1. Look. Make eye contact and use other attentive body language so that the complainant can see you're listening. If the complaint is being made over the telephone, "look" with your words: Use plenty of uh-huh's and I see's.

A Word to the Wise

Be grateful for complaints. Treat them as important information from someone who cares. See them as opportunities to get your "house in order" and build customer loyalty.

Foot in Mouth

If you're tempted to cut the customer off because you think you know what he's going to say—don't! Having his say is just as important as having his way.

2. Listen. Listen carefully. Really hear what the person is trying to tell you. Sift what you're hearing into the four Fs—Fact, Fantasy, Folklore and Feelings.

3. Affirm. As we saw in Chapter 15, "Listen, Listen, Listen," affirmative listening, or nodding and grunting while the person is talking, can get us twice as much information as "stunned mullet" listening.

4. Restate what you've understood. Use reflective listening skills to prove you've heard and understood, to calm the person down if necessary, and to clear up any misunderstandings. Restate both facts and feelings.

5. Ask the right questions. The right question might be "How can I best help you now?" Or it might be "Can you explain that a bit more to me, please?" Or "When did that actually happen?" It depends on the situation.

6. Act. Take responsibility for putting matters right or for making sure someone else puts them right. Don't fob the customer off with "Well, this isn't my job" or "You'll have to put your complaint in writing" or "You'll have to speak with the boss."

L-L-A-R-A-A helps us gather good information professionally and lets customers have their say, the first step in winning with a complaint. It leads us into our crystal clear communication pattern of Gathering Good Information, Giving Good Information, and Making Progress.

Gather Good Information

Does it surprise you that the first five of the six steps above deal with gathering good information? This reflects the importance of listening in winning with a complaint.

A Word to the Wise

After thanking the customer for their feedback, explain what you will do to sort it out—right now and, if appropriate, in the long term.

Give Good Information

When it's our turn to give good information, we do two things:

➤ First, thank the customer for telling us about the problem, and commiserate with them if the situation warrants it.

➤ Then, focus on the future. Customers aren't interested in excuses. They want to know what will happen because they bothered to spend their valuable time letting us know they experienced a problem.

Returning to the lost baggage example from above, the operator at the flight center who spoke with Karin could have said:

Thank	"Thank you for telling me about that.
Restate facts	and I'm sorry your suitcase didn't arrive as it should have.
Restate feelings	I'm sure you didn't need a hassle like that to end your day.
Ask the right questions	Let me note down a few details
Act	so I can pass this on to our baggage-handling manager. What flight were you on?"

Wouldn't that have been much more courteous and professional? Wouldn't a response like that have earned Karin's loyalty?

Notice that the various elements are combined in a different order. Flexibility is the key.

Make Progress

Agree and act are the two key aspects of making progress. Once you've settled on what to do, summarize it and make sure the customer concurs. Then do it.

The flight center operator who spoke to Karin could have finished their conversation like this:

A Word to the Wise

Because behavior breeds behavior, keep your locus of control inside so that you are in charge of the interaction, not the customer (see Chapter 3, "We Reap What We Sow").

Thank	"Thank you again for taking the time to alert us to this."
Act	I'll pass this information on to our baggage-handling manager so hopefully other passengers on stand-by won't be inconvenienced as you were.
Agree	"Does that sound acceptable to you?"

How much better that would have been for everyone concerned.

Dealing With Angry Customers

Have you ever tried to make your point to someone and become angry and upset because they weren't listening?

Have you ever heard someone say to an angry person, "Now just calm down and we'll talk about this sensibly" or "Don't you use that kind of language with me!" They may mean well, but unfortunately, commands like this make people more angry not less.

A Word to the Wise

Use your reflective listening skills and attentive body language to show the angry person you're listening.

When people are angry, their biggest need is to be heard. We can help them "get it off their chest."

Angry people are on the Emotions Side of Mt. Anger. Telling them to "calm down" ensures they'll stay there. In fact, every time we fail to listen to them, we dig them further into the Emotions Side of the mountain.

To help them crest the mountain and reach the Progress Side, we need to let them have their say and show we've heard it.

This may seem like an invitation for them to shout all the more but, actually, once the angry person has "had their say" and we've shown we've heard it by summarizing it back, they will be ready to move on.

Here's what the mnemonic for dealing with an angry person looks like now:

L-L-A-R-A-S.

> Look
>
> Listen
>
> Affirm
>
> Restate what you've understood, both facts and feelings
>
> Ask questions
>
> Summarize

When the angry person has finished and you have asked any questions you need to gather good information, summarize both their feelings and the facts as you've understood them. This helps them climb Mt. Anger. It brings them up the Emotions Side of the mountain and helps them climb over to the Progress Side.

Consider how the following L-L-A-R-A-S could have helped poor Tony out of the following mess:

Charlotte needed a new set of tires. She telephoned several tire stores, eventually settling on Tony's Tires, where she made an appointment for 2 o'clock the following Wednesday. "Bring your car in then and leave it with us for an hour," Tony said.

Charlotte took a day off work and planned it meticulously. She needed her car for a number of errands in the morning. After lunch, she'd leave the car with Tony for an hour, do a few local errands on foot, collect the car, and drive to the local cinema where she planned to meet a friend to catch the matinee. A rare treat!

At the appointed time, Charlotte brought the car into Tony's. "Come back in an hour and your car will be ready," he said.

Charlotte returned at 3 o'clock. "Ah," said Tony, "have a seat. I'll just go and start on your car; I won't be long."

"What? You said my car would be ready at 3 o'clock!"

"Yes I know, I've been really busy and haven't had a chance to get to it. Just sit down and I'll have it ready for you in 10 minutes."

"But I'm expected somewhere else now! You said my car would be ready!"

Back and forth went the conversation between Charlotte and Tony, Charlotte becoming more and more angry while Tony kept repeating that she should sit down and he'd get started on her car.

In the end, they spent far longer than 10 minutes arguing and Charlotte was furious! Tony had broken a promise and didn't seem to understand how he'd upset her carefully made plans for one of her few days off.

Poor Tony. He didn't know it, but all he was doing by repeatedly telling her to sit down was blocking Charlotte's path up Mt Anger. This made her even angrier!

Not a happy situation for either Charlotte or Tony. Both lost—Charlotte was late for her matinee and Tony had to deal with an angry customer (and almost certainly one he would never see again). Let's see how the L-L-A-R-A-S formula would have turned the situation around.

After listening to Charlotte without interrupting her, Tony could have summarized like this:

"I'm really sorry your car isn't ready when I said it would be. I understand how inconvenient this delay is for you, and I know you need to be on your way. Can you give me 10 more minutes?"

This would have acknowledged both Charlotte's feelings and the facts. She would have felt heard. She would have felt no need to carry on trying to make her point. Instead, she could have sat down and let Tony get on with the job.

It's the *way* we deal with people that counts. In the example above, nothing would change the fact that the car wasn't ready as promised and Charlotte would be delayed. But if Tony had dealt with Charlotte professionally, he wouldn't have lost a customer and she wouldn't have been delayed as long.

Dealing With Habitual Complainers

Some people were born to complain. If one of them is a customer of yours, here's what to do:

1. Thank them.
2. Say you'll pass on their comments.
3. Do something to placate the customer now, if this is feasible.

Remember the Latin motto:

Non tu bastardi carborundum.

(Don't let the "difficult customers" grind you down.)

The Least You Need to Know

➤ Welcome complaints as important feedback, warnings, and opportunities.

➤ The *way* you deal with a complaint matters more to the customer than the actual outcome.

➤ Use the L-L-A-R-A-A mnemonic to deal with complaints.

➤ Calm angry people down by showing you've listened and understood their point(s).

➤ Use the L-L-A-R-A-S mnemonic to deal with angry people.

Chapter 28

Fix It!

In This Chapter

➤ Using S-O-L-V-E to solve problems and make decisions

➤ Involving others

➤ Avoiding your brain's traps

➤ Plugging into your creativity

Wouldn't it be great if we never had any problems, and all our decisions were easy ones! For those times when you have a thorny problem to unravel and put right, or when you need to select between alternatives, this chapter will help smooth the process.

How Much Effort?

The first question when we have a problem to solve or a decision to make is: How much effort does it deserve?

At one extreme are routine, insignificant, and inconsequential problems and decisions. These don't merit much time or energy. At the other extreme are the very complex, momentous, or crucial problems and decisions. These warrant all the time, effort, and creativity we can muster.

Here are some questions to help you assess how much time and effort to put into a decision.

➤ How much risk is involved?

➤ How significant are the potential consequences if I get it wrong or right?

➤ What would happen if I do nothing?

➤ Who else is involved or interested?

➤ How much time do I have available?

➤ Is anyone's safety or security at stake?

➤ What resource costs are involved (e.g., money, time, goodwill, property) in ignoring the problem? In fixing it?

➤ Do I have much freedom in dealing with this or are my actions prescribed to some extent?

A Word to the Wise

On a scale of 1 to 10, how much time, effort, and trouble is the decision or problem worth? Invest accordingly.

Approach Problems Positively

As we do in other areas of our communications and our life, we need to put the self-fulfilling prophecy to work for us. So approach problems and decisions with a positive expectation that you can and will resolve them.

SOLVE it! The mnemonic device S-O-L-V-E makes it easy to remember how to solve problems.

State the problem

Outline the problem

List your options

Visualize your options

Evaluate your results

State the Problem

Have you ever thought you had solved a problem only to find that it came back again in a slightly different form? Or that all your efforts made no difference at all?

You might have succumbed to the first of problem solving's three most common mistakes—jumping in too quickly. We feel good because we're doing something, but in our haste, our prompt action is directed at the wrong problem or at only a symptom of the real problem.

Before taking any action, take the time to think it through thoroughly and find out what you're dealing with. Develop a clear and accurate description of the problem. This puts the focus on the real problem, so you can find practical solutions. It helps to make sure you don't waste your time and effort solving "symptoms" while the real problem continues or worsens.

Choose words that are clear, concrete, complete, and correct when describing the problem. Vagueness is useless. Go for a precise portrait, not a fuzzy sketch, of the problem.

Solve problems not symptoms is a good motto. This will ensure that you don't succumb to the second most common mistake in problem solving.

Symptoms are results of problems. Solving a symptom can be tempting because it is quick and easy, but it's like taking aspirin for a headache when the headache is caused by shortsightedness. Only eyeglasses will stop the headache at its source—aspirin merely masks the problem.

Here are two good questions to help uncover the real problem and distinguish it from symptoms:

1. How do I know I have a problem? Examine the evidence that tells you a problem exists.

2. Why does the problem exist? Ask yourself this question five times, and you'll probably uncover the real problem. State your problem, then keep asking why it exists until you reach its root cause.

Silver Tongue

"The greatest challenge to any thinker is stating the problem in a way that will allow a solution."

—Bertrand Russell

A Word to the Wise

Develop a statement that captures the essence of the problem and is short enough to say in one breath.

The third most common mistake in problem solving is to bite off more than you can chew and try to solve a complex problem without breaking it down into smaller problems. This only leads to frustration and failure. Break big problems down into their components and solve each one at a time. This leads to satisfaction and success.

Outline the Problem

Now flesh out the problem statement. Probe the problem from all angles to discover as much as possible about it. Use the four Fs to help you gather good information about the problem.

Facts	What are the facts?
Fantasy	What is your opinion? What do others think?
Folklore	Is there any useful information "on the grapevine"?
Feelings	What does your intuition tell you? What "hunches" do others have?

Here are some points to ponder when outlining the problem:

➤ *What is* the problem? *What isn't* it?

➤ *When is* it occurring? *When isn't* it occurring?

➤ *Where is* the problem located? *Where is it not* located?

➤ *Who is* involved? *Who is not* involved that you might expect to be?

➤ *How* many, *how* much, *how* often, *how* regularly does the problem occur?

➤ *How* is it affecting others?

➤ *How much* is it costing in time, money, effort, or other resources?

➤ *What* is involved? What isn't?

➤ *What* is the nature of the problem?

➤ *What* was happening before? What has *changed*?

➤ *Which* customers are involved? *Which* equipment is involved? *Which* aren't involved that you might expect to be?

➤ Are things *improving* or *worsening*?

➤ *How* do I usually respond to the problem? *What* happens when I respond this way?

Sometimes past experience can limit our thinking and cause us to miss important information or overlook unexpected solutions. The questions above help to explore problems and analyze them carefully.

Know when enough is enough. People who get carried away collecting information suffer paralysis by analysis! We might as well resign ourselves to the fact that we'll never find out everything. We need to learn as much as we reasonably and realistically can. Then we need to know when the time has come to stop investigating and start focusing on solutions.

Silver Tongue

"The voyage of discovery consists not in seeking new landscapes but in having new eyes."

—Marcel Proust

A Word to the Wise

Take off blinders and relinquish preconceived ideas. Listen to your intuition. Think it through logically. Ask others for their input. Ferret out the facts.

Having said that, the more time we spend outlining the problem, the more we improve our chances of understanding and solving it. A thorough analysis stops us working on symptoms or charging off in the wrong direction. It can save a lot of time and trouble, so consider the time you spend on a proper analysis time well spent. In fact, a thorough analysis often points directly to a solution.

Search for the cause. What does the information suggest could be the cause of the problem? Once you know why a problem is occurring, the bulk of your work is probably done.

List Your Options

First, establish goals. What should the solution you are about to generate do for you? What do you want to achieve? How will you know whether your solution is working?

Next, list alternatives. Develop a list of possible solutions—the more solution you generate, the better. How can you remove the source of the problem entirely? How can you lessen its effects? Could you rechannel its effects so that they are less harmful or neutral, or even beneficial? If none of these options is possible, how can you learn to live with your problem more comfortably?

Since good ideas seldom jump up and bite us on the nose, use your own, and others', thinking power to develop possible solutions.

Work out some options using logical thinking. Develop others using your creative thinking abilities. Listen to your intuition.

It's a big mistake to evaluate each idea as it comes. It may take a bit of willpower, but it's far better to list all your ideas first, then evaluate them.

Having trouble?

Try a different approach:

➤ Look at the problem from a bigger perspective, or a smaller one.

A Word to the Wise

Don't settle for the first idea that pops into your head. Don't settle for obvious—or neat and simple—solutions just because they're easy.

Silver Tongue

"Nothing is more dangerous than an idea when it's the only one you have."

—Emile Chartier

A Word to the Wise

Doing nothing is an option. Think of it as an action.

Silver Tongue

"The human race is governed by its imagination."

—Napoleon Bonaparte

➤ Keep focused on a solution that will be acceptable to everyone and will meet your needs.

➤ Keep your mind open.

➤ Rewrite your problem statement, redefine the problem, or look at it from a different angle.

➤ Switch to a completely different activity to give your brain a break.

➤ Close your eyes, relax, and breathe deeply. Listen to your hunches.

➤ Gather your information, then sleep on it.

Visualize Your Options

The next step is to visualize your options in operation. This helps you evaluate them against the criteria you developed earlier and alerts you to potential problems.

There is seldom "one best answer" to a problem. More often, you need to work within the constraints of reality—budgets, other people, time. Sometimes it will make sense to combine two or three options and find a way to make them work. At other times you will need to find ways to optimize a less than ideal solution. Visualizing can help.

Picture each possible solution in operation. How well does it meet your criteria? How can you adjust it to make it work even better? What potential difficulties are there and how can you avoid them?

When you visualize your solutions in operation, you can look for what could go wrong, what you'll need to do to ensure the solution works, who needs to be involved, the resources you'll need, and/or what methods will work best. This helps to safeguard your solution and gives it the best possible chance of working.

Visualizing your options also helps you select the most suitable one. You can implement it with confidence because you've selected it against meaningful criteria, visualized it in action, and made any needed adjustments.

Evaluate Your Results

We don't pop a delicious steak on the barbecue and leave it until we want to eat, do we? We watch it, turn it, and nurture it along so that we end up with a wonderful meal. Similarly, we don't just implement our solution and walk away! We watch it to see how it's succeeding. Is it meeting our expectations? Are there any snags? Are our success criteria being realized or do we need to do some fine-tuning? Work with your solution to make it succeed.

Making Decisions

Essentially, decision making is the final three steps in the S-O-L-V-E system. Before you begin listing options, establish your goals. These give you good selection criteria on which to base your decision. Before reaching a decision, visualize your options in operation. Once the decision is made and put into effect, evaluate it to make sure it is working as expected. Sometimes you'll need to make adjustments, sometimes it will be working well, and sometimes you'll need to go back to the drawing board and begin the process again.

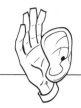

Listen to This

Do you base your decisions more on emotions or on fact? Both overly emotional and overly logical decisions can be difficult to implement. The best solutions balance both. Balanced decisions are easier to implement.

Involving Others

The famous inventor, Thomas Edison, was once asked why he had a team of 21 assistants. He replied, "If I could solve all problems myself, I would."

In most cases, the adage that *two brains are better than one* is true. Of course, this is only true if the two brains contain different perspectives, insights, experience, and knowledge. As Walter Lippman, the US journalist, said: "Where we all think alike, no one thinks very much."

Involve others ...

Foot in Mouth

If options are presented to you for you to make the final decision, don't just accept them—ask yourself whether any other options should be considered.

➤ when they will be involved in implementing or executing your decision or the solution to your problem.

➤ when they will be affected by your decision or the solution to your problem.

➤ when they show interest.

➤ when you need them to understand or support your decision.

➤ when you feel you need support or encouragement.

➤ when the problem or decision is complex and others can add their perspective, opinions, judgment, experience, or expertise.

➤ when others want to be involved and feel they have something to contribute or to learn.

Don't Let Your Brain Trip You Up!

Our brains can sabotage us. They use unconscious routines, called heuristics, when dealing with complexity. These shortcuts save us working things out step by step. They can also undermine our ability to arrive at the most effective conclusion. Here are six ways to guard against the most common heuristics:

Foot in Mouth

Don't involve others just so you can have someone to "share the blame with" or just to confirm your own thoughts and ideas.

➤ Beware first impressions. Always view problems and reach decisions from different perspectives.

➤ Don't select the *status quo* as default. Only do nothing if it really is the best option, not just because it's easier or safer.

➤ Set aside past poor choices and don't base future decisions on an attempt to recover past losses. Prolonging mistakes only compounds them.

➤ Remain flexible and open-minded when collecting information, interpreting it, and weighing it. Don't accept evidence that confirms your opinions without question.

➤ The way you state your problem can distort it. Make several initial problem statements from different points of view to make sure you end up working with an objective problem statement.

➤ Be disciplined when making guesstimates. Consider both ends of the spectrum to avoid becoming anchored by your initial estimate.

Capitalize on Your Creativity

Has a good idea ever popped into your head out of the blue? Have you ever had a sudden understanding or insight into something? That's your creative mind at work. While we usually think of creativity as a sudden flash of insight, it can also result from systematic, analytical thinking.

Creativity is a natural ability that gets rusty if we don't use it. And while some of us are more creative than others, we all have at least some ability to think creatively, and we can all increase our creativity through practice.

A dose of creativity enriches our solutions to problems and helps us to reach high-quality, workable decisions. Here are six things you can do to boost your creativity.

Know Your Stuff

Sir Isaac Newton had been pondering the puzzle of gravity for quite a while before he watched the apple fall. When asked how he made this and other creative and groundbreaking mathematical discoveries, he replied, "by thinking about them."

No matter how creative we are, if we don't have the underlying knowledge and experience, we will not be able to create workable, yet unique, solutions or recognize them when we see them.

Silver Tongue

"Genius is 1% inspiration and 99% perspiration."

—Thomas Edison

Stick With It

Expertise alone is not enough. We also need perseverance and a genuine desire to come up with a creative solution. If our first set of ideas didn't produce a great solution, persistence, willingness, and the sheer determination to produce another set of ideas will ensure that we sit down and take the time and effort to think through the problem some more. Great inventors do this over and over again until they "crack it."

Creativity is actually hard work. Following S-O-L-V-E and the creativity techniques discussed here supply the necessary ingredients, which you can supplement with your own expertise, perseverance, and motivation.

Brainstorm

Brainstorming has been around since the 1930s. It improves problem solving and decision-making, communication, fluency (our ability to produce original or novel ideas), and flexibility (our ability to come up with lots of ideas). Brainstorm by yourself or, better still, with others. Come up with as many ideas as you can—the wilder the better. Evaluate them afterward.

Work Backward

What would your perfect solution be? This becomes your goal. Now work backward step-by-step to figure out how to get there. Keep asking yourself, "How do I make that happen?"

Imagine

Use guided imagery, such as symbols, analogies, and metaphors, to challenge assumptions, find a different perspective, and generate ideas. How

Silver Tongue

"Let us learn to dream, gentlemen. Then perhaps we shall discover the truth."

—Friedrich Kekule

301

would someone else—a surgeon, an artist, a scientist, or a crime writer—solve the problem? How would someone you know and respect solve it?

Famous Last Words

As you are falling asleep, review what you know about a problem you are trying to solve, a decision you are trying to make, or something that is puzzling you, and what you want to happen or find out. Then go to sleep and let your subconscious go to work. This is called **incubating**.

Sleep On It

Many of our most creative ideas come to us as if from nowhere, when we are thinking about something else, when we are day-dreaming, even in our dreams, if we can recall them.

Using a technique known as *incubating,* we can review the problem we want to solve as we're falling asleep, remind ourselves of our solution criteria and, literally, sleep on our problem. Eight out of ten times, our creative subconscious will produce some sort of an answer for us within three nights of incubation.

Creative people have learned to place their dilemmas, quandaries, and problems in their subconscious and let it work on them while they are relaxing, daydreaming, or working on other matters. Provided the skill and knowledge is there to support the subconscious, this technique works very well.

Put your great communication skills to work for you in tough situations and with tough problems.

The Least You Need to Know

➤ Invest time to gather information, clearly define your problem, establish goals, and explore alternatives.

➤ Don't waste time solving symptoms—rectify the cause of problems.

➤ Use the S-O-L-V-E system to reliably solve problems and make decisions.

➤ Involving others improves results and increases commitment.

➤ Use your intuition and the available facts to decide.

➤ Practice creativity and pay attention to your dreams.

Self-Talk as an Indicator of Self-Esteem

The silent messages we continually give ourselves have enormous influence on our behavior, so much so that they become self-fulfilling prophecies. How does your self-talk guide your behavior?

Compare the answers you gave in the exercise in Chapter 2, "Where It All Begins: Your Beliefs" with the examples below. Which do they match more closely?

Situation	Indicators of Low Self-Esteem	Indicators of High Self-Esteem
You've made a mistake in front of your co-workers	"Now they'll *know* I'm useless!"	"Next time, I'll ..."
You're doing something for the first time and finding it difficult	"I'm so stupid; I can never learn anything!"	"I've learned things like this before; I'll get it if I keep at it."
You've forgotten to do something you'd promised to do	"I'm so stupid and forgetful!"	"That's not like me. This is how I'll fix this."
You walk into a meeting with people you've never met before	"I hate this; I'm terrible with strangers."	"This will be a challenge; I'll keep calm and everything will be fine."

continues

continued

Situation	Indicators of Low Self-Esteem	Indicators of High Self-Esteem
The boss calls you in and you don't know why	"I'm in for it now; I must have made a mistake again."	"I wonder what's up?"
You trip walking down the road to the sandwich bar	"What a clod I am; I can't even walk without making a fool of myself."	"Goodness! I'd better pay more attention to where I'm going!"
You're running late for an important appointment	"Trust me to be late again. I'm always late. I make a mess of everything."	"This isn't like me to be late. I'd better get to a telephone to warn them."
You can't get your checkbook to balance	"I'm hopeless at this kind of stuff. I'll never get it right."	"I know I can do this if I concentrate."
You've done something particularly well	"Miracles can happen! That was lucky."	"I'm really good at this."

Body Language Practice

The only way we can ever be sure about what peoples' body language means is to ask them or check our interpretation of it with them. That's a good way to build your confidence at reading body language, too.

Meanwhile, did you practice reading the body language examples from Chapter 11, "Other People's Body Language"? The most likely meaning of these common signal clusters is shown below along with some suggestions for how to respond. As I pointed out in the chapter, though, the context is important, and so is the baseline that you've already established for the individual's body language.

Body Language	Possible Meaning	My Response
The speaker is constantly clearing his throat; speaking rapidly with changes in pitch; making jerky, rapid gestures.	This person is uncertain and uneasy.	Make him comfortable. Be supportive and reassuring. Act naturally, relieve the tension, possibly through humor.
During a meeting, a man takes off his jacket and hangs it over the back of his chair.	His is comfortable with you, open, and cooperative.	Take off your own jacket and indicate your willingness to be candid and accommodating also.
A woman takes off her glasses, pinches the bridge of her nose, looks up at the ceiling, then closes her eyes and becomes quiet.	She is thinking something through, evaluating what has been said.	Give her time; stay quiet and be ready to answer any questions.

continues

continued

Body Language	Possible Meaning	My Response
A man leans fully back in his chair, clasps his hands behind his head, puts one foot on the table, and allows his other leg to fall sideways.	This person is feeling dominant and superior.	Maintain your level of confidence. Echo the posture or some aspects of it if appropriate. Try to equalize the relationship.
A colleague abruptly takes glasses off and throws them to the table or flings pen down onto table.	This indicates a strong negative reaction to what you've just said.	Probe to find out what the objection is; change your approach.
Open palm is placed over the heart.	This person is expressing sincerity, honestly.	Respond in kind if appropriate.
Hand partially covers a person's mouth while she's speaking.	This person may not be sure or convinced about what she is saying, or she might be deceiving you.	Probe to make sure you are uncovering all of the facts.
A man continually folds and unfolds the arms of his eyeglasses.	He may be bored.	Try to find a topic of mutual interest to discuss.
A woman strides decisively and quickly into the room.	This person is confident and self-assured.	Project similar levels of poise.
A man clasps his hands tightly behind his back and locks his ankles together. Later, he clenches his jaw.	This person may be holding back from saying something; keeping himself "in check."	Encourage self-expression. Ask open questions and listen reflectively (see Chapter 16, "The Ten Deadly Sins of Communication").

Turning Closed Questions into Open Questions

Your ideas will probably be different, so these are just suggestions for the questions in Chapter 17, "Step Off with the Right Foot."

To test whether you have succeeded in turning the closed questions into open questions, ask yourself whether you could answer your reworded question with a simple "yes," "no," or a short statement of fact. If you can, they are still closed questions.

When did that happen?	What led up to that?
Was your trip successful?	What did you manage to accomplish on your trip?
Did you like that candidate?	In what ways do you think that candidate meets our needs?
Did you have a good meeting?	What happened at the meeting?
Why did that happen?	What do you suppose could have caused that?

Some Ideas for Frames

Did you think of some short frames for the situations in Chapter 17, "Step Off with the Right Foot"? Here are some possibilities:

1. "Peter, I'd like to have a word with you about our committee meetings. I've noticed that you often talk quietly to the person next to you, and this bothers me because I really want everyone's attention and input."

   (You've decided not to mention Peter's whispering as annoyance to others because this is only a guess on your part. You've told Peter what you do want, not what you don't want.)

2. "Carla, have you got a minute? I'd like to have a chat about something that bothers me a lot."

   (At this point, you might deliver an "I" statement see Chapter 22, "Ask Don't Tell." You can't force Carla to change her work habits, but you can point out how they affect you.)

3. "Thanks for getting together with me, Manny. We both know that management wants everyone to do more in less time. I was thinking that between us we could come up with a plan to do that."

   Manny agrees.

   "I thought we might bounce a few ideas around ourselves about how our teams could work together to reduce lead times and then perhaps we could call a joint meeting to see what ideas our teams have. What do you think?"

   (The key here is working together to make improvements.)

4. "Thanks for seeing me about my expenditure proposal, Sean. I'd like to spend a few minutes on why I've put it to you and summarize it for you. Then I thought we could work out the pros and cons and list any concerns you might still have. What I'd hoped for is to make sure you have all the information you need to make a decision on it."

   (We're trying to put gentle pressure on Sean without making him feel defensive, uncomfortable, or rushed.)

5. "Thank you for coming. I've asked you here to get some ideas on how we can speed up getting the figures out to each of our customer departments. I've spoken with each of the department managers, who agree that a reduction in turnaround from three weeks to two would be very helpful to them. I'd like to make that our goal.

   I thought we'd begin by brainstorming the things that slow us down. Who can suggest anything?"

   (Notice the tone is not "You'll have to do it faster or better"; it's "How can we improve?" This is more likely to lead to cooperation and ideas.)

6. "Ellen, it's missed-deadline discussion time again, I'm sorry to say. When we discussed this at your performance appraisal and again last month, you said that you felt you needed to be more organized. I'd like to hear what changes you've made to your working habits and see if there's anything I can do to help. We've really got to come to grips with this."

   (We're treating this as a problem to be solved together; what, if anything, has she done to improve her self-organization? What help might she need from you? If she has improved her self-organization, is there some other explanation for missed deadlines?)

WIFMs

Here are some WIFMs you could bring out early in the discussion:

1. More respect or acceptance from other committee members, not getting hassled by you.

2. Smoother flow of work through the department; personal pride in meeting deadlines; helping you out (it might not have occurred to Carla that she was causing you a problem). At the very least, you'll feel better for having aired your concern.

3. You'll both gain some kudos with senior management for improved results; team participation is good for morale.

4. Approval will mean better results from your department, which in turn will

make Sean look good. He will feel quite comfortable with his decision because he will have all the facts he needs.

5. By cutting out wasted effort, repeated work, bottlenecks, and so on, their jobs will become much easier and more hassle-free; they'll have an opportunity to participate in improving the overall process of the way they work.

6. A chance for Ellen to improve the one poor area of her performance and become excellent in all aspects of her job; an opportunity to improve a key job skill (self-organization).

Some Word Meanings: *Order* and *Strike*

When you think of how many meanings these two simple words can have, it's easy to appreciate the need for making sure we choose our words carefully and check that others have understood our intended meaning!

Order

align	edict	rank
arrange	genus	religious fraternity
array	grouping	requisition
assemble	instruction	reserve
category	line	row
command	mandate	sequence
contract	method	suitable
demand	normal	to book
dictate	pattern	

Strike

ambush	delete	picket
assault	dispute	punch
attack	hit	raid
blow	impose	smite
boycott	knock	stamp
coin	mint	walkout
cuff		

How to Score the Neuro-Linguistic Programming Quiz

To find out which representational systems you prefer and which you need more practice in to increase the number of languages you speak, add up the ticks in each column from the quiz in Chapter 19, "Speak the Other Person's Language." The more ticks, the more you use this language.

Eight or more ticks indicates a strong preference to use this mode while four or fewer ticks indicates a strong preference not to use it.

Visual	The top right box shows your tendency to take in, organize, and communicate information visually. Are you an "eye" person?
Auditory	The lower right box shows your tendency to take in, organize, and communicate information in an auditory fashion. Are you an "ear" person?
Kinaesthetic	The top left box shows your tendency to take in, organize, and communicate information kinaesthetically. Are you a "feeling" person?
Digital	The lower left box shows your tendency to take in, organize, and communicate information digitally. Are you a "words" person?

Glossary

affirmation   A performance-enhancing technique of subconsciously embedding through repetition a short, positive, first person, and present-tense statement stating a desired characteristic.

affirmative listening   Using attentive body language to show we are listening.

aggressive communication   Putting one's own wants and needs ahead of everyone else's and often ignoring or belittling other people's concerns.

apathy   A lack of feeling, interest, or concern.

assertive communication   A learned set of verbal and nonverbal communication skills based on mutual respect that results in clear, open communication. Assertive communicators can express their own point of view, listen to others' points of view, and work towards outcomes that satisfy everyone

broken record   Calmly repeating your main message, like a broken record, until it gets through.

bullying   Continual aggressive and demeaning remarks and behavior that ignores and undermines the victim's rights to be treated with respect and consideration.

clarifying question   A question used to make a point or detail clear or more specific.

closed question   A question that can be answered with a "yes," "no," or a short statement of fact.

cluster   A group of postures, movements, expressions, or gestures that reveal a person's inner thoughts and impulses.

coercive question A leading question that narrows or limits the possible answers and traps the other person into giving the answer we want.

cognitive dissonance Feelings of acute discomfort and confusion that occur when we are faced with information that contradicts our deeply held beliefs. One function of our subconscious is to reduce cognitive dissonance by ignoring or reinterpreting such information.

comfort zone That nice, safe place where we do the same old, comfortable things, and communicate in the same old, comfortable ways.

communication barriers Factors in the environment that prevent communication or make it more difficult.

communication filters Screens, such as stereotypes, prejudices, and fixed ideas, that we carry around with us to eliminate information we don't expect or want.

communication incompatibilities Barriers that exist between ourselves and another person, such as a difference in values, which lead to misunderstandings and even conflict.

compliment Praise or kind words about things that are within a person's control and usually about something they've done (as opposed to flattery, which is about things people have little or no control over).

difficult person A person whom others, not just you, find trying and tiresome.

empathy The ability to grasp, or participate in, another's experience, feelings, or thoughts without taking them fully on board.

energy The intensity and enthusiasm with which a person speaks.

extrovert A doer who uses the outside world as a reference point.

feedback Finding out the effect of our actions; explaining the effect of others' actions.

flag A type of frame used during a conversation that highlights what you are about to do (for example, "Let me ask you a question," or "To summarize, then ...")

fogging A "yes, maybe that's so" technique to curtail unjustified or unwanted criticism without starting an argument.

frame A short statement that introduces a conversation by stating what you want to discuss.

frame of reference The way we view the world, the sum of our beliefs, values, experiences, background, personality style, mind-sets, and paradigms.

general question Usually an open question that introduces a topic or highlights the one we wish to pursue further.

Gotcha! question   A question used to indirectly, and seemingly innocently, point out a weakness in someone or show up mistakes they have made.

hypothetical question   An indirect, backdoor way of making a statement that asks the other person to imagine himself to be in a situation that he is not in.

"I" statement   A clear, succinct, and blame-free statement of another's actions, their effect on you, and your preferred outcome.

imperative question   A demand or command veiled as a request for information or action.

incubating   "Sleeping on" a problem, decision, or dilemma to allow our subconscious mind to work on it.

inflection   The way voices rise and fall.

introvert   A thinker who lives his or her world primarily inside his or her head.

Law of Psychological Reciprocity   The principle that behavior breeds behavior, or people tend to treat us as we treat them.

leading   Shifting your position or altering your energy level or voice to see whether the other person follows your lead as a way of testing for rapport.

leading question   A question that hints at and encourages the answer you are looking for or expect.

limbic system   Part of our primitive brain; involved in basic emotions and feelings, including the fight-flight response, which is the source of aggressive and passive communication styles.

locus of control   The location of the impulses that guide our behavior; it can be internal or external.

matching   Communicating in similar ways to the person we're with, both verbally and nonverbally; a sign of rapport.

mirroring   Cross-over, or back-to-front matching—just like looking in a mirror.

mnemonic device   A formula used to remember something.

moralizing   Explaining or interpreting things from an excessively moralistic, "right and wrong" or "good and bad" point of view.

multiple question   A string of questions, often culminating in a weak one, which is, unfortunately, the one that is usually answered.

negative assertion   Agreeing with a justified criticism in order to curtail the discussion.

negative inquiry   Asking questions to draw out more information concerning a criticism.

neural pathways   The specific connection of cells associated with a thought.

neuro-linguistic programming   A discipline that studies the way we take in, deal with, and convey information.

neurons   Brain cells.

open question   A question that encourages a full response, not just a "yes," "no," or short statement of fact.

optimist   Someone who is inclined to favorably interpret events and to anticipate the best, not the worst, outcome.

paradigms   Ways of looking at the world.

passive communication   Putting the wants and needs of others ahead of one's own.

passive-aggressive cycle   Generally passive communication and behavior with occasional outbursts of aggressive communication and behavior.

patronizing   Communicating in a condescending way.

pitch   How high or low a person's voice is.

probing question   A question used to explore a topic further.

projection   An unconscious process whereby, rather than admit we have a characteristic or quality, we cast, or project, it onto someone else.

pseudo question   A statement disguised as a question.

rapport   The feeling of being in sync or in harmony with another person. When we have rapport with someone, we feel comfortable with him or her and communication flows.

reflective listening   Briefly restating your understanding of the speaker's feeling and/or meaning.

rhythm   The tempo with which a person speaks.

sarcasm   A cutting, contemptuous, or caustic comment; or hostile, disparaging, acrimonious, and mocking remarks and put-downs.

screened question   A way of reaching agreement by asking someone her opinion without revealing our thoughts or what we want first.

self-esteem   Our feelings of respect and self-worth. How we value ourselves.

self-fulfilling prophecy   The process by which our beliefs, values, and world views influence the way we perceive the world and others, and our behavior; we tend to perceive what we expect, which reinforces our beliefs.

self-image   How we see ourselves; the view we hold of ourselves that describes us and defines us.

self talk   The often unconscious messages we give ourselves about ourselves that shape our behavior.

set-up question   A double-whammy question that rebounds on the victims and puts them in a difficult or embarrassing situation.

subconscious   Thoughts and beliefs below the threshold of our awareness.

submissive communication   See passive communication.

sympathy   Such a close affinity that what affects one person similarly affects the other. What one thinks or feels, so does the other.

tone   The quality of the sound of our voice, its expressiveness, or color.

unspoken question   A question asked nonverbally, for example, by lifting an eyebrow or leaning slightly forward towards the speaker.

values   Deeply and strongly held beliefs and principles about what is right and wrong, good and bad, important and unimportant, what should and shouldn't be.

visualization   A performance enhancing technique of mentally seeing and feeling something so clearly that the body accepts its reality and performs accordingly.

For Further Reading

Getting to Yes, by Roger and Ury W. Fisher, Hutchinson Better Business Guides, 1981.

Looks at how to communicate on a win–win basis, particularly in negotiation situations.

Gifts Differing, by Isabel Myers, Consulting Psychologists Press, Inc., 1986.

Provides a clear description of the 16 Myers-Briggs personality types, which the types and temperaments we looked at in Chapter 24, "Tune In to the Same Wavelength," are based on.

Influencing with Integrity, by Genie Z. Laborde, Syntony Publishing, 1984.

An inspiring book.

Leader Effectiveness Training, by Dr. Thomas Gordon, Bantam Books, 1980.

There are several editions of this book under different publishers. All are good. It contains some of the earliest and most clearly explained techniques for communicating well.

People Skills, by Robert Bolton, Simon & Schuster Australia, 1987.

A good overview of communication.

Seven Habits of Highly Effective People, by Stephen R. Covey, Simon & Schuster Fireside Books, 1989.

A really terrific book that covers a multitude of skills.

Smart Choices: A Practical Guide to Making Better Decisions, by John S. Hammond, Ralph L. Keeney, and Howard Raiffa, Harvard Business School Press, 1998.

A clearly written book that reviews the latest scientific research into problem solving and decision making.

Supervision: The Theory and Practice of Front-Line Management, by Kris Cole, Prentice Hall, 2001.

Gives in-depth information on problem solving and decision-making, written communications, and assertiveness.

Unlimited Power, by Anthony Robbins, Simon & Schuster, 1986.

An in-depth, yet easy-to-read, explanation of many personal and communication skills.

Index

A

accommodation, 264
achievement needs, 250-251
Act As If principle, 34-35
action, taking, 32
  Act As If principle, 34-35
  comfort zones, 33
  "faking it until you make it," 34
  viewing mistakes as learning experiences, 33-34
action plans, 42-43
affiliation needs, 250-251
affirmations, 63-65
affirmative listening, 135, 156
aggressive communication, 211-212
  fight-flight response, 210-211
  passive-aggressive cycle, 210-211
analogies, 194
analysts, 257
analytical language. *See* digital language
anger, 84, 289-291
apathy (versus empathy and sympathy), 85-87
appearance (first impressions), 95-96
asking (versus telling), 230
assertive communication, 211-213
  asking versus telling, 230
  avoiding distracters
    broken record technique, 222
  Change/Time/Consequence formula, 234-235
  dealing with criticism, 222
  ending a conversation, 225
  fogging technique, 224-225
  negative assertion, 223-224
  negative inquiry technique, 223
  DELWAC acronym, 234
  development tips, 215
  handling bullies, 227-228
  "I" statements, 230-234
  identifying, 213-215
    nonverbal cues, 214
    verbal cues, 213-214
  persuading versus pressuring, 235-238
  saying "no" graciously, 225-227
  talking about yourself, 220
    opening up, 221-222
    owning your feelings, 220-221
    owning your message, 220
    speaking only for yourself, 220
assumptions, 217
attentiveness, 107-108
auditory language, 200, 205
avoidance, 263-264
"avoiding"
  metaprograms, 251-252
  sins, 171
    diverting, 171-172
    vagueness, 171

B

back-stabbers, 280
behavior
  body language, 28
    body-mind experiment, 29-30
    mood link, 28
    self-esteem link, 30
  choosing your behavior, 83-84
  dealing with anger, 84
  Law of Psychological Reciprocity, 82-83
  professional approach, 85
beliefs, 4-5, 10, 14. *See also* thoughts, values
  about others, 20-21
    projection, 22-24
  about ourselves, 14-15
    self-esteem, 15-17
    self-image, 17-18
    self-talk, 18-20
  about the world
    paradigms, 24-25
  self-fulfilling prophecies, 6-7
  Success Sequence, 5-6
body language, 28, 94-95
  body-mind experiment, 29-30
  first impressions, 96-97
  impact, 103-104
  interpretations and responses, 305-306
  main aspects
    SO CLEAR acronym, 104-111
  matching, 121
  mood link, 28
  reading, 114-115
    movements, 116
    negative signals, 116-117

positive signals,
117-118
signal clusters, 115-116
self-esteem link, 30
boundaries, establishing,
179
broken record technique,
222
bullies, 227-228, 282-283

C

Change/Time/Consequence
formula, 234-235
clarifying questions,
146-147
clarity, 193
closed questions
situations to avoid, 134,
142
turning into open ques-
tions, 307
useful applications,
136-139
clusters, body language,
115-116
coercive questions, 142
cognitive dissonance, 6-7
collaborative conflict management, 262-263
comfort zones, 33
commanding, 169-170
commonalities, identifying,
123
communication
basic modes, 198-202
answers to identifica-
tion quiz, 315
applications, 204-206
auditory, 200
digital, 201
identification quiz,
202-203
kinaesthetic, 200-201
visual, 199-200
word examples,
204-206
"dance" of communica-
tion
five-part tempo, 71-76

Four Fs, 215-217
impact, 70-71
obstacles, 76
external barriers, 79
filters, 76-78
incompatibilities,
79-80
styles, 211
aggressive, 211-212
assertive, 212-215,
220-238
passive, 212
Communicator's Pledge, 89
complainers, 279-280
complaints
handling, 287
agreeing and acting,
289
angry people, 289-291
gathering good infor-
mation, 288
giving good informa-
tion, 288-289
habitual complainers,
292
L-L-A-R-A-A acronym,
287-288
purpose identification,
286
feedback, 286-287
opportunities for
improvement, 287
warnings, 287
compliments, 48
compromise, 264-265
conflict management, 262
approach styles, 262
accommodation, 264
avoidance, 263-264
collaboration, 262-263
compromise, 264-265
force, 263
resolution tips, 266-271
source recognition,
265-267
win-win behaviors, 266
conscientious thinkers, 257
contact, eye, 109-110
control (internal locus),
30-31

conversations
appealing to individual
motivators, 250
need for achievement,
250-251
need for affiliation,
250-251
need for power,
250-251
asking versus telling, 230
assertive communication
avoiding distracters,
222
dealing with criticism,
222-225
developing, 215
handling bullies,
227-228
identifying, 213-215
saying "no" graciously,
225-227
talking about yourself,
220-222
assumptions, 217
Change/Time/Conse-
quence formula,
234-235
communicating with
panache, 193
clarity, 193
demonstrations, 194
examples, metaphors,
and analogies, 194
incorporating names,
193-194
matching idiolect of
listeners, 194-195
using the listeners'
"language," 195
visual aids, 194
communication styles,
211
aggressive, 211-212
assertive, 212-213
passive, 212
DELWAC acronym, 234
feedback, 240
negative, 240-242
no feedback, 242
offering, 242-245
positive, 240

receiving, 245-248
requesting, 244-245
flagging, 182-183
Four Fs, 215-217
framing, 178
    example statements,
        309-310
    practice exercises,
        180-181
    statement types, 179
    "I" statements, 230-234
    metaprogram adapta-
        tions, 251
        avoiders and seekers,
            251-252
        "just knowing" and
            needing to be told,
            252-253
        lone rangers and mus-
            keteers, 253
        matchers and mis-
            matchers, 252-253
    neuro-linguistic program-
        ming (NLP), 197-198
        applications, 204-206
        language types,
            198-203, 315
        word examples,
            204-206
    perception and process-
        ing differences, 254
        feelers, 255
        intuitors, 255
        sensors, 255
        thinkers, 254
    persuading versus pressur-
        ing, 235-238
    WIFM (What's In It For
        Me?) factor, 181-182
        example statements,
            310-311
    word selection, 187-188
        neutral words, 188-189
        positive words,
            189-190
        specific words, 190-192
        strong words, 192-193
    words
        power of words,
            185-187

working with different
    personality types,
    253-257
        analysts, 257
        conscientious thinkers,
            257
        dominant directors,
            255-256
        empathists, 258
        interacting socializers,
            256
        introverts and extro-
            verts, 253-254
        legalists, 257
        realists, 258
        steady relaters, 256
        task focused or people
            focused, 254
cooperative work style, 253
creative problem-solving
    methods, 300-302
credibility, 236
criticism, 222
    curtailing conversation
        assertively ending a
            conversation, 225
        fogging technique,
            224-225
        negative assertion,
            223-224
    handling, 247-248
        negative inquiry tech-
            nique, 223
cycle, improvement, 50-51

D

"dance" of communication
    (five-part tempo), 71-72
    "approach, not intention
        is reality," 74
    "communication is a two-
        way street," 75-76
    "delivery always affects
        how the message is
        received," 74
    "everything we do is
        communication," 72-73

"message beginnings
    often determine the out-
    come," 73
decision-making, 299
degrees, listening, 155
    affirmative, 156
    "Half-An-Ear," 155-156
    reflective, 156-163
    "Stunned Mullet,"
        156-157
delivery, message, 193
    clarity, 193
    demonstrations, 194
    examples, metaphors,
        and analogies, 194
    incorporating names,
        193-194
    matching idiolect of lis-
        teners, 194-195
    neuro-linguistic program-
        ming (NLP), 197-198
        applications, 204-206
        language types,
            198-202
        answers to identification
            quiz, 315
        identification quiz,
            202-203
        word examples,
            204-206
    using the listeners' "lan-
        guage," 195
    visual aids, 194
DELWAC acronym, 234
demonstrations, 194
difficult people
    handling
        general principles,
            274-277
        strategy steps, 277-279
    types, 279
        back-stabbers and gos-
            sips, 280
        bullies, 282-283
        complainers, 279-280
        power-seekers, 282
        sarcastic people, 281
        showoffs, 281
        unreliable people,
            281-282

digital language, 201, 206
disagreeing, 276
diverting, 171-172
dominant directors, 255-256

E

EARS acronym (gathering
   information), 134-136
empathists, 258
empathy
   development tips, 89
   frame of reference appli-
      cations, 87-88
   versus sympathy and
      apathy, 85-87
emphasis, 100
energy
   matching, 122
   vocal, 100-101
evaluating, 167
examples, 194
extroverts, 253-254
eye contact, 109-110

F

facts, 215-217
fantasy, 215-217
feedback, 240
   complaints, 286-287
   negative, 240-242
   no feedback, 242
   offering, 242-244
      Keep-Stop-Start
         approach, 245
      More-Less-Same
         approach, 245
   positive, 240
   receiving, 245-246
      accepting praise, 248
      handling criticism,
         247-248
   requesting, 244-245
feeling language. *See* kinaesthetic language
feelings, 215-217, 220-221
feelings-based information
   processing, 255

fight-flight response,
   210-211
filters, 76-78
first impressions, 95
   appearance, 95-96
   body language, 96-97
   voice, 97
flagging, 136-137, 182-183
focus, improving, 131-133
focused concentration,
   107-108
fogging technique, 224-225
folklore, 215-217
force (conflict management
   approach), 263
Four Fs of communiation,
   215-217
frame of reference, 87-88
framing, 178
   example statements,
      309-310
   practice exercises,
      180-181
   statement types, 179
      boundaries, 179
      history, 179
      problem, 179
      process, 179
      purposes, 179
further reading resources,
   323-324

G

gathering information
   closed questions, 136-139
   complaints, 288
   EARS acronym, 134-136
   evaluating received mes-
      sages, 150
   focusing on the speaker,
      131-133
   listening
      degrees of listening,
         155-157
      reflective listening,
         157-163
      true listening, 153-155
   neutral questioning, 145

question types to avoid,
   141-142
   leading questions, 144
   multiple questions,
      144-145
   pseudo questions,
      142-144
ten deadly sins, 166, 169,
   171
   commanding, 169-170
   diverting, 171-172
   evaluating, 167
   giving unsolicited
      advice, 170-171
   labeling, 168-169
   moralizing, 167-168
   railroading, 170
   sarcasm, 169
   threatening, 170
   vagueness, 171
tips for success, 147
   analyzing compar-
      isons, 150
   asking for specificity,
      148
   clarifying jargon,
      148-149
   examining generaliza-
      tions, 149-150
   making "assumptions
      and rules" explicit,
      149
useful question types, 146
   clarifying questions,
      146-147
   general questions, 146
   open questions, 146
   probing questions,
      146-147
   unspoken questions,
      147
general questions, 146
giving information
   appealing to individual
      motivators, 250
      need for achievement,
         250-251
      need for affiliation,
         250-251
      need for power,
         250-251

asking versus telling, 230
assertive communication
  avoiding distracters, 222
  dealing with criticism, 222-225
  developing, 215
  handling bullies, 227-228
  identifying, 213-215
  saying "no" graciously, 225-227
  talking about yourself, 220-222
assumptions, 217
Change/Time/Consequence formula, 234-235
communicating with panache, 193
  clarity, 193
  demonstrations, 194
  examples, metaphors, and analogies, 194
  incorporating names, 193-194
  matching idiolect of listeners, 194-195
  using the listeners' "language," 195
  visual aids, 194
communication styles, 211
  aggressive, 211-212
  assertive, 212-213
  passive, 212
complaints, 288-289
DELWAC acronym, 234
feedback, 240
  negative, 240-242
  no feedback, 242
  offering, 242-245
  positive, 240
  receiving, 245-248
  requesting, 244-245
flagging conversations, 182-183
Four Fs, 215-217
framing conversations, 178
  example statements, 309-310

practice exercises, 180-181
statement types, 179
"I" statements, 230-234
metaprogram adaptations, 251
  avoiders and seekers, 251-252
  "just knowing" and needing to be told, 252-253
  lone rangers and musketeers, 253
  matchers and mismatchers, 252-253
neuro-linguistic programming (NLP), 197-198
  applications, 204-206
  language types, 198-203, 315
  word examples, 204-206
perception and processing differences, 254
  feelers, 255
  intuitors, 255
  sensors, 255
  thinkers, 254
persuading versus pressuring, 235-238
power of words, 185-187
pre-conversation questions to ask yourself, 177-178
WIFM (What's In It For Me?) factor, 181-182
  example statements, 310-311
word selection, 187-188
  neutral words, 188-189
  positive words, 189-190
  specific words, 190-192
  strong words, 192-193
working with different personality types, 253, 255, 257
  analysts, 257
  conscientious thinkers, 257

  dominant directors, 255-256
  empathists, 258
  interacting socializers, 256
  introverts and extroverts, 253-254
  legalists, 257
  realists, 258
  steady relaters, 256
  task focused or people focused, 254
goals, 42
  peak performers' approach, 52
  STAR goals, 38-39
    A equals achievability, 40-41
    R equals results and activities needed to get there, 41-42
    S equals setting simple and specific goals, 39-40
    T equals target dates, 40
gossips, 280
Gotcha! questions, 143-144

H

habits (poor listening), 129-130
habitual complainers, 292
"Half-An-Ear" listening, 155-156
hearing language. *See* auditory language
heuristics, 300
history, establishing (framing statements), 179
hypothetical questions, 142

I

"I" statements, 230-234
idiolect, 194-195
impact, 70-71
imperative questions, 142-143

329

impressions, first, 95
appearance, 95-96
body language, 96-97
voice, 97
improvement cycle, 50-51
incompatibilities, 79-80
incubating problems, 302
independent work style, 253
inflections, voice, 99
information
gathering
closed questions,
136-139
complaints, 288
EARS acronym,
134-136
evaluating received
messages, 150
focusing on the
speaker, 131-133
listening, 153-163
neutral questioning,
145
question types to
avoid, 141-145
ten deadly sins,
166-172
tips for success,
147-150
useful question types,
146-147
giving
appealing to individual
motivators, 250-251
asking versus telling,
230
assertive communica-
tion, 213-215,
220-228
assumptions, 217
Change/Time/
Consequence for-
mula, 234-235
communicating with
panache, 193-195
communication styles,
211-213
complaints, 288-289
DELWAC acronym,
234

feedback, 240-248
flagging conversations,
182-183
Four Fs, 215-217
framing conversations,
178-181, 309-310
"I" statements,
230-234
metaprogram adapta-
tions, 251-253
neuro-linguistic pro-
gramming (NLP),
197-206, 315
perception and pro-
cessing differences,
254-255
persuading versus pres-
suring, 235-238
power of words,
185-187
pre-conversation ques-
tions to ask yourself,
177-178
WIFM (What's In It For
Me?) factor, 181-182,
310-311
word selection,
187-193
working with different
personality types,
253-258
interacting socializers, 256
internal factors
beliefs, values, and
thoughts, 4-5, 7-10, 14
beliefs about others,
20-24
beliefs about ourselves,
14-20
beliefs about the
world, 24-25
self-fulfilling prophe-
cies, 6-7
Success Sequence, 5-6
locus of control, 30-31
interpretations (body language), 305-306
introverts, 253-254
intuition-based information
processing, 255

involving others (problem-
solving), 299-300
irony, 169

J-K

jargon, clarifying, 148-149

Keep-Stop-Start feedback
approach, 245
kinaesthetic language,
200-201, 205-206

L

L-L-A-R-A-A acronym,
287-288
labeling, 168-169
language
body, 94-95
first impressions, 96-97
impact, 103-104
interpretations and
responses, 305-306
main aspects (SO
CLEAR acronym),
104-111
matching, 121
reading, 114-118
NLP types, 198-202
answers to identifica-
tion quiz, 315
applications, 204-206
auditory, 200
digital, 201
identification quiz,
202-203
kinaesthetic, 200-201
visual, 199-200
word examples,
204-206
Law of Psychological
Reciprocity, 82-83
leading questions, 144
leaning, 108
legalists, 257
limbic system, 210-211
listening
affirmative, 135, 156
bad habits, 129-130

degrees, 155
  affirmative, 156
  "Half-An-Ear," 155-156
  reflective, 156-157
  "Stunned Mullet,"
    156-157
EARS mnemonic device,
  134-136
reflective, 135, 156-158
  applications, 159-160
  guidelines, 158-159
  techniques, 160-163
  when to avoid, 160
tips
  focusing on the
    speaker, 131-133
  true listening, 153-155
locus of control, 30-31
logical language. *See* digital
  language

M

management, conflict, 262
  approach styles, 262
    accommodation, 264
    avoidance, 263-264
    collaboration, 262-263
    compromise, 264-265
    force, 263
  resolution tips, 266-271
  source recognition,
    265-267
  win-win behaviors, 266
matching, 121
  body language, 121
  energy, 122
  metaprograms, 252-253
  voice, 121-122
mental involvement,
  131-132
messages, owning, 220
meta-messages, 169
metaphors, 194
metaprograms, 251
  avoiders and seekers,
    251-252
  "just knowing" and need-
    ing to be told, 252-253

lone rangers and muske-
  teers, 253
matchers and mismatch-
  ers, 252-253
mirroring, 122-123
mismatching metaprograms,
  252-253
mistakes, embracing, 57
moods (body language link),
  28
moralizing, 167-168
More-Less-Same approach,
  245
motivators, 250
  need for achievement,
    250-251
  need for affiliation,
    250-251
  need for power, 250-251
movements (interpreting
  other people's body language), 116
multiple questions, 144-145

N

needs, psychological, 250
  need for achievement,
    250-251
  need for affiliation,
    250-251
  need for power, 250-251
negative
  assertion, 223-224
  feedback, 240-242
  inquiry technique, 223
  signals, 116-117
neural pathways, 9
neuro-linguistic program-
  ming (NLP), 197-198
  applications, 204-206
  language types, 198-199,
    201-202
    answers to identifica-
      tion quiz, 315
    auditory, 200
    digital, 201
    identification quiz,
      202-203

kinaesthetic, 200-201
visual, 199-200
word examples
  auditory words, 205
  digital words, 206
  kinaesthetic words,
    205-206
  visual words, 204-205
neutral
  questioning, 145
  words, 188-189
NLP (neuro-linguistic programming), 197-198
  applications, 204-206
  language types, 198-202
    answers to identifica-
      tion quiz, 315
    auditory, 200
    digital, 201
    identification quiz,
      202-203
    kinaesthetic, 200-201
    visual, 199-200
  word examples
    auditory words, 205
    digital words, 206
    kinaesthetic words,
      205-206
    visual words, 204-205
"no" (saying), 225-227
non-verbal communication
  body language, 28, 94-95
    body-mind experi-
      ment, 29-30
    first impressions, 96-97
    impact, 103-104
    interpretations and
      responses, 305-306
    main aspects, 104-111
    matching, 121
    mood link, 28
    reading, 114-118
    self-esteem link, 30
  unspoken questions, 147

O

obstacles, 76
  external barriers, 79
  filters, 76-78
  incompatibilities, 79-80
open
  body language, 106-107
  communication, 221-222
  questions, 134-135
    turning closed questions into open questions, 307
owning
  feelings, 220-221
  messages, 220

P

paradigms, 24-25
paraphrasing, 161
passive
  communication, 211-212
    fight-flight response, 210-211
    passive-aggressive cycle, 210-211
  listening, 156-157
passive-aggressive cycle, 210-211
patronizing communication methods, 166
  evaluating, 167
  labeling, 168-169
  moralizing, 167-168
  sarcasm, 169
peak performers' approaches to life
  building self-esteem in others, 47-50
  embracing mistakes, 57
  focusing on goals, 52
  focusing on solutions, not problems, 57-59
  focusing on worthwhile efforts, 56-57
  high standards, 50-51
  self-affirmations, 63-65
  self-esteem, 46-47

taking responsibility, 51, 56
visualizing success, 59-63
working with others, 52
people focused personalities, 254
persistence, 43
personal space, 105-106
personality types, 253, 255, 257
  analysts, 257
  conscientious thinkers, 257
  dominant directors, 255-256
  empathists, 258
  interacting socializers, 256
  introverts and extroverts, 253-254
  legalists, 257
  realists, 258
  steady relaters, 256
  task focused or people focused, 254
persuasion (versus pressuring), 235-238
pitch (voice), 99
plans, action, 42-43
positive
  feedback, 240
  signals, 117-118
  words, 189-190
power needs, 250-251
power-seeking people, 282
praise, 48-50, 248
pressuring (versus persuading), 235-238
probing questions, 146-147
problem-solving
  creativity elements, 300-302
  effort assessment guidelines, 293-294
  involving others, 299-300
  making decisions, 299
  preventing heuristics, 300
  S-O-L-V-E acronym, 294
    E equals evaluate your results, 298

    L equals list your options, 297-298
    O equals outline the problem, 295-297
    S equals state the problem, 294-295
    V equals visualize your options, 298
problems, identifying (framing statements), 179
process, explaining (framing statements), 179
professional approach, 85
projection, 22, 24
  situations, 23
  unrecognized characteristics in ourselves, 22-23
  unrecognized desires in other people, 24
prophecies, self-fulfilling, 6-7
pseudo questions, 142, 144
  coercive questions, 142
  Gotcha! questions, 143-144
  hypothetical questions, 142
  imperative questions, 142-143
  screened questions, 143
  set-up questions, 144
psychological needs, 250
  need for achievement, 250-251
  need for affiliation, 250-251
  need for power, 250-251
purpose, establishing (framing statements), 179

Q

questions
  closed
    situations to avoid, 134, 142
    turning into open questions, 307
    useful applications, 136-139

evaluating received messages, 150
neutral questioning approach, 145
open, 134-135
tips for information gathering, 147
  analyzing comparisons, 150
  asking for specificity, 148
  clarifying jargon, 148-149
  examining generalizations, 149-150
  making assumptions and "rules" explicit, 149
unhelpful types to avoid, 141-142
  leading questions, 144
  multiple questions, 144-145
  pseudo questions, 142-144
useful types, 146
  clarifying questions, 146-147
  general questions, 146
  open questions, 146
  probing questions, 146-147
  unspoken questions, 147

R

railroading, 170
rapport, 120
  identifying commonalities, 123
  matching, 121
    body language, 121
    energy, 122
    voice, 121-122
  mirroring, 122-123
  testing, 124-125
reading body language, 114-115
  movements, 116
  negative signals, 116-117

positive signals, 117-118
signal clusters, 115-116
realists, 258
reflective listening, 110, 135, 156-158
  applications, 159-160
  guidelines, 158-159
  techniques, 160
    imagining out loud, 162-163
    paraphrasing meanings, 161
    reflecting feelings, 161
    summarizing content, 161-162
    synthesizing, 162
  when to avoid, 160
resolution, conflict, 262
  approach styles, 262
    accommodation, 264
    avoidance, 263-264
    collaboration, 262-263
    compromise, 264-265
    force, 263
  source recognition, 265-267
  tips for success, 266-271
  win-win behaviors, 266
resources (further reading), 323-324
responses, body language, 305-306
responsibility
  peak performers, 51
  taking responsibility, 56
rhythm, vocal, 100-101

S

S-O-L-V-E acronym, 294
  E equals evaluate your results, 298
  L equals list your options, 297-298
  O equals outline the problem, 295-297
  S equals state the problem, 294-295
  V equals visualize your options, 298

sarcasm, 169
sarcastic people, 281
saying "no," 225-227
screened questions, 143
seeing language. *See* visual language
seeking metaprograms, 251-252
self-esteem, 15-17
  body language link, 30
  peak performers, 46-50
  self-talk influences, 303-304
self-fulfilling prophecies, 6
self-image, 17-18
self-talk, 18-20
  affirmations, 63-65
  self-esteem indicators, 303-304
"sending signals" sins, 169
  commanding, 169-170
  giving unsolicited advice, 170-171
  railroading, 170
  threatening, 170
sensory-based information processing, 255
set-up questions, 144
showoffs, 281
signal clusters, 115-116
silence, 135-136
sins (communication), 166
  avoiding sins, 171
    diverting, 171-172
    vagueness, 171
  patronizing sins, 166
    evaluating, 167
    labeling, 168-169
    moralizing, 167-168
    sarcasm, 169
  sending signals sins, 169
    commanding, 169-170
    giving unsolicited advice, 170-171
    railroading, 170
    threatening, 170
SO CLEAR acronym (body language), 104-111
Socratic irony, 143

solving problems
  creativity elements, 300-302
  effort assessment guidelines, 293-294
  involving others, 299-300
  making decisions, 299
  preventing heuristics, 300
  S-O-L-V-E acronym, 294
    E equals evaluate your results, 298
    L equals list your options, 297-298
    O equals outline the problem, 295-297
    S equals state the problem, 294-295
    V equals visualize your options, 298
space, personal, 105-106
specific words, 190-192
specificity, 148
speed, vocal, 99-100
standards (peak performers), 50-51
STAR goals, 38-39
  A equals achievability, 40-41
  R equals results and activities needed to get there, 41-42
  S equals setting simple and specific goals, 39-40
  T equals target dates, 40
statements, "I", 230-234
steady relaters, 256
strong words, 192-193
"Stunned Mullet" listening, 156-157
styles, 211
  aggressive, 211-212
  assertive, 212-213
    asking versus telling, 230
    avoiding distracters, 222
    Change/Time/Consequence formula, 234-235
    dealing with criticism, 222-225

DELWAC acronym, 234
    developing, 215
    handling bullies, 227-228
    "I" statements, 230-234
    identifying, 213-215
    persuading versus pressuring, 235-238
    saying "no" graciously, 225-227
    talking about yourself, 220-222
  passive, 212
subconscious, 6-7
success
  Success Sequence, 5-6, 14, 28, 38
  three steps to success, 42
    action plan development, 42-43
    goal setting, 42
    persistence, 43
  visualizing, 59-63
summarizing, 161-162
sympathy (versus empathy and apathy), 85-87
synthesizing, 162

T

taking action, 32
  Act As If principle, 34-35
  comfort zones, 33
  "faking it until you make it," 34
  viewing mistakes as learning experiences, 33-34
task focused personalities, 254
telling (versus asking), 230
ten deadly communication sins, 166
  avoiding sins, 171
    diverting, 171-172
    vagueness, 171
  patronizing sins, 166
    evaluating, 167
    labeling, 168-169

moralizing, 167-168
    sarcasm, 169
  sending signals sins, 169
    commanding, 169-170
    giving unsolicited advice, 170-171
    railroading, 170
    threatening, 170
thought-based information processing, 254
thoughts, 4-5, 9-10. *See also* beliefs, values
  self-fulfilling prophecies, 6-7
  Success Sequence, 5-6
threatening, 170
tone (voice), 98-99
touching language. *See* kinaesthetic language
true listening, 153-155

U

unreliable people, 281-282
unsolicited advice, 170-171
unspoken questions, 147

V

vagueness, 171
values, 4-5, 7-8. *See also* beliefs, thoughts
  self-fulfilling prophecies, 6-7
  Success Sequence, 5-6
visual
  aids, 194
  language, 199-200
  words, 204-205
visualizations
  step-by-step guide, 61-63
  success, 59
    brain reprogramming, 59-60
    process steps, 60-62
voice
  communication impact, 97-98
  emphasizing specific words, 100

energy and rhythm,
  100-101
first impressions, 97
inflections, 99
matching, 121-122
pitch, 99
speed, 99-100
tone, 98-99

W-X-Y

WIFM (What's In It For
  Me?) factor, 181-182,
  310-311
words
  auditory, 205
  digital, 206
  kinaesthetic, 205-206
  meanings
    order versus strike, 313
  power of words, 185-187
  selecting, 187-188
    neutral words, 188-189
    positive words,
      189-190
    specific words, 190-192
    strong words, 192-193
  visual, 204-205

Z

zones, comfort, 33